CAMBRIDGE LIBRARY COLLECTION

Books of enduring scholarly value

Philosophy

This series contains both philosophical texts and critical essays about
philosophy, concentrating especially on works originally published in the
eighteenth and nineteenth centuries. It covers a broad range of topics including
ethics, logic, metaphysics, aesthetics, utilitarianism, positivism, scientific
method and political thought. It also includes biographies and accounts of
the history of philosophy, as well as collections of papers by leading figures.
In addition to this series, primary texts by ancient philosophers, and works
with particular relevance to philosophy of science, politics or theology, may be
found elsewhere in the Cambridge Library Collection.

Studies in Hegelian Cosmology

John McTaggart (1866–1925) was a Cambridge philosopher, famous for
his metaphysical theory that time is not real and that temporal order is an
illusion. Although best known for his contributions to the philosophy of time,
McTaggart also spent a large part of his career expounding Hegel's work. In
this book, first published in 1901, he discusses which views on a range of
topics in metaphysics and ethics are compatible with Hegel's logic and idea of
'the Absolute'. Some early work on theories for which McTaggart later became
well known can be found in this work, such as his beliefs that humans are
immortal, that the Absolute is not in any sense a person, and that love is the
relation that binds people together. In this book he also discusses punishment,
sin, morality and whether Hegel could be considered a Christian.

T0381833

Studies in
Hegelian Cosmology

JOHN MCTAGGART ELLIS MCTAGGART

CAMBRIDGE
UNIVERSITY PRESS

CAMBRIDGE UNIVERSITY PRESS

Cambridge, New York, Melbourne, Madrid, Cape Town,
Singapore, São Paolo, Delhi, Tokyo, Mexico City

Published in the United States of America by Cambridge University Press, New York

www.cambridge.org
Information on this title: www.cambridge.org/9781108037945

This edition first published 1901
This digitally printed version 2011

ISBN 978-1-108-03794-5 Paperback

STUDIES

IN

HEGELIAN COSMOLOGY.

𝔏𝔬𝔫𝔡𝔬𝔫: C. J. CLAY AND SONS,
CAMBRIDGE UNIVERSITY PRESS WAREHOUSE,
AVE MARIA LANE.
𝔊𝔩𝔞𝔰𝔤𝔬𝔴: 50, WELLINGTON STREET.

𝔏𝔢𝔦𝔭𝔷𝔦𝔤: F. A. BROCKHAUS.
𝔑𝔢𝔴 𝔜𝔬𝔯𝔨: THE MACMILLAN COMPANY.
𝔅𝔬𝔪𝔟𝔞𝔶: E. SEYMOUR HALE.

STUDIES

IN

HEGELIAN COSMOLOGY

BY

JOHN McTAGGART ELLIS McTAGGART, M A.

FELLOW AND LECTURER OF TRINITY COLLEGE IN CAMBRIDGE,
AUTHOR OF " STUDIES IN THE HEGELIAN DIALECTIC."

CAMBRIDGE:
AT THE UNIVERSITY PRESS.
1901

Cambridge:

PRINTED BY J. AND C. F. CLAY,

AT THE UNIVERSITY PRESS.

PREFACE.

CHAPTERS V. and VII. of this book appeared, nearly in their present form, in the International Journal of Ethics. (July 1896, and July 1897.) The other chapters have not been previously published.

In referring to Hegel's works I have used the Collected Edition, the publication of which began in 1832. For purposes of quotation I have generally availed myself of Wallace's translation of the Encyclopaedia, of Dyde's translation of the Philosophy of Law, and of Spiers' and Sanderson's translation of the Philosophy of Religion.

I am much indebted to Mr G. L. Dickinson, of King's College in Cambridge, and to my wife, for their kindness in reading this book before its publication, and assisting me with many valuable suggestions.

TABLE OF CONTENTS.

CHAPTER I.

INTRODUCTION.

CHAPTER II.

HUMAN IMMORTALITY.

A.

B.

D.

CHAPTER III.

THE PERSONALITY OF THE ABSOLUTE.

A.

CHAPTER IV

THE SUPREME GOOD AND THE MORAL CRITERION.

A.

B.

CHAPTER V

PUNISHMENT.

CHAPTER VI.

SIN.

CHAPTER VII.

THE CONCEPTION OF SOCIETY AS AN ORGANISM.

CHAPTER VIII.

HEGELIANISM AND CHRISTIANITY.

A.

D.

CHAPTER IX.

THE FURTHER DETERMINATION OF THE ABSOLUTE.

A.

CHAPTER I.

INTRODUCTION.

1. By Cosmology I mean the application, to subject-matter empirically known, of à *priori* conclusions derived from the investigation of the nature of pure thought. This superficial element clearly distinguishes Cosmology from the pure thought of Hegel's Logic. On the other hand, it is clearly to be distinguished from the empirical conclusions of science and every-day life. These also, it is true, involve an à *priori* element, since no knowledge is possible without the categories, but they do not depend on an explicit affirmation of à *priori* truths. It is possible for men to agree on a law of chemistry, or on the guilt of a prisoner, regardless of their metaphysical disagreements. And a man may come to correct conclusions on these subjects without any metaphysical knowledge at all. In Cosmology, however, the conclusions reached are deduced from propositions relating to pure thought. Without these propositions there can be no Cosmology, and a disagreement about pure thought must result in disagreements about Cosmology.

Of this nature are the subjects treated of in this book. The conception of the human self is a conception with empirical elements, and there is therefore an empirical element in the question whether such selves are eternal, and whether the Absolute is a similar self. So too the conceptions of Morality, of Punishment, of Sin, of the State, of Love, have all empirical elements in them. Yet none of the questions we shall discuss can be dealt with by the finite sciences. They cannot be settled by direct observation, nor can they be determined by induction. In some cases the scope of the question is so vast, that an induction based on instances within the sphere of our observation would not give even the slightest rational presumption in favour of any solution. In other cases the question relates to a state of things so different to our present experience that no relevant instances can be found. The only possible treatment of such subjects is metaphysical.

2. Hegel gives a very small part of his writings to Cosmological questions—a curious fact when we consider their great theoretical interest, and still greater practical importance. When he passes out of the realm of pure thought, he generally confines himself to explaining, by the aid of the dialectic, the reasons for the existence of particular facts, which, on empirical grounds, are known to exist, or, in some cases, wrongly supposed to exist. The Philosophy of Nature, the greater part of the Philosophy of Spirit, and nearly the whole of the Philosophy of Law, of the Philosophy of History, and of the Aesthetic, are taken up by this. The same thing may be said of the Second Part of the Philosophy of Religion, the First and Third Parts of which contain almost the only detailed discussion of cosmological problems to be found in his works.

This peculiarity of Hegel's is curious, but undeniable. I do not know of any possible explanation, unless in so far as one may be found in his want of personal interest in the part of philosophy which most people find more interesting than any other. When I speak in this book of Hegelian Cosmology, I do not propose to consider mainly the views actually expressed by Hegel, except in Chapter VIII, and, to some extent, in Chapter V. Elsewhere it will be my object to consider what views on the subjects under discussion ought logically to be held by a thinker who accepts Hegel's Logic, and, in particular, Hegel's theory of the Absolute Idea. I presume, in short, to endeavour to supplement, rather than to expound.

It is for this reason that I have devoted so much space to discussing the views of Lotze, of Mr Bradley, and of Professor Mackenzie. Since we have so little assistance on this subject from Hegel himself, it seemed desirable to consider the course taken by philosophers who held the same conception of the

Absolute as was held by Hegel, or who supported their opinions by arguments which would be equally relevant to Hegel's conception of the Absolute.

3. The subject-matter of those problems which can only be treated by Cosmology is varied, and the following chapters are, in consequence, rather disconnected from each other. But they illustrate, I think, three main principles. The first of these is that the element of differentiation and multiplicity occupies a much stronger place in Hegel's system than is generally believed. It is on this principle that I have endeavoured to show that all finite selves are eternal, and that the Absolute is not a self. These two conclusions seem to me to be very closely connected. As a matter of history, no doubt, the doctrines of human immortality and of a personal God have been rather associated than opposed. But this is due, I think, to the fact that attempts have rarely been made to demonstrate both of them metaphysically in the same system. I believe that it would be difficult to find a proof of our own immortality which did not place God in the position of a community, rather than a person, and equally difficult to find a conception of a personal God which did not render our existence dependent on his will—a will whose decisions our reason could not foresee.

My second main principle is that Hegel greatly over-estimated the extent to which it was possible to explain particular finite events by the aid of the Logic. For this view I have given some reasons in Chapter VII of my Studies in the Hegelian Dialectic. Applications of it will be found in Chapters IV and VII of the present work, and, in a lesser degree, in Chapters V and VI.

Thirdly, in Chapter IX, I have endeavoured to demonstrate the extent to which the Logic involves a mystical view of reality—an implication of which Hegel himself was not, I think, fully conscious, but which he realised much more fully than most of his commentators.

CHAPTER II.

HUMAN IMMORTALITY.

4. EXPERIENCE teaches us that there exist in the Universe finite personal spirits[1]. I judge myself, in the first place, to be such a finite personal spirit—to be something to which all my experience is related, and so related, that, in the midst of the multiplicity of experience, it is a unity, and that, in the midst of the flux of experience, it remains identical with itself. And I proceed to judge that certain effects, resembling those which I perceive myself to produce, are produced by other spirits of a similar nature. It is certain that this last judgment is sometimes wrong in particular cases. I may judge during a dream that I am in relation with some person who does not, in fact, exist at all. And, for a few minutes, an ingenious automaton may occasionally be mistaken for the body of a living person. But philosophy, with the exception of Solipsism, agrees with common sense that I am correct in the general judgment that there do exist other finite personal spirits as well as mine.

These spirits are called selves. And the problem which we have now to consider is whether there is a point in time for each self after which it would be correct to say that the self had ceased to exist. If not, it must be considered as immortal,

---

[1] Throughout this chapter, I shall employ the word finite, when used without qualification, to denote anything which has any reality outside it, whether its determination is merely external, or due to its own nature. Hegel himself speaks of the self-determined as infinite. But this is inconvenient in practice, though it is based on an important truth. For it leaves without a name the difference between the whole and a part of reality, while it gives the name of infinity to a quality which has already an appropriate name—self-determination.

whether as existing throughout endless time, or as having a timeless and therefore endless existence.

5. Hegel's own position on this question, as on so many other questions of cosmology, is not a little perplexing. He asserts the truth of immortality in several places[1], and he never denies it. But his assertions are slight and passing statements, to which he gives no prominence. And in the case of a doctrine of such importance, a merely incidental assertion is almost equivalent to a denial.

When we pass to the applications of the dialectic, the perplexity becomes still greater. For the doctrine of immortality is quietly ignored in them. Hegel treats at great length of the nature, of the duties, of the hopes, of human society, without paying the least attention to his own belief that, for each of the men who compose that society, life in it is but an infinitesimal fragment of his whole existence—a fragment which can have no meaning except in its relation to the whole. Can we believe that he really held a doctrine which he neglected in this manner?

On the other hand we have his explicit statements that immortality is to be ascribed to the self. To suppose these statements to be insincere is impossible. There is nothing in Hegel's life or character which would justify us in believing that he would have misrepresented his views to avoid persecution. Nor would the omission of such casual and trifling affirmations of the orthodox doctrine have rendered his work appreciably more likely to attract the displeasure of the governments under which he served.

6. The real explanation, I think, must be found elsewhere. The fact is that Hegel does not appear to have been much interested in the question of immortality. This would account for the fact that, while he answers the question in the affirmative, he makes so little use of the answer. It is the fundamental doctrine of his whole system that reality is essentially spirit. And there seems no reason whatever to accuse him of supposing that spirit could exist except as persons. But—rather

[1] Cp. *Philosophy of Religion*, i. 79, ii. 268, 313, 495 (trans. i. 79, iii. 57, 105, 303).

illogically—he seems never to have considered the individual persons as of much importance. All that was necessary was that the spirit should be there in some personal form or another. It follows, of course, from this, that he never attached much importance to the question of whether spirit was eternally manifested in the same persons, or in a succession of different persons.

No one, I imagine, can read Hegel's works, especially those which contain the applications of the dialectic, without being struck by this characteristic. At times it goes so far as almost to justify the criticism that reality is only considered valuable by Hegel because it forms a schema for the display of the pure Idea. I have tried to show elsewhere[1] that this view is not essential to Hegel's system, and, indeed, that it is absolutely inconsistent with it. But this only shows more clearly that Hegel's mind was naturally very strongly inclined towards such views, since even his own fundamental principles could not prevent him from continually recurring to them.

Since Hegel fails to emphasise the individuality of the individual, his omission to emphasise the immortality of the individual is accounted for. But it remains a defect in his work. For this is a question which no philosophy can be justified in treating as insignificant. A philosopher may answer it affirmatively, or negatively, or may deny his power of answering it at all. But, however he may deal with it, he is clearly wrong if he treats it as unimportant. For it does not only make all the difference for the future, but it makes a profound difference for the present. Am I eternal, or am I a mere temporary manifestation of something eternal which is not myself? The answer to this question may not greatly influence my duties in every-day life. Immortal or not, it is equally my duty to pay my bills, and not to cheat at cards, nor to betray my country. But we can scarcely exaggerate the difference which will be made in our estimate of our place in the universe, and, consequently, in our ideals, our aspirations, our hopes, the whole of the emotional colouring of our lives. And this is most of all the case on Hegelian principles, which declare that

[1] *Studies in the Hegelian Dialectic.*

existence in time is inadequate, and relatively unreal. If we are immortal, we may be the supreme end of all reality. If time made us, and will break us, our highest function must be to be the means of some end other than ourselves.

7. To determine the true relation of Hegel's philosophy to the doctrine of immortality, we must go into the matter at greater length than he has thought it worth while to do himself. We must take Hegel's account of the true nature of reality, and must ask whether this requires or excludes the eternal existence of selves such as our own. Now Hegel's account of the true nature of reality is that it is Absolute Spirit. And when we ask what is the nature of Absolute Spirit, we are told that its content is the Absolute Idea. The solution of our problem, then, will be found in the Absolute Idea.

8. We are certain, at any rate, that the doctrine of the Absolute Idea teaches us that all reality is spirit. No one, I believe, has ever doubted that this is Hegel's meaning. And it is also beyond doubt, I think, that he conceived this spirit as necessarily differentiated. Each of these differentiations, as not being the whole of spirit, will be finite. This brings us, perhaps, nearer to the demonstration of immortality, but is far from completing it. It is the eternal nature of spirit to be differentiated into finite spirits. But it does not necessarily follow that each of these differentiations is eternal. ·It might be held that spirit was continually taking fresh shapes, such as were the modes of Spinoza's Substance, and that each differentiation was temporary, though the succession of differentiations was eternal. And, even if it were established that spirit possessed eternal differentiations, the philosophising human being would still have to determine whether he himself, and the other conscious beings with whom he came in contact, were among these eternal differentiations.

If both these points were determined in the affirmative we should have a demonstration of immortality. But the conclusion will be different in two respects from the ordinary form in which a belief in immortality is held. The ordinary belief confines immortality to mankind—so far as the inhabitants of this planet are concerned. The lower animals are not supposed, by most people, to survive the death of their present bodies. And even those who extend immortality to all animals commonly hold that much of reality is not spiritual at all, but material, and that consequently neither mortality nor immortality can be predicated of it with any meaning. But if we can deduce immortality from the nature of the Absolute Idea, it will apply to all spirit—that is to say to all reality—and we shall be led to the conclusion that the universe consists entirely of conscious and immortal spirits.

The second peculiarity of the conclusion will be that the immortality to which it refers will not be an endless existence in time, but an eternal, *i.e.*, timeless existence, of which whatever duration in time may belong to the spirit will be a subordinate manifestation only. But this, though it would separate our view from some of the cruder forms of the belief, is, of course, not exclusively Hegelian but continually recurs both in philosophy and theology.

We have to enquire, then, in the first place, whether our selves are among the fundamental differentiations of spirit, whose existence is indicated by the dialectic, and, if this is so, we must then enquire whether each of these differentiations exists eternally.

9. The first of these questions cannot be settled entirely by pure thought, because one of the terms employed is a matter of empirical experience. We can tell by pure thought what must be the nature of the fundamental differentiations of spirit. But then we have also to ask whether our own natures correspond to this description in such a way as to justify us in believing that we are some of those differentiations. Now our knowledge of what we ourselves are is not a matter of pure thought—it cannot be deduced by the dialectic method from the single premise of Pure Being. We know what we ourselves are, because we observe ourselves to be so. And this is empirical.

Accordingly our treatment of the first question will fall into two parts. We must first determine what is the nature of the differentiations of spirit. This is a problem for the dialectic, and must be worked out by pure thought. And then we must apply the results of pure thought, thus gained, by enquiring how far our selves can or must be included in the number of those differentiations.

10. Hegel's own definition of the Absolute Idea is, "der Begriff der Idee, dem die Idee als solche der Gegenstand, dem das Objekt sie ist[1]." This by itself will not give us very much help in our present enquiry. But, as Hegel himself tells us, to know the full meaning of any category, we must not be content with its definition, but must observe how it grows out of those which precede it. We must therefore follow the course of the dialectic to see how the Absolute Idea is determined. It would be too lengthy to start with the category of Pure Being, and go through the whole chain of categories, and it will therefore be necessary to take some point at which to make a beginning. This point, I think, may conveniently be found in the category of Life. There seems to be very little doubt or ambiguity about Hegel's conception of this category as a whole, although the subdivisions which he introduces into it are among the most confused parts of the whole dialectic. And it is at this point that the differentiations of the unity begin to assume those special characteristics by which, if at all, they will be proved to be conscious beings. For both these reasons, it seems well to begin at the category of Life.

According to that category reality is a unity differentiated into a plurality (or a plurality combined into a unity) in such a way that the whole meaning and significance of the unity lies in its being differentiated into that particular plurality, and that the whole meaning and significance of the parts of the plurality lies in their being combined into that particular unity.

We have now to consider the transition from the category of Life to that of Cognition. We may briefly anticipate the argument by saying that the unity required by the category of Life will prove fatal to the plurality, which is no less essential to the category, unless that plurality is of a peculiar nature;

---

[1] *Encyclopaedia*, Section 236.

and that it is this peculiarity which takes us into the category of Cognition[1].

11. The unity which connects the individuals is not anything outside them, for it has no reality distinct from them. The unity has, therefore, to be somehow *in* the individuals[2] which it unites. Now in what sense can the unity be *in* the individuals ?

It is clear, in the first place, that it is not in each of them taken separately. This would be obviously contradictory, since, if the unity was in each of them taken separately, it could not connect one of them with another, and, therefore, would not be a unity at all.

12. The common-sense solution of the question would seem to be that the unity is not in each of them when taken separately, but that it is in all of them when taken together. But if we attempt to escape in this way, we fall into a fatal difficulty. That things can be taken together implies that they can be distinguished. For, if there were no means of distinguishing them, they would not be an aggregate at all, but a mere undifferentiated unity. Now a unity which is only in the aggregate cannot be the means of distinguishing the individuals, which make up that aggregate, from one another. For such a unity has only to do with the individuals in so far as they are one. It has no relation with the qualities which make them many. But, by the definition of the category, the whole nature of the individuals lies in their being parts of that unity. Consequently, if the unity does not distinguish them, they will not be distinguished at all, and therefore will not exist as an aggregate.

In the case of less perfect unities there would be no difficulty in saying that they resided in the aggregate of the individuals, and not in the individuals taken separately. A regiment, for example, is not a reality apart from the soldiers,

---

[1] Sections 11—19 are taken, with some omissions, from a paper on Hegel's Treatment of the Categories of the Idea, published in *Mind*, 1900, p. 145.

[2] I use the word Individual here in the sense given it by Hegel (cp. especially the Subjective Notion). To use it in the popular sense in which it is equivalent to a person would be, of course, to beg the question under discussion.

neither is it anything in each individual soldier, but it is a unity which is found in all of them when taken together. But here the differentiations are not entirely dependent on the unity. Each man would exist, and would be distinguishable from the others, if the regiment had never been formed. In the category of Life, however, no differentiations can exist independently of the unity. And therefore the unity must be found in them, not only in so far as they are not taken as differentiated, but also in respect of all their differentiation. The unity cannot, indeed, as we saw above, be in each individual as a *merely* separated individual. But it must, in some less crude way, be found in *each* of the united individuals, and not merely in the sum of them. For those separate characteristics which differentiate the individuals can have no existence at all, unless the unity is manifested in them.

13. It might be suggested that we could overcome this difficulty by the idea of mutual determination. If each individual is in relation with all the rest, then its character is determined by these relations, that is, by the unity of which the individuals are parts. Thus, it may be said, the unity will be manifested in the separate nature of each individual, since that nature will be what it is by reason of the unity of all the individuals.

But this is only going back to the category of Mechanism, and the same difficulties which compel us to regard that category as inadequate will recur here. Are we to regard the individuals as possessing any element of individuality which is not identical with their unity in the system? To answer this question in the affirmative is impossible. Such an inner reality, different from the external relations of the individual, though affected by them, would take us back to the Doctrine of Essence. And therefore it would be quite incompatible with our present category, which demands, not only that the individuals shall not be independent of their unity, but that they shall have no meaning at all but their unity. And therefore there cannot be any distinct element of individuality[1].

---

[1] It will be seen later that this does not mean that the individuality is subordinated to the unity, but that both moments are completely united in the concrete conception of reality, from which they are both abstractions.

On the other hand, if we answer the question in the negative, our difficulties will be as great. The individuals are now asserted not to possess any elements of individuality, which are not identical with their unity in the system. But this, while it is no doubt the true view, is incompatible with the conception that the unity in question is simply the unity of the mutual determination of the individuals. As we saw when Absolute Mechanism transformed itself into Chemism, "the whole nature of each Object lies in the relation between it and the other Objects. But each of these relations does not belong exclusively, *ex hypothesi*, to the Object, but unites it with the others. The nature of wax consists, for example, partly in the fact that it is melted by fire. But this melting is just as much part of the nature of the fire. The fact is shared between the wax and the fire, and cannot be said to belong to one of them more than the other. It belongs to both of them jointly....... The only subject of which the relation can be predicated will be the system which these two Objects form. The qualities will belong to the system, and it will be the true" individual. "But again, two Objects cannot form a closed system, since all Objects in the universe are in mutual connexion. Our system of two Objects will have relations with others, and will be merged with them, in the same way that the original Objects were merged in it—since the relations, which alone give individuality, are found to be common property, and so merge their terms instead of keeping them distinct. The system, in which all the Objects, and all their relations, are contained, becomes the reality—the only true Object, of which all the relations contained in the system are adjectives. The individual Objects disappear[1]."

This explanation also, therefore, must be rejected. For it destroys the individual in favour of the unity, while our category asserts that the individuality and the unity are equally essential. And such a victory would be fatal to the unity also, since it converts it into a mere undifferentiated blank, and therefore into a nonentity.

The impossibility of taking the connection required by the

[1] *Mind*, 1899, p. 47.

category of Life to be the mutual determination of individuals comes, it will be seen, from the intensity of the unity in that category. Any individuality not identical with the unity is incompatible with it. And in mutual determination the individuality is not identical with the unity. Each individual has qualities which are not part of its relations to others, and which are therefore not the unity between them. (From one point of view it may be said that this ceases to be true when mutual determination becomes perfect. But then it ceases to be mutual determination, and we return once more to the difficulties, quoted above, of Chemism.)

14. We are forced back to the conclusion that it is necessary that in some way or another the whole of the unity shall be in each individual, and that in no other way can the individuals have the requisite reality. Yet, as we saw above, to suppose that the unity exists in the individuals *as isolated*, is to destroy the unity. The unity must be completely in each individual. Yet it must also be the bond which unites them. How is this to be? How is it possible that the whole can be in each of its parts, and yet be the whole of which they are parts?

The solution can only be found by the introduction of a new and higher idea. The conception which, according to Hegel, will overcome the difficulties of the category of Life, is that of a unity which is not only *in* the individuals, but also *for* the individuals. (I am here using "in" and "for" rather in their customary English meanings than as the equivalents of Hegel's technical terms "an" and "für.") There is only one example of such a category known to us in experience, and that is a system of conscious individuals.

Accordingly Hegel calls his next category, to which the transition from Life takes us, Cognition (Erkennen). This does not seem a very fortunate name. For the category is subdivided into Cognition Proper and Volition, and Cognition is scarcely a word of sufficient generality to cover Volition as a sub-species. If the category was to be named from its concrete example at all, perhaps Consciousness might have been more suitable.

15. If we take all reality, for the sake of convenience, as limited to three individuals, *A*, *B*, and *C*, and suppose them to be conscious, then the whole will be reproduced in each of them. *A*, for example, will, as conscious, be aware of himself, of *B*, and of *C*, and of the unity which joins them in a system. And thus the unity is within each individual.

At the same time the unity is not in the individuals as isolated. For the whole point of saying that the unity is *for A*, is that it exists both out of him and in him. To recur to our example, the essence of consciousness is that the contents of consciousness purport to be a representation of something else than itself. (In the case of error, indeed, the contents of consciousness have no external counterpart. But then it is only in so far as consciousness is not erroneous that it is an example of this category.)

Thus the unity is at once the whole of which the individuals are parts, and also completely present in each individual. Of course it is not in the individuals in the same manner as the individuals are in it. But this is not to be expected. The dialectic cannot prove that contraries are not incompatible, and, if it did, it would destroy all thought. Its work is to remove contradictions, and it succeeds in this when it meets the demand that the unity shall be in the individuals, and the individuals in the unity, by showing that both are true, though in different ways.

The unity is now, as it is required by the category to be, the whole nature of each individual. In so far as we regard the individual as merely cognitive, and in so far as his cognition is perfect (and both these conditions would be realised when we were judging him under the category of Cognition), his whole nature would consist in the conscious reproduction of the system of which he is a part. This does not involve the adoption of the view that the mind is a *tabula rasa*, and that it only receives passively impressions from outside. However the cognition may be produced, and however active the part which the mind itself may take in its production, the fact remains that the cognition, when produced, and in so far as perfect, is nothing but a representation of reality outside the knowing self.

16. We must, of course, remember with Cognition, as with Mechanism, Chemism, and Life, that the dialectic does not profess to deduce all the empirical characteristics of the concrete state whose name is given to the category, but merely to deduce that pure idea which is most characteristic of that particular state. But the case of Cognition has a special feature. We can recall and imagine instances of the categories of Mechanism and Life outside the spheres of Mechanics and Biology, and this helps us to realise the difference between the concrete state and the category which Hegel calls after it. But of the category of Cognition there is no example known to us, and, as far as I can see, no example imaginable by us, except the concrete state of cognition. We cannot, I think, conceive any way in which such a unity should be for each of the individuals who compose it, except by the individuals being conscious. This introduces a danger which does not exist in so great a degree with the other categories of Mechanism, Chemism, and Life—namely, that we should suppose that we have demonstrated more of the characteristics of cognition by pure thought than in fact we have demonstrated. And great care will be needed, therefore, when we come to apply the conclusions gained in this part of the dialectic to cosmological problems.

17. The pure idea of Cognition, to which the process of the dialectic has now conducted us, is free from any empirical element either in its nature or its demonstration. It is true that it is suggested to us by the fact that there is part of our experience—the existence of our own consciousness—in which the category comes prominently forward. It is possible that we might never have thought of such a category at all, if we had not had such an example of it so clearly offered us. But this does not affect the validity of the transition as an act of pure thought. The manner in which the solution of a problem has been suggested is immaterial, if, when it has been suggested, it can be demonstrated.

Is the transition from Life to Cognition validly demonstrated? It will have been noticed, no doubt, that, though these two categories form the Thesis and Antithesis of a triad, the passage from one to the other resembles closely the transition to a Synthesis. Certain difficulties and contradictions arise in the category of Life, which forbid us to consider it as ultimately valid, and the claim of the category of Cognition to validity lies in the fact that it can transcend and remove these contradictions. But this gradual subordination of the triadic form to a more direct movement is a characteristic to be found throughout the Logic, and one which by no means impairs its validity[1]

The transition must therefore be judged as a transition to a Synthesis. Now the evidence for such a transition is always in some degree negative only. We have reached a category to which the dialectic inevitably leads us, and which we cannot therefore give up, but which presents a contradiction, and which we cannot therefore accept as it stands. The contradiction must be removed. Now the necessity of the proposed Synthesis lies in the fact that it can do this, and that no other idea can, so that our choice lies between accepting the Synthesis in question and asserting a contradiction. So far, therefore, the proof of the validity of the Synthesis is in a sense incomplete. For it is never possible to prove that no other idea could be proposed which could remove the contradiction. All that can be done is to consider any particular idea which may be put forward for that purpose.

So, in this case, our justification in asserting the claim of Cognition to be a category of the Logic lies in the belief that no other solution can be found for the difficulties of the category of Life. But, until some other solution *has* been found, or at least suggested, it would be futile to doubt the validity of the transition because of such a bare possibility. It is abstractly possible that there is some simple logical fallacy in the fifth proposition of Euclid, which has escaped the notice of every person who has ever read it, but will be found out to-morrow. But possibilities of this sort are meaningless[2].

We must remember, too, that any idea which involves any of the previous categories of the Logic, except in a transcended

---

[1] I have endeavoured to prove this in *Studies in the Hegelian Dialectic*, Chap. IV.

[2] Cp. Mr Bradley's *Logic*, Book I. Chap. VII.

form, can be pronounced beforehand inadequate to solve the problems offered by the category of Life, by which all such categories have themselves been transcended. And this confines the field, in which an alternative solution could appear, to very narrow limits.

18. We may sum up the argument as follows, putting it into concrete terms, and ignoring, for the sake of simplicity of expression, the possibility of the category of Cognition having other examples than consciousness—examples at present unknown and unimagined by us. The Absolute must be differentiated into persons, because no other differentiations have vitality to stand against a perfect unity, and because a unity which was undifferentiated would not exist.

Any philosophical system which rejected this view would have to adopt one of three alternatives. It might regard reality as ultimately consisting partly of spirit and partly of matter. It might take a materialistic position, and regard matter as the only reality. Or, holding that spirit was the only reality, it might deny that spirit was necessarily and entirely differentiated into persons. Of each of these positions it might, I believe, be shown that it could be forced into one of two untenable extremes. It might not be in earnest with the differentiation of the unity. In that case it could be driven into an Oriental pantheism, referring everything to an undifferentiated unity, which would neither account for experience nor have any meaning in itself. Or else—and this is the most probable alternative at the present time—it might preserve the differentiation by asserting the existence, in each member of the plurality, of some element which was fundamentally isolated from the rest of experience, and only externally connected with it. In this case it would have fallen back on the categories of Essence, which the dialectic has already shown to be untenable.

19. Lotze, also, holds the view that the differentiations of the Absolute cannot be conceived except as conscious beings. His reason, indeed, for this conclusion, is that only conscious beings could give the necessary combination of unity with change[1]. This argument would not appeal to Hegel. But he

---

[1] *Metaphysic*, Section 96.

also points out[1] that we can attach no meaning to the existence
of anything as apart from the existence of God, unless we
conceive that thing to be a conscious being. Here, it seems to
me, we have the idea that consciousness is the only differentiation which is able to resist the force of the unity of the
Absolute. Lotze, however, destroys the Hegelian character of
his position (and, incidentally, contradicts the fundamental
doctrines of his own Metaphysic) by treating the individuality of
the conscious beings as something which tends to separate them
from God, instead of as the expression of their unity with him.

20. The subdivisions of the category of Cognition do not
concern us here. The transition from Cognition to the Absolute
Idea itself is simple. In Cognition we had a harmony—a
harmony of each part with the whole, since the nature of each part
is to reproduce the nature of the whole. Now harmonies are
of two different kinds. One side may be dependent on the
other, so that the harmony is secured by the determining side
always being in conformity with the determining side. Or,
again, neither side may be dependent on the other, and the
harmony may be due to the fact that it is the essential nature
of each to be in harmony with the other, so that neither of
them needs any determination from without to prevent its
divergence.

The harmony which we have found to be the nature of
reality must be of the latter kind. The nature of the whole is
not determined by the nature of the individuals, nor the nature
of the individuals by the nature of the whole. For if either of
these suppositions were true then the determining side—whether
the whole or the individuals—would be logically prior to the
other. If, however, the whole was logically prior to the
individuals, we should be back in the category of Chemism.
And if the individuals were logically prior to the whole, we
should be back in the category of Mechanism. Both of these
categories have been transcended as inadequate. In the category
of Life we saw that the two sides implied one another on a
footing of perfect equality. The plurality has no meaning

[1] *Metaphysic*, Section 98. *Microcosmus*, Book ix. Chap. iii (iii. 533
trans. ii. 644).

except to express the unity, and the unity has no meaning except to unify the plurality. The passage from Life into Cognition contained nothing which could destroy this equality of the two sides, which, therefore, we must still regard as true. And thus we must consider the harmony produced in Cognition to be one in which the two sides are harmonious, not by the action of one or the other, but by the inherent nature of both. Knowledge and will cease therefore to be adequate examples. For harmony is secured in knowledge when the content of the individual is in accordance with the content of the whole. And the harmony of will is produced when the content of the whole harmonises with that of the individual. But here the subordination of one side to the other must disappear.

21. This brings us to the Absolute Idea. And the meaning of that idea may now be seen in greater fulness than in Hegel's own definition. Reality is a differentiated unity, in which the unity has no meaning but the differentiations, and the differentiations have no meaning but the unity. The differentiations are individuals for each of whom the unity exists, and whose whole nature consists in the fact that the unity is for them, as the whole nature of the unity consists in the fact that it is for the individuals. And, finally, in this harmony between the unity and the individuals neither side is subordinated to the other, but the harmony is an immediate and ultimate fact.

It will be noticed that there is nothing in the transition to the Absolute Idea which can affect our previous conclusion that reality must be a differentiated unity, and that the unity must be for each of the individuals who form the differentiations. The transition has only further determined our view of the nature of the relation between the individuals and the whole. It still remains true that it is that particular relation of which the only example known to us is consciousness.

This is as far as pure thought can take us. We have now to consider the application of this result to the question of the immortality of the selves which are known to each of us, in himself and others.

22. Taken by itself, our conclusion as to the nature of Absolute Reality may be said to give some probability to the

proposition that our selves are some of the fundamental differentiations of the reality. For we have learned that those fundamental differentiations must be of a certain nature. We know nothing which possesses that nature except our selves, and we cannot even imagine anything else to possess it except other selves.

That this gives a certain presumption in favour of the fundamental nature of óur selves cannot, I think, be fairly denied. For the only way of avoiding such a conclusion would be either to suppose that selves like our own were fundamental, while our own were not, or else to take refuge in the possibility of the existence of other ways in which the whole might be for the part—ways at present unimaginable by us. And neither of these seems a very probable hypothesis.

But, after all, they are both possible. It is possible that the fundamental differentiations may be some unimaginable things other than selves, or that they may be selves other than our own. In that case our selves would be degraded to an inferior position. They would have some reality, but they would not be real as selves, or, in other words, to call them our selves would be an inadequate expression of that reality. The case would only differ in degree, from that, for example, of a billiard-ball. There is some reality, of course, corresponding to a billiard-ball. But when we look on it as material, and bring it under those categories, and those only, which are compatible with the notion of matter, we are looking at it in an inadequate way. It is not utterly and completely wrong, but it is only a relative truth. It is possible that this is the case with our selves. The view of the universe which accepts the reality of me and you may be one which has only relative truth, and practical utility in certain circumstances. The full truth about the reality which I call me and you may be that it is not me and you, just as the full truth about what we call a billiard-ball would be that it was not a piece of matter.

23. We must look for a more positive argument. We have shown so far, if we have been successful, that our selves have certain characteristics which they would have if they were some of the fundamental differentiations of reality. What is now

required is to show, if possible, that our selves have characteristics which they could *not* have, *unless* they were some of
the fundamental differentiations of reality. And something, I
think, can be said in support of this view.

24. One of the most marked characteristics of our selves is
that they are finite, in the ordinary sense of the word. There
are few things which appear so certain to the plain man as the
fact that he is not the only reality in the universe. Yet when
I enquire as to the division which exists between myself and
any other reality, I find it quite impossible to draw the line. If
I am to distinguish myself from any other reality, then, obviously,
I must be conscious of this other reality. But how can I be
conscious of it without it being in me? If the objects of consciousness were outside me, they would make no difference to
my internal state, and, therefore, I should not be conscious of
them. And, also, if they were outside me, I should not exist.
For the pure I, though doubtless an essential moment of the
self, is only a moment, and cannot stand alone. If we withdraw
from it all its content—the objects of cognition and volition—
it would be a mere abstract nonentity.

25. The common-sense solution of the difficulty is that the
objects which exist outside me, and not in me, produce images
which are in me and not outside me, and that it is these images
which I know. But this theory breaks down. No one, of
course, would assert that something I knew—my friend, for
instance—existed in my mind in the same way that he existed
for himself. But it is equally untenable to assert that he exists
exclusively outside me, and that I only know an image of him
which exists exclusively in me. For then I should only know
the image—not him at all—and therefore should not know it
to be an image, since nothing can be known to be a copy unless
we are aware of the existence of its archetype. Now we are
aware of the existence of images in our minds; we recognize
them as such; we distinguish them from the reality that they
represent; and we make judgments about the latter. I say
that I have an image of my friend in my mind, and also
that he really exists. The subject of this second assertion is
clearly not an image in my mind. For the second assertion is

additional to, and contrasted with, a statement about such an image. It can only be taken as a statement about my friend himself. Let us assume it to be true (as some such statements must be, except on the hypothesis of Solipsism). Then its truth shows that my friend exists, and not merely as my mental state, that is, that he exists outside me. And yet he is an object of my consciousness. And how can he be that, unless he is also inside me ?

Thus the theory that we only know images refutes itself, for, if it were so, we should never know them to be images. It is possible—the question does not concern us here—that we only know reality other than ourselves through inferences based on images which are simply in our minds. But that we do know something more than images is proved by the fact that we know images to be such. And this something more must be outside us to make our knowledge true, and inside us to make our knowledge possible.

26. Again, while the self can never say of any reality that it is only outside it, it is equally impossible for it to say of any reality that it is only inside it. By the very fact of saying " I know it," I make a distinction between the I who know, and the thing which is known. The only reality of which it could be asserted that it was not separated from the self by the self's consciousness of it is the pure I. And this is a mere abstraction. Without it the self would not exist. But taken by itself it is nothing.

This discrimination of the self from the object of knowledge increases with the increase of knowledge. In proportion as I know a thing more completely, I may, from one point of view, be said to have it more completely in myself. But it is equally true to say that, as I more thoroughly understand its nature, it takes more and more the form of a completely and clearly defined object, and, in proportion as it does this, becomes more emphatically not myself. The same course may be traced with will and emotion. My will can only find satisfaction in anything in proportion as it appears a distinct, though harmonious, reality. If it should become something which I could not distinguish from myself, the sense of satisfaction would vanish into a mere

emptiness. And, in the same way, while nothing draws us so
close to others as intense emotion, nothing enables us to
appreciate more clearly the fact that those others exist in their
own right, and not merely as phenomena subordinate to our own
reality.

27. Thus the nature of the self is sufficiently paradoxical.
What does it include? Everything of which it is conscious.
What does it exclude? Equally—everything of which it is
conscious. What can it say is not inside it? Nothing. What
can it say is not outside it? A single abstraction. And any
attempt to remove the paradox destroys the self. For the two
sides are inevitably connected. If we try to make it a distinct
individual by separating it from all other things, it loses all
content of which it can be conscious, and so loses the very
individuality which we started by trying to preserve. If, on
the other hand, we try to save its content by emphasising the
inclusion at the expense of the exclusion, then the consciousness
vanishes, and, since the self has no contents but the objects of
which it is conscious, the content vanishes also. Locke tried the
first alternative, and left the fact that we know anything
inexplicable. Green, on the other hand, came very near to the
second alternative, and approached proportionally nearly to the
absurdity of asserting knowledge without a knowing subject.

28. The idea of the self need not be false because it is
paradoxical. Hegel has taught us that the contradictions
which the abstract understanding finds in an idea may be due
to the idea being too concrete, that is, too true, to be adequately
measured by the abstract terms of merely formal thought. But
a contradiction is very far from being a sign of truth. On the
contrary, as Hegel fully recognized, an unreconciled contradiction is a sign of error. The abstract understanding would
pronounce the category of Life and the idea of a four-sided
triangle to be equally contradictory. Hegel would agree with
the non-speculative understanding in taking this as a sign of
error in the idea of the triangle. But of the category he
would say that the contradiction only showed it to be too deep
and true for the abstract understanding to comprehend.

How is the distinction to be explained? The explanation

is that no idea which is contradictory, according to the canons
of the understanding, is to be accepted as true unless the idea
can be deduced in such a way as to explain and justify the
contradiction. It is in this manner that we gain the right to
believe in the successive Syntheses of the dialectic, each of
which is contradictory to the abstract understanding, since
each of them unites two contradictory extremes—a union which
the understanding declares to be contradictory. The dialectic
starts from a beginning, the validity of which the understanding
cannot deny. From this it is led into a contradiction, when it
is seen that the truth of this first Thesis involves the truth
of the contradictory Antithesis. From this it proceeds to a
Synthesis, which unites and reconciles the two sides. This
reconciliation is a paradox and a contradiction to the non-
speculative understanding, because it unites contradictions.
But the understanding has lost its right to be regarded in this
matter. For the course of the triad has shown that if we trust
to the understanding alone we shall be left with an *unreconciled*
contradiction—since we shall have to acknowledge the truth
both of the Thesis and the Antithesis, and they contradict each
other. The Synthesis is the only way out of the unreconciled
contradiction to which the course of thought inevitably leads us,
and if we adhered to the canons of the non-speculative understanding, which would reject the Synthesis, our result would
not be less contradictory from the standpoint of those canons,
while we should have lost the reconciliation of the contradiction
which a higher standpoint gives us. The understanding has
no right to reject the solution when it cannot escape the
difficulty.

But with the four-sided triangle the case is very different.
There is no course of reasoning which leads us up to the
conclusion that four-sided triangles must exist, and therefore we
take the contradictory nature of the idea as a proof, not of the
inadequacy of the understanding to judge of the matter, but of
the falseness of the idea.

The idea of the self is paradoxical—contradictory for the
understanding. Then we have two alternatives. We may
treat it like the idea of the four-sided triangle, and consider it

as completely erroneous, and to be got rid of as soon as possible. Or else we shall have to justify it by showing that the necessary course of thought leads us to it, that it is the only escape from an unreconciled contradiction, and that it must therefore be considered as too deep a truth to be judged by the understanding. Whether it is to be taken as a relative or as the absolute truth would depend on whether it did or did not develop contradictions which, in their turn, needed transcending by a fresh idea.

29. To dismiss the idea of self as completely erroneous— as a pure and simple mistake—would be the course which Hume would take. Such a course would necessarily conduct us to a scepticism like his. It would be too great a digression to recapitulate here the arguments to prove that such a scepticism is untenable, and that the idea of the self cannot be summarily rejected in this way. Nor is it necessary to do so. For we are now endeavouring to determine what must be thought of the self on Hegelian principles, and it is certain that, on those principles, or on those of any idealistic system, it would be impossible to treat the idea of the self as a mere delusion, even if it is not considered as an adequate expression of reality.

30. The only remaining course is to justify the idea of the self by showing that the characteristics by which it offends the laws of the abstract understanding are the result of the inevitable nature of thought, and are therefore marks, not of the error of the idea, but of the inadequacy of the laws. If we take the selves to be the fundamental differentiations of reality, which the dialectic, as we saw, requires, we have obtained the necessary explanation. For each of those differentiations was shown to contain in itself the content of the whole, though, of course, not in the same way that the whole itself contains it. Thus if we ask what is contained in each individual differentiation, the answer is Everything. But if we ask what is contained in each differentiation in such a way as not to be also outside it, the answer is Nothing. Now this is exactly the form that the paradox of the self would take, if we suppose a self whose knowledge and volition were perfect, so that it knew and acquiesced in the whole of reality. (I shall consider later on the objection that the knowledge and volition of the actual selves which we know are by no means so perfect.)

And thus the paradox of the self would be justified. But how is it to be justified on any other view? If we are to take the idea of the self, not as a mere error, yet as less than absolute truth, we must find some justification of it which will show that the necessary course of thought leads up to it, and also over it—that it is relatively true as transcending contradictions which would otherwise be unreconciled, but relatively false as itself developing fresh contradictions which must again be transcended. Can such a deduction be found? We cannot say with certainty that it never will be, but at any rate it does not seem to have been suggested yet. Most attempts to deal with the self endeavour to get rid of the paradox by denying one side or the other—either denying that the self includes anything which is external to it, or denying that it excludes what it includes. Mr Bradley, who fully recognizes the paradox, and does not admit the absolute validity of the idea, gives no explanation which will enable us to see why the idea is to be accepted as having even relative truth.

To sum up—the self answers to the description of the fundamental differentiations of the Absolute. Nothing else which we know or can imagine does so. The idea of the self has certain characteristics which can be explained if the self is taken as one of the fundamental differentiations, but of which no explanation has been offered on any other theory, except that of rejecting the idea of the self altogether, and sinking into complete scepticism. The self is so paradoxical that we can find no explanation for it, except its absolute reality.

31. We now pass on to the second branch of the subject. If we are to accept the selves that we know as some of the fundamental differentiations of the Absolute, does this involve that the selves are eternal? The Absolute, no doubt, is eternal, and must be eternally differentiated. But is it possible that

it should be differentiated by means of an unending succession
of individuals, each of whom has only a limited existence in
time? There are, I think, two objections to the possibility
of this. In the first place it does not seem possible that the
differentiations in question should change at all, and, secondly,
if they did change, it would still be impossible that any of them
should cease completely, and be succeeded by others.

32. Can we then conceive the selves—which we have now
identified with the fundamental differentiations—as changing
at all? The content of each, we learn from the dialectic, is
simply a reproduction of the content of the whole[1]. It will,
therefore, be impossible for any individual self to suffer any
change, unless the Absolute itself likewise changes.

Can the Absolute change as a whole? The Absolute, as
I have pointed out elsewhere[2], must be considered as having
two moments in it. One of these is pure thought, the nature
of which is determined in the dialectic process, and described
in the Absolute Idea. The other is the unnameable but equally
real element, which is the immediate which thought mediates,
the existence of which makes the difference between the still
partially abstract Absolute Idea and the completely concrete
Absolute Spirit.

33. Now, of these two elements, the element of pure
thought cannot possibly change. If the dialectic has proved
anything, it has proved that nothing can be an adequate
description of reality but the Absolute Idea. But if the
element of pure thought in reality should change, then something more, or less, or at any rate different from the Absolute
Idea would be, at one time, an adequate description of reality.
This would destroy the whole of Hegel's Logic. The dialectic
process from category to category is not one which takes place,
or is reflected, in time. For the point of each transition to
a Synthesis, the only thing which makes the transition valid

---

[1] The word reproduction seems the best we can employ, but it is rather
misleading, as it may be taken to imply that the whole is active in this
harmony, and the individual passive. This, as we saw from the transition
to the Absolute Idea, is not the case.

[2] *Studies in the Hegelian Dialectic*, Sections 14, 15.

at all, is the demonstration that, as against the Thesis and Antithesis, the Synthesis is the only reality, and that these terms, in so far as they differ from the Synthesis, are unreal and erroneous. Thus to suppose that the dialectic process advanced in time would be to suppose that at one time—indeed till the end of the process was reached—the unreal existed, and gradually produced the real, which would be obviously absurd[1].

The element of pure thought in absolute reality, then, cannot change. But would it not be possible that absolute reality should change in respect of the other element? All that the dialectic tells us about this is that it must be such as to be mediated by the element of pure thought, and to embody it. May not several different states of this element answer to this description, and in this case would not a change in absolute reality be possible, in so far as the element of immediacy passed from one of these stages to the other?

We must however remember how completely and closely the two elements are connected. They are not two separate things, out of which absolute reality is built, but two aspects which can be distinguished in absolute reality. And while, on the one side, pure thought has no existence except in so far as it is embodied in the element of immediacy, on the other side the element of immediacy has no existence, except in so far as it embodies pure thought. It is not like the material with which an artist works, which, while it embodies an artistic idea, has yet an independent existence, with various qualities irrelevant to the idea embodied. A block of marble has a certain commercial value, a certain legal ownership, a certain temperature, a certain history. But all these qualities might vary, without making it less fit to express the sculptor's purpose. The element of immediacy, on the other hand, only exists in so far as it embodies the element of pure thought.

Now if this element were to change—say from XY to XZ—while the element of pure thought, of course, remained the same, it would mean that the difference between XY and XZ was

---

[1] *Studies in the Hegelian Dialectic*, Section 147.

immaterial to the embodiment of pure thought, since the unchanged pure thought would be equally embodied in both of them. And this would be contrary to what we had previously determined—that the element of immediacy had reality only in so far as it embodied the pure thought. Of course, in ordinary life we often see a thing change its qualities, and yet, by means of those very changing qualities themselves, continue to embody some purpose or meaning. But in all these cases, we have to conclude that the difference between those changing qualities is irrelevant to what is manifested. And here we have a union between the two sides which is so close that we are forbidden to think anything in the one irrelevant to its relation to the other. The conclusion would seem to be that the element of immediacy can change no more than the element of pure thought, and that therefore absolute reality as a whole must be regarded as unchanging.

Another difficulty is that if we conceive change without causation we reduce the universe to chaos—which is certainly not compatible with the Absolute Idea. But, if change is to be determined, it must be either from without or from within. Now there is nothing outside the whole of reality to determine it to change. But we know by the Absolute Idea that all reality must be conceived as absolutely harmonious. In that case, can there be a cause inside it to determine it to move to another state, even if another could be found which was equally harmonious?

34. But even if it were possible for the selves to change, would it be possible for any of them to perish? It is not sufficient that the unity should be, in a general way, differentiated into *some* selves. The nature of the unity consists simply in its differentiation into the parts which compose it, and, as it has a definite nature, that nature must determine the precise nature of the individuals. Or, to put it the other way round, the nature of the individuals is simply to embody the unity. And, therefore, if the nature of the unity did not determine the precise nature of the individuals, the nature of the individuals would not be determined at all, and the individuals would not exist.

Each individual, then, has its definite nature, by means of which it manifests the unity. If one perished, then another must take its place. Now can we conceive, even if we allow the possibility of change, that one self could in this way take the place of another? For, although they might resemble one another in certain ways, still, by the hypothesis, they are different individuals. They differ then in respect of their individuality. And here there is a complete break between the two. For, if there was not, there would not be the death of one individual, and the creation of another. Such a breach in the continuity of the manifestation must imply a similar breach in the continuity of what is manifested. Now this reduces the supposition to an absurdity. For, supposing the Absolute to be able to change at all, it must at any rate change continuously. If there was a breach in the continuity of the Absolute, it would have to be an absolutely complete one—for there is nothing behind the Absolute to bridge over the separation. Reality would be divided into two unconnected parts—which is impossible, since they would not then both be reality. And this necessary continuity in the Absolute, involving a similar continuity in the manifestation, will, therefore, forbid us to suppose that any of the selves who form that manifestation can ever perish.

35. It may be objected to this that a breach of continuity in the manifestation need not mean a breach of continuity in what is manifested. One king dies, and another succeeds him. Here then is a break between the one person and the other, but the same sovereignty passes from one to the other without a break. But in such a case as this the transfusion of manifested and manifestation is not complete. A man is a king only in respect of certain aspects of his nature. And these he may have in common with his successor, although they are· different people. But the selves have no existence except in so far as they manifest the unity of the Absolute. All their characteristics do this, and therefore there can be no breach in the continuity of any of the characteristics without a breach in the continuity of what is manifested. On the other hand, to suppose that one self could succeed another without a breach in the continuity of characteristics, would be to reduce the self to a mere *Ding an sich*, which would be entirely incompatible with what we have already determined about it.

Of course this line of argument would not hold with such a view of the Absolute as Lotze's. For there the Absolute is to be taken as something more and deeper than the unity of its differentiations, so that, while there is nothing in them which is not in it, there is something in it which is not in them. In that case a breach in the unity of the differentiations would not necessarily imply a breach in the unity of the Absolute, because the unity might be preserved by that part of the Absolute which lay behind the differentiations. But then this is not Hegel's view. He reaches in the category of Life a result from which he never departs in the subsequent categories—that the unity and plurality are in an absolutely reciprocal relation, so that, while the plurality is nothing but the differentiation of the unity, the unity is nothing but the union of the plurality.

In many cases in ordinary life we find that, although a sudden and simultaneous change of *all* the parts of the whole would destroy its continuity, yet, if they change successively, they may all have their continuity broken without the continuity of the whole suffering. But these are cases in which every part is not necessary to manifest the whole, but it is possible for the manifestation to vary within certain limits. A regiment, for example, cannot exist without soldiers. But each soldier does not fulfil a definite and unique function without which the regiment would cease to be a regiment. Thus the breach of continuity between any one soldier and his successor does not mean a breach in the continuity of the regiment because the other soldiers, who are not discharged at the same moment, are sufficient to keep up the continuity. But with the differentiations of the Absolute it is different. For it is the nature of the Absolute to be manifested in precisely those differentiations in which it is manifested, and so a breach in the continuity anywhere could not be compensated for by unbroken continuity elsewhere. The Absolute requires each self, not to make up a sum, or to maintain an average, but in respect of the self's special and unique nature.

36. Up to a certain point indeed, it is a mark of relatively high reality when anything can change, and yet remain the same. In the lowest categories of all—those of Quality—there is no such thing as change possible. For, so long as we confine ourselves to them, a thing must either remain exactly the same, or cease to exist. The moment the slightest variation is introduced, the previously existing thing is destroyed, and a quite fresh thing substituted in its place. For reality is not yet separated into moments in such a way that one varies while the other remains the same, and till then we can have no change, but only the substitution of one reality for another. The first possibility of true change comes in with the categories of Quantity. And that possibility develops as we reach the categories of Essence, while it is greatest, perhaps, in the category of Matter and Form.

But, although the dialectic starts below the possibility of change, it reaches, towards the end, a point above that possibility. Change only became possible when the first anticipations of Essence intruded themselves into Being. It ceases to be possible as the last traces of Essence die out of the Notion. For change, as has been said, we require to look at the reality as consisting of moments, of which one may change without affecting the other. Now this independence of the two sides is the mark of Essence. When we reach the final subdivision of Teleology, we have at last left this fully behind. This we saw at the beginning of this chapter, while defining the category of Life, which has the same content as the last form of Teleology. The unity has no meaning except its expression in the plurality, the plurality has no meaning except its combination in the unity. The independence of the two sides has gone, and with it the possibility of change.

If we consider what are the cases in which we can say that a thing changes and yet remains the same, we shall find that we regard them all from the point of view of Essence. Either the manifestation, or what is manifested, or both of them, must be taken as having something in it which is not concerned with the relation between the two sides, and which can consequently change while the other side is constant, or be constant while

the other side changes. In the instance which we considered
above, when the sovereignty passes unchanged through different
kings, the kings were conceived as having characteristics other
than their royalty, so that the men were different, while
manifesting themselves in the same sovereignty. In technically
Hegelian language, this is a case of Essence as Appearance,
since we disregard the change in what is manifested, and only
regard the manifestation, which does not change. On the other
hand, when we say that a man is the same man as he was
yesterday, though he may be thinking quite different thoughts,
and doing quite different things, we are at the stand-point of
Essence as Ground. For here our answer depends on the unchanged state of what is manifested, and the change in the
manifestation is disregarded. Both alike are cases of Essence,
and both therefore are inapplicable to our present subject-
matter.

37. The view that selves are manifestations of the Absolute,
in such a way that they change and perish while the Absolute
remains unchanged, is one which has always had an attraction
for mystics. It is especially prominent among Oriental thinkers.
The most frequent metaphors by which this thought is expressed
are those of a drop of water returning to the ocean, and of
a ray of light returning to the sun. They show that the
relation which was conceived to exist between the Absolute
and the self was substantially that of Matter and Form. The
Absolute was formless—or relatively formless—itself, but a part
of it assumed form and limitation and became a self. At death,
or in the mystic vision of true wisdom, the form disappeared,
and the matter dropped back into the undifferentiated mass of
the Absolute. Such a view involves the indifference of the
Absolute to the form it assumes. For all the changes in the
forms do not affect the changelessness of the Absolute.

It is unnecessary to repeat here Hegel's demonstration of
the inadequacy of Matter and Form, since it is quite clear that
such a category could never apply to the selves which we are
now considering. These selves we have determined as the
fundamental differentiations of the Absolute, and we know that
the Absolute is not indifferent to the nature of these differen-

tiations—on the contrary, that its whole nature consists in manifesting itself in just these differentiations.

Such a view moreover is incompatible with what we know of the self by observation. For it would compel us to regard each self as the form of a certain amount of matter[1], which would continue to exist when the form was destroyed, and the self, as a self, had ceased to exist. This conception, as applied to the self, seems to be meaningless. The self, no doubt, can be differentiated into parts. But they are parts of such a nature that they would cease to exist when the self ceased to exist. To regard the self as built up of parts, which could exist after it, and be recombined like the bricks from a house which has been pulled down, is to render it impossible to explain consciousness.

38. It may be objected to the preceding arguments that in order to identify the selves which we know with the fundamental differentiations of the Absolute, we have given to them a perfection which those selves notoriously do not possess, and so reduced our arguments to an absurdity. We have proved that they must be changeless, while in point of fact they do continually change. We have identified their consciousness with the manner in which the whole exists for each of the fundamental differentiations. But, if this is so, it would seem to follow that every self must be in complete and conscious harmony with the whole of the universe. This is not in accordance with facts. Our knowledge is limited, it is often erroneous, and when we do know facts, our desires are often not in harmony with the facts which we know.

39. The difficulty is no doubt serious enough. But it is not, I think, any objection to our interpretation of Hegel, because it is a difficulty which applies equally to all idealistic theories, however interpreted. It is nothing less than the old difficulty of the origin of evil. And for this, as I have tried to show elsewhere[2], idealism has no definite solution. All that can be done is to show that the difficulties are as serious if we

---

[1] Matter is, of course, used here as the contrary of Form, not of Spirit.

[2] Cp. *Studies in the Hegelian Dialectic*, Chap. v.

deny reality to be perfect, as they are if we affirm it, and to point out a direction in which it is not altogether unreasonable to hope for the advent of some solution at present unimaginable by us. This is certainly not much, but it does not seem that we are entitled at present to any more.

The Absolute, according to Hegel, is timeless and perfect. In this conclusion most idealistic systems would agree. We find around us and in us, however, a world which changes in time, and which is far from perfect. Yet the Absolute is the only reality of this world. How, then, are we to account for the change and the imperfection? It is in this form that the problem of evil presents itself to idealism.

If we take the selves to be the fundamental differentiations of the Absolute, and therefore timeless and perfect, the question will of course be raised why, in that case, the selves appear as changeable and imperfect. And to this question no answer has been given. But we shall not avoid the difficulty by giving up our theory. For the selves, whether fundamental or not, still exist, and have to be accounted for. The only reality is the Absolute, which is timeless and perfect. The question will now take this form—Why does a timeless and perfect Absolute appear as changeable and imperfect selves? And it is as impossible to return any answer to this question as to the other. The gap between the perfect and imperfect has to come in somewhere. The difficulty is the same whether we place the true nature of the selves on the side of perfection, and find the gulf between that and their appearances, or whether we take the selves as imperfect, and then find the gulf between them and the Absolute.

Since this difficulty, then, applies to any idealist theory, it can be no special reason against ours. And we can therefore rest, as before, on the considerations that the selves, if they perfectly realised the nature which they possess, would correspond to the differentiations of the Absolute, which nothing else that we know or can imagine does, and also, that the selves, in spite of their imperfections, show characteristics which are inexplicable if they are not among those differentiations. And thus our proper conclusion would seem to be that all selves are timeless and perfect, as the Absolute is, but that they, like the Absolute of which they are the differentiations, appear under the forms of time and imperfection.

40. Another difficulty which may be raised is that the activities most prominent in ourselves are knowledge and will. Now neither of these, it may be said, are examples of the Absolute Idea at all, but rather of the previous category which Hegel names Cognition. For in the Absolute Idea the harmony is not produced by the subordination of one side to the other. It is the essential nature of each side to be in such a harmony, and the idea of subordination becomes meaningless. This is not the case with knowledge and will. In knowledge we condemn our thought as false if it does not correspond to the reality outside it, and the harmony is thus produced by the subordination of the individual to the whole. In will, on the other hand, we condemn the reality as unsatisfactory if it does not correspond to our desires, and the harmony is thus produced by the subordination of the whole to the individual.

To this it may be answered, in the first place, that, besides knowledge and will, emotion is also an activity of the self, and that it may be plausibly maintained that in a harmony produced by emotion neither side is subordinated to the other, but the harmony is the essential nature of each. But, besides this, the dialectic demonstrates, by the transition from Cognition to the Absolute Idea, that, if the whole does exist for any individual, it must be by means of that reciprocal and equal harmony which is expressed by the Absolute Idea[1]. We may therefore reasonably infer, since our souls show on observation a harmony under the category of Cognition, that they are really in harmony in the deeper manner characteristic of the Absolute Idea.

41. The results we have reached may throw some light on the difficult question of personal identity. The self is not, as sceptics maintain, a mere delusion. Nor is it a mere collection of adjectives, referring to no substance except the Absolute.

---

[1] Cp. Section 20.

It is, on the contrary, itself a substance, existing in its own right. This does not mean, of course, that any self could exist independently, and in isolation from all others. Each self can only exist in virtue of its connection with all the others, and with the Absolute which is their unity. But this is a relation, not of subordination, but of reciprocal dependence. If each self is dependent on the others, they in turn are dependent on it. If the self has no meaning, except as manifesting the Absolute, the Absolute has no meaning except as manifested in that self. The self is not an isolated substance but it may be properly called a substance.

In the identity of the substance lies, it seems to me, the personal identity. This is a rather unfashionable mode of expression, and it will be necessary to remember that we are speaking of the substance as it really is, and not of any abstraction of substantiality, and, moreover, that we are speaking of the personal identity itself, and not of the signs by which we may infer its existence.

42. It would be absurd to place personal identity in the imaginary identity of substance regardless of any continuity of attributes. The substance taken apart from its attributes could never be the basis of personal identity. For all substances, if abstraction were made of their attributes, are absolutely indistinguishable, and the distinction between persons would be non-existent. And, indeed, we may go further, for a substance without attributes is inconceivable, and if personal identity rested in this it would vanish. But when we talk of an identity of substance we do not mean any such imaginary *Ding an sich.* Substance is nothing apart from its attributes, as the attributes are nothing apart from the substance, and when we place personal identity in the identity of the substance, we speak of a substance manifesting itself in its attributes.

Why, then, emphasise the substance ? The reason for this is as follows—all attributes must be referred to some substance. But, according to some idealistic systems, a self is merely a bundle of attributes, whose substance is the Absolute. The self has no substance of its own, but is merely a phenomenon of the Absolute. On this view the identity of the self could not be an identity of substance, as all selves are attributes of the same substance. We have taken a view which puts the self higher, and makes each self, not an attribute of one sole self-subsistent substance, but itself a self-subsistent substance, though not an isolated one. (True self-subsistence is incompatible with isolation. We can only get self-determination by means of determination by others.) This view is brought out by calling the personal identity an identity of substance.

Since substance and attributes are only two aspects of the same reality, the identical substance will have identical attributes. It might seem at first sight as if identity of attributes was not a condition of personal identity. For the whole question of that identity can only arise when there is change of some sort, and, if a thing changes, how can its attributes be identical? In all the changes, however, which the character of a thing or a person may undergo, there is an aspect which is permanent and unchanging, and it is on that aspect that our attention is fixed when we speak of identity of attributes through change. For example, a man who was honourable in his youth meets with certain temptations, and becomes a scoundrel in old age. From one point of view this is a considerable change in his attributes. But from another they are unchanged. For, while he was still an honourable man, it was part of his character that, under certain circumstances, he would become a scoundrel. And, after that has occurred, it is still part of his character— still a predicate which may be applied to him and may help to describe him—that, before those circumstances occurred, he was an honourable man. It is this identity of attributes which is involved, I think, in personal identity.

There is a very real difference, certainly, between a potential and an actual characteristic, and the permanent element which persists all through change does not explain that change away, or render it less perplexing. But the permanent element does exist, and it is in respect of that element that, in spite of the change, we ascribe personal identity to the changed person. The question presents itself—unfortunately without an answer —how a permanent and changeless character comes to develop itself in time and change. But this is only part of the larger problem—equally insoluble—how change of any sort is possible, when the ultimate reality is a timeless Absolute.

43. This view seems to avoid several difficulties which stand in the way of the theory that personal identity consists in memory. Personal identity, no doubt, is the identity of a conscious being, but it does not at all follow from this that it must be an identity of which the possessor is conscious. Such a theory, to begin with, makes personal identity something which continually fluctuates. I may have completely forgotten some past episode in my life, and then be vividly reminded of it by discovering an old letter. If identity lies simply in memory, we must hold that I had ceased to be identical with the person who had taken part in those events, and that, after I had found the letter, I became identical with him again.

We do not only forget what is insignificant. We often forget events which make a profound difference to the whole of our future lives, because we were too young or too dull to appreciate their significance. And no man could possibly remember all the acts or forbearances, each by itself trifling, which helped to form his character. And yet it was surely he who did them. If the man who instinctively acts unselfishly in an emergency were not the same man whose forgotten choices of unselfishness have determined that instinctive action, would personal identity have any meaning at all?

And if the past cannot form part of our personal identity unless it is remembered, what about a past that is remembered, but has never taken place? George the Fourth said, and apparently in good faith, that he remembered that he had fought at Waterloo. Similar delusions can be produced by hypnotism. The belief in the patient's mind is exactly the same as if it were a case of truthful memory. If, then, it is this belief on which personal identity hangs, it would seem that personal identity must be admitted here. And yet would any one be prepared to say that, if A could be made by hypnotism to "remember" B's past, he would thereupon become identical with B?

Nor does personal identity seem to have much meaning if it loses its connection with the special and unique interest which we feel in our own future as distinguished from that of anyone else. Our interest in the well-being of others may be as real as our interest in our own, it may even be stronger, but it is never the same. Now suppose a man could be assured that in a short time he would lose for ever all memory of the past. Would he consider this to be annihilation, and take no more interest in the person of similar character who would occupy his old body than he would in any stranger? Or would a man approaching the gate of hell lose all selfish regret for his position if he was assured that memory, as well as hope, must be left behind on his entrance? It is not, I think, found that believers in transmigration are indifferent to their fate after their next death. And yet they believe, in the majority of cases, that the next death will, for the time at least, break the chain of memory as completely as the last did.

44. Another theory which has been held on this subject is that personal identity consists simply in continuity of character. We must hold a and β to be successive states of the same person, if the effect of the circumstances in which a occurred would be to change a into β by the time we observe β. This theory is prominent in Buddhist metaphysics. Its practical results are the same as those of the theory I have advocated above—that is, it would affirm and deny personal identity wherever the other theory affirmed or denied it. For identity of substance, we saw, was only the other side of identity of attributes, and identity of attributes must reveal itself in time as an ordered succession of changes, of which each determines the next. So that, admitting that personal identity lay in identity of substance, our way of determining whether two states belonged to the same person would be to endeavour to trace a causal relation between them. The difference between the two theories is one of explanation, not of application. The theory as held by Buddhists is involved in all the difficulties of extreme sensationalism. For it denies the existence of all substance, and makes the self into a bundle of attributes, which are attributes of nothing.

45. In attempting, as I have attempted, to demonstrate the immortality of the self as a consequence of an idealist system, it is impossible to forget that the latest idealist system considers immortality to be improbable. Mr Bradley's authority on this point is very great. He does not call himself a Hegelian. But few professed Hegelians, if any, understand the secret of Hegel's philosophy so well. And few professed Hegelians, I will venture to say, are so thoroughly Hegelian in spirit. His definition of the Absolute, too, has much resemblance to Hegel's. It is therefore of the greatest importance to us that he should have come to a negative decision about immortality[1].

His main reason for doing so is his belief that the idea of the self cannot be considered as an adequate representation of reality. He discusses, from this point of view, several meanings which may be given to the word self[2]. With regard to all of these meanings but one, few people, I think, would disagree with his conclusion that they are too confused and contradictory to be accepted as adequate to reality. But when we come to the self as the subject of knowledge, the reasons given for rejecting it do not seem so satisfactory.

He objects that we cannot find in the self any content which is always subject and never object. Or, if we can, at most it is the pure I, which, taken by itself, is completely trivial, indeed unmeaning, and cannot be accepted as a key to the nature of all reality. Whatever is object, however, is not-self, and thus the self dwindles away on examination. If we take what is pure self only, we have an unmeaning abstraction. If we take in any content, we find that it is—at any rate potentially—not-self[3].

46. All this is doubtless quite true. The only element in self which is self and nothing else is an abstraction, which, taken by itself, is a nonentity. And the self had only reality by including in itself that which is just as much not-self. But it is not clear why this should be considered as affecting the adequacy of the idea of self.

If any person, indeed, were to assert that the self was an adequate representation of reality, and at the same time to

---

[1] *Appearance and Reality*, Chap. xxvi. p. 501. My references are to the edition of 1897.

[2] *op. cit.* Chaps. ix and x.

[3] *op. cit.* Chap. ix. pp. 88—96.

identify the self with the pure I, taken in abstraction from anything else, his position would be absolutely untenable. But the knowing self is not at all identical with the pure I, which, if taken in abstraction, neither knows anything nor is anything. The knowing self is a concrete whole of which the pure I is one abstract element. It is doubtless an indispensable element. It is doubtless meaningless when taken in abstraction. But between these two facts there is no contradiction. Whenever one element of a concrete whole is taken in abstraction the same thing recurs. Taken by itself it is meaningless, for it is only an element, and can only exist in combination with the other element. But it is also essential, for, if it is withdrawn, it leaves nothing but another abstract element, and this by itself would also be meaningless.

The other element, besides the pure I, which is found in the knowing self is the not-self. Why should this not be so? It is doubtless paradoxical in the highest degree, as has been pointed out above. The self can only exist in so far as its content is both in and outside it. By the very act of knowledge it at once accepts the content as part of itself, and repels it as an independent reality. And thus no limits can be put to the self. For if we exclude whatever is not self, the self shrinks to a point, and vanishes altogether. On the other hand, if we include all that is self, it includes all of which we are conscious, and, in the ideal self, would include the whole of reality.

But is there any reason why this should induce Mr Bradley to reject the idea of self as inadequate? His own idea of the Absolute is highly paradoxical, and yet he rightly declines to see in this any objection to its truth[1]. And if the idea of the Absolute is paradoxical, it is surely to be expected that, if we are able to arrive at an adequate idea of the differentiations of the Absolute, that idea will also be paradoxical. If the abstract understanding cannot accept the truth about the unity, is it probable that it will be able to accept the truth about the plurality which adequately expresses

---

[1] Cp. e.g. *op. cit.* Chap. xv. pp. 175—183.

that unity? It would seem that it is rather the absence of paradox than its presence that should be looked upon with suspicion here.

The adequacy of the idea, of course, is not in the least proved by its paradoxical nature. It could only be proved by a detailed deduction from the nature of the Absolute, of the kind which I have attempted above. What I contend here is, that the idea is not proved to be false because it is paradoxical.

47. Treating more directly of immortality, Mr Bradley points out that our desire for immortality affords no reasonable ground for believing in it[1]. This cannot be denied. An idealistic theory of the universe may perhaps justify us in believing that the fundamental nature of spirit will eventually gain its full realisation, and that all desires which really express that fundamental nature will be gratified. But then what human desires *do* really express the fundamental nature of spirit? That could only be settled by an investigation into the nature of reality so thorough that it would probably settle the question of immortality in a less circuitous fashion by directly deducing its necessity or impossibility. Our field of observation is too small to make induction of the least value. A large proportion of the western world, no doubt, desire immortality. But even if the whole human race had done so from the beginning of history (and this is notoriously not the case), this would have no more force than the desire entertained by a certain proportion of them that the wicked should spend their eternal life in everlasting torment.

48. Mr Bradley seems to doubt if immortality would give the relief for the sake of which it is demanded[2]. He says, with profound truth, that the partings made by life are harder to bear than those made by death. But are not the partings of life one of those troubles for which the help of immortality is most passionately demanded? In proportion as love has prospered on earth, its cessation at death seems less intolerable. For in such fruition, however short, there is an element of

---

[1] *op. cit.* Chap. xxvi. p. 507.
[2] *op. cit.* Chap. xxvi. p. 509.

eternity, which, so far as it goes, makes its cessation in time irrelevant[1]. It is when the mischances either of life or death have interfered between the birth and the fulness of emotion that our longing for another chance is strongest and deepest. These however are questions which philosophy can presume neither to neglect nor to discuss at length[2].

And would immortality help us? On this point, also, Mr Bradley seems doubtful. Much depends, no doubt, on whether we are to hold that time, taking reality as a whole, brings progress with it. The point is too large to be discussed in passing. Of course, on Hegel's system, we cannot regard progress as ultimately real. But then neither can we, on that system, regard time or imperfection as ultimately real. And the more probable conclusion seems to be that progress is as real as the imperfection for the removal of which it is needed[3].

Even, however, if this were not so, and we had reason to suppose the world not to be progressing in time, but to be on a dead level, that dead level, I think, would be higher if selves were immortal than if they were not. For the deepest longings of our nature are also the most persistent. It is easy enough, as experience shows, for unfavourable circumstances to thwart them for the space of a single life. But it would be far more improbable that the circumstances should never become favourable to them throughout a duration indefinitely prolonged. And,

[1] It is not, I think, justifiable to carry this line of thought so far as to assert that a state of consciousness can ever rise so high that its duration or extinction in time should be *completely* irrelevant. It is true that if such a state reached absolute perfection, it would not matter if it were extinguished immediately afterwards. But why is this? Only because a perfect state is an eternal one, and the eternal does not require duration in time for its perfections to be displayed in. But then the eternal is the timeless, and therefore its end in time is not only unimportant, but impossible. On the other hand, if a state does end in time, it is not completely eternal, or completely perfect, and then its end in time is not absolutely irrelevant.

If we deny that a perfect state is eternal, we have no reason to suppose that a perfect state is indifferent to its duration. But if the perfect is the eternal, it seems quite clear that no state, which is imperfect enough to cease in time, can be perfect enough to entirely disregard its cessation.

[2] A more adequate consideration of this subject than is possible in prose will be found in "The Lost Leader," and "Evelyn Hope."

[3] Cp. *Studies in the Hegelian Dialectic*, Section 175.

in matters of this kind, gain, once achieved, is not altogether cancelled by a subsequent loss.

49. Lotze adds another to the list of the idealists who consider that we have no evidence for immortality. We have only "this general idealistic conviction; that every created thing will continue, if and so long as its continuance belongs to the meaning of the world; that everything will pass away which had its authorised place only in a transitory phase of the world's course. That this principle admits of no further application in human hands hardly needs to be mentioned. We certainly do not know the merits which may give to one existence a claim to eternity, nor the defects which deny it to others[1]."

50. Lotze's philosophy, as has been generally admitted, bears a resemblance on many points to Hegel's. His opinion, however, need not inspire any doubts in us as to the Hegelian character of a belief in immortality, for he differs from Hegel on the very point which is of cardinal importance for this belief, namely the relation of the differentiations of the unity to the unity itself.

In his Metaphysic he demonstrates that the universe must be fundamentally one. But what he does not demonstrate is that it is also fundamentally many. In demonstrating its fundamental unity he started from the point of view of common sense and physical science which regards the universe as a manifold only externally connected. And he seems to have assumed that so much of this view was true as made the universe a manifold, and to have thought it only necessary to correct it by showing that it was equally really a unity. But it is not safe to trust in metaphysics to the uncritical beliefs of common life. They must in a sense be our starting-point, but only to be criticised, not to be accepted in their own right. And as Lotze had just been proving that half of the common-sense view, the merely external connection of the manifold, was erroneous, it is curious that he should not have seen that the other half, if it was to be retained, would require demonstration. Thus the result of his treatment in the

[1] *Metaphysic*, Section 245.

Metaphysic is that the unity is in a position of greater importance and security than the differentiation. For it has been
demonstrated that the universe must be fundamentally one,
but not that it must be fundamentally many.

When we pass to Lotze's treatment of the Philosophy of
Religion we find this unity changed in its character. In the
Metaphysic it had no name but M. It was scarcely suggested
that it was spiritual. Its main function was to permit inter-
action between its various manifestations. But now it has
been transformed into a personal God. There is no reason to
doubt that Lotze's mature judgment held this transition to be
valid. His fullest treatment, indeed, of the unity as a personal
God, is in the Microcosmus, which is earlier than the Metaphysic.
But the Lectures on the Philosophy of Religion take the same
line as the Microcosmus. And we must therefore take the M of
the Metaphysic as only a provisional stage in the process of
determining all reality as a personal God.

This change in the nature of M rendered it very desirable
that Lotze should be able to consider the unity as deeper than
its plurality of manifestations, and as not exhausted by them.
It *might* be possible to consider a unity as personal, even if it
was completely manifested in a system of persons[1]. (It must
be remembered that Lotze held that we could not conceive the
finite manifestations of the Absolute except as conscious.) But
it is clear that it would be much easier to conceive it as personal,
if it were taken as being more than could be expressed in such
manifestations, and as being logically prior to them, instead of
being simply their complement. Moreover, for ethical and
religious reasons Lotze was anxious to make his God something
higher than the world of plurality, and, therefore, something
more than the unity of that plurality.

This he was enabled to do, because, as we have seen, he had,
in his determination of M in the Metaphysic, left, perhaps
unconsciously, the unity in a much stronger position than the
plurality, having proved the necessity of the one, and not of
the other. And, now, when M had developed into a personal
God, the same characteristic was preserved. His God is not

[1] This will be discussed in the next Chapter, Section 88.

quite the God of ordinary theology. For he is not merely the highest reality, but the only reality, and (in spite of various occasional expressions to the contrary) Lotze appears still to take the finite world as God's manifestation rather than his creature. But there is no logical equality between the unity which is Lotze's God and the plurality which is his world. The plurality is dependent on the unity, but not the unity on the plurality. The only existence of the world is in God, but God's only existence is not in the world.

51. We have not to enquire if this theory is tenable. It is sufficient that it is Lotze's theory, and that it would make any demonstration of immortality quite impossible. Our only guarantee of the immortality of a self would be a demonstration that the existence of that self was essential to the Absolute. And this could only be the case if it were a necessity for the Absolute to manifest itself in that particular self. Now the personal God who is Lotze's Absolute has no such necessity as part of his nature. He exists otherwise than as he is manifested. And from this Lotze is justified in drawing the conclusion that he could exist with different manifestations from those which he at present has. For the present manifestations could cease without God being changed. And it is only his nature of whose permanence we are assured.

But all this is based on one of the points where Lotze differs from Hegel,—the elevation of the unity of the Absolute above its differentiation as more fundamental. And consequently Lotze's rejection of immortality cannot give us the least reason to suppose that a similar rejection would be consequent on, or compatible with, Hegel's philosophy. For with Hegel the unity and the plurality are strictly correlative. The plurality has no meaning except to be combined into the unity. But the unity has no meaning except to be differentiated into the plurality. And not into some plurality or the other, but into that particular plurality. And so we must reject the foundation of Lotze's argument—the possibility of changing the plurality without affecting the unity.

52. Lotze has another objection to immortality. He is considering the argument for immortality which might be derived from the view of the soul as a "stable atom" in a world whose unity is only external. Of this reasoning he says, "we might be glad to accept its guarantee for immortality...but the other conclusion which is forced on us at the same time, the infinite pre-existence of the soul before the life we know, remains, like the immortality of the souls of all animals, strange and improbable[1]." The conception of the self as a stable atom is not, of course, the one which we have put forward. But our view also seems to involve the pre-existence of the self in time. The universe was certainly manifesting itself in time before I was born. And to suppose that parts of reality could be in time, while other parts were not, scarcely seems compatible with the unity of all reality. The more probable hypothesis is that the whole of reality, in itself timeless, is manifested throughout the whole of time. The *infinite* pre-existence of the self would not necessarily follow from this. For, at any rate, there is no greater contradiction in supposing time to have begun, than in supposing that an infinite series has elapsed. But its pre-existence throughout time would be a fair inference. Nor is there anything about the present existence of each of us which would suggest the view that it was, in each case, the first of a series destined to be indefinitely prolonged.

53. Our lives indeed are so fragmentary that, in trying to explain them, we are almost tied down to two alternatives—either they mean nothing, or they are episodes in a long chain. That they should mean nothing—or at least nothing except as a means to something else—is not compatible with the view of the self which we have been led to adopt. And any attempt to give them meaning would seem to require that they should not be the only manifestations in time of the selves which experience them, but should form part of a longer process, stretching before as well as after.

Neither this nor any other hypothesis can explain for us the ultimate mystery why any evil or unhappiness exists. But this hypothesis might at any rate enable us to see some possibility of an explanation why they seem to us, who can only

---

[1] *Metaphysic*, Section 245.

see one life of each self at once, to be so unequally distributed. The evidence which we could gain by such empirical observation, indeed, could never by itself be strong enough to give any reason for belief in our pre-existence. But what little weight it has, will be on that side.

Lotze calls this belief strange and unsatisfactory. If he means by its strangeness that it is unusual, he has made no very serious objection. And it is only unusual if we limit ourselves to the western world. For its strangeness, if strangeness means extravagance, and for its unsatisfactoriness, he does not give any arguments. And till some are given, the mere assertion is not of much importance. There seems to be an implication that the idea of pre-existence is one that we should not accept willingly. But this would prove nothing against its truth. A system of idealism, indeed, may lay claim to so much optimism as to believe that the universe is bound to honour all the demands made on it by the true nature of the human spirit. But the present and past desire of most, or even of all people, who now exist on this earth, or are known to us through history, would not necessarily be an inevitable and permanent demand of the human spirit.

54. But why should the belief in pre-existence be held to be unsatisfactory? Mainly, I think, for this reason. We do not now remember anything of any previous life, and if, nevertheless, we have lived previously, there seems no reason to expect that we shall be able to remember our present lives during subsequent lives. And an existence thus cut up into comparatively isolated lives, none of which can remember anything but itself, may be thought to have no value from a practical standpoint. We might as well be mortal, it may be maintained, as immortal without a memory beyond the present life.

It is quite true that a life which remembers so small a part of itself must be rather fragmentary. But then this is an objection to all life in time, whether it could all be remembered or not, for all life in time declares itself, by that very fact, to be imperfect. If time is itself a transitory form, and one with which eternity will some day[1] dispense, then the reality which now forms a time-series will be timelessly present in a way which would render memory quite superfluous. But if time is to continue in a never-ending duration, then an infinite series of lives forgetful of the past would not be more meaningless, and would certainly be less dreary, than a single unending life cursed with a continually growing memory of its own false infinity. If we can get rid of time, we can dispense with memory. If we cannot get rid of time, memory would become intolerable.

55. If each life had no effect on its successors, then, indeed, there would be little point in calling them all lives of the same person. But no one has suggested that this would be the case. If the same self passes through different lives, it is certain that whatever modifications in its nature took place in one life would be reproduced in the next. For this is involved in that continuity of attributes, which, as we have seen above, is the form which personal identity takes *sub specie temporis*. Death and rebirth, no doubt, are in themselves facts of sufficient importance to modify a character considerably, but they could only work on what was already present, and the nature with which each individual starts in any life would be moulded by his actions and experiences in the past.

The different lives of each self, too, must be regarded not only as bound together in a chain of efficient causality, but as developing towards an end according to final causality. For all change in time, for the individual as well as for the universe, must be taken as ultimately determined by the end of developing as a series the full content of the timeless reality, with no other incompleteness or imperfection than that which is inseparable from the form of a series in time. The steps of such a process would surely form more than a merely nominal unity.

56. To such a view as this the objection has been made that the rebirth of a self without a memory of its previous life

---

[1] The expression is no doubt flagrantly contradictory. But the contradiction may perhaps be only a necessary consequence of considering time as a whole from inside time, and thus be no evidence against the possibility of time's eventual disappearance.

would be exactly equivalent to the annihilation of that self, and the creation of a new self of similar character. Now, it is argued, I should not regard myself as immortal, if I knew that I was to be annihilated at death, even if I knew that an exactly similar individual would then be created. And therefore, it is urged, rebirth without memory cannot be considered as real immortality of the self.

But the objection supposes an impossibility. There could not be another self of exactly similar character to me. For the self is not a *Ding an sich*, which can change independently of its qualities. The self is a substance with attributes, and the substance has no nature except to express itself in its attributes. If, therefore, the attributes were exactly the same, so would the substance be, and I should not be annihilated at all. But if there were a new self, there must be a breach in the continuity of the attributes, caused by the annihilation and the creation. Then the new self would not be exactly similar to me, and the parallel to rebirth fails, since with rebirth there is no interruption whatever in the continuity of the attributes. Thus the continuity of the attributes is always sufficient to preserve personal identity, not because it would be sufficient if the substance changed, but because it proves that the substance remains unchanged.

But can we, it may be asked, suppose that a series of lives, under different circumstances and with different surroundings, could ever form a continuous development? There is no reason that I know of for supposing that successive lives should show sudden and discontinuous variations, even in their outer circumstances. But, if they did, they might yet be part of a continuous development. For such outer circumstances are only of significance as means and expressions for the growth of the persons who live in them, and a continually developing end may avail itself of discontinuous variations of the means. What could be more irrationally discontinuous than the movements of the members of an orchestra would seem to a deaf man? And yet the music which they produce may be a living unity revealing itself in a continuous scheme.

If indeed we suppose that the circumstances of our successive lives are determined by chance, or by laws of merely efficient causation, the probability that they could be made subservient to a continuous development would be infinitesimal. But, if the dialectic has taught us anything, it has taught us that chance does not exist, and that efficient causation is a category of merely relative truth, which must be transcended when we seek to know reality adequately. The circumstances of our respective lives can only be determined by the true nature of the Absolute, and can therefore afford no hindrance to the development of the true nature of the Absolute. Nor, since the whole is perfectly in every part, can they afford any hindrance to the development of the true nature of each self. For any hindrance to the development of any self would be a hindrance to the development of the Absolute.

Thus we may lay down a general principle as to the continuity of external circumstances from life to life. In so far as it is necessary to the continuous development of the self, it will be present. In so far as it is not present, we may be sure that it is not required for the continuous development of the self.

57.   The true nature of reality has been shown to be the manifestation of the Absolute in individuals, or the unity of individuals in the Absolute—in other words, the relation of self to self. But, if the relations between selves are the only timeless reality, and the establishment of these relations the only progress in time—how, it may be asked, can progress be made in a series of separate lives? If what is experienced before each death is forgotten after it, how can any personal relation survive? Shall we not be for ever limited to the amount which can be developed in a single life, and be doomed continually to form fresh relations to be continually swept away by death?

We are certain of this, at any rate—that the personal relations of one life must have much to do in determining the personal relations of the next. The relations which men form with one another depend ultimately on two things—on their characters, and on the circumstances into which they are born. Now a man's character at rebirth would be clearly influenced by the personal relations he had previously formed. With regard to the causes that would determine rebirth we could only know that they would proceed from the nature of the Absolute in so far as it was manifested in that individual at that time. The personal relations he had formed immediately previously would certainly be a part of the way in which the Absolute was manifesting itself just then in that individual. On our theory, indeed, they would be by far the most important and significant part, since in them alone would the true meaning of reality become more or less explicit. It is clear then that they would have much to do in determining the circumstances of rebirth.

58. "And yet," it may be replied, "though they might be determined by them, they would be different from them. The new relations would not be the old ones, and thus it would still be true that the continuity was broken at each death." Of course, without memory the relations could not be *known* to be the same. But they might, nevertheless, be the same. At all events, the more intimate of our relations have a depth of significance which is often absurdly disproportionate to those causes of which we are conscious. These relations, ultimate facts as they doubtless are *sub specie. aeternitatis*, must, as arising in time, have antecedents. Is it rash to suggest that the most probable antecedent to love is love, and that, if our choices appear unreasoned, it is only because the memories which would justify them have condensed into an instinct which despises justification? Analogous cases may be found in the power to diagnose a disease, or to pronounce on the authenticity of a picture. These powers are often gained by long practice, and yet their possessors are often unable to give any reasons for perfectly correct decisions, because—in this case without the break of death—the memory of past experience has ceased to be memory, and has become an instinct.

Whether this be so or not, we may at any rate expect that a relation, once established, would not only determine the course of future lives, but would be reproduced in them. For we have seen that the only eternal reality is related persons. And if a personal relation exists in time, it would seem difficult to account for it except by supposing that that very relation between those very persons was ultimate and eternal—though of course in far greater perfection than is possible in its temporal manifestation[1]. And if its significance is ultimate and eternal, its appearance in time must be persistent, or at least recurrent. For how could the individual develop in time, if an ultimate element of his nature was destined not to recur in time? The length of the intervals which may elapse between two recurrences does not, of course, admit of prediction. But we know that nothing can be lost. And we know that personal relations cannot be transcended, because there is nothing higher. They must therefore be preserved as themselves, and preservation, *sub specie temporis*, means persistence and recurrence.

59. Thus everything is not lost with the loss of memory. We may go further. Can anything be eventually lost? If the only reality is an eternal system of personal relations, then any event can only be an inadequate way of expressing part of that system. And so, in such a system of personal relations, all the meaning and all the value of every event would exist—synthesised, transcended, but not lost.

Something closely analogous to this does unquestionably exist within the limits of a single life, and can be perceived by direct observation. When a personal relation has existed for many years, many of the events which formed its temporal content, and had importance and significance at the time, are completely forgotten. But we do not regard them as lost, for we recognize that each of them has done its part in moulding the relationship which exists at present. And so they are preserved—preserved indeed far more perfectly than they could be in memory. For, in memory, each of them would be a mere potentiality, except in the moment when it was actually thought of, while, as factors of disposition, they are all permanently real.

60. I am not denying—it would certainly be useless to deny—that, to a man who is living a particular life in time,

---

[1] This might require some qualification about every form of personal relation except that form which we found reason to consider absolutely adequate. Cp. Chap. IX.

the prospect that he will cease to remember that life—even by transcending memory—will always *appear* a loss and a breach of continuity. Arguments may convince him that this is a delusion, but they will not remove the feeling. Nor is it to be expected that this should be otherwise. A Synthesis can only be seen to preserve the true value of its terms in so far as we have attained to the standpoint of the Synthesis. And so a process towards perfection can never be perfectly painless. For the surrender of imperfection could only be quite painless to the perfect individual, and till the process is completed he is not perfect.

CHAPTER III.

THE PERSONALITY OF THE ABSOLUTE.

61. THE question whether there is a God has attracted much attention, for the ordinary definition of God makes the question both important and doubtful. But, according to Hegel's use of the word God, it ceases to be either doubtful or important. For he defines God as the Absolute Reality, whatever that reality may turn out to be. To question the existence of such a God as this is impossible. For to deny it would mean the denial that there was any reality at all. This would be contradictory, for what, in that case, would happen to the denial itself? But the same reasons which make the existence of such a God quite certain make it also quite trivial. For it tells us nothing except that there is some reality somewhere. We must know of what nature that reality is, if our conviction of its existence is to have any interest, either for theory or practice.

Thus Hegel's treatment of God's existence and nature will proceed differently from that which is generally employed. The common plan is to use the word to connote certain definite attributes, and then to enquire if a being answering to this description really exists. But Hegel defines God to mean whatever really exists, and then the important question is to determine the nature of this reality. Instead of " Is there a God ? " we must ask " What is God's nature ? "

In ordinary usage, and in the usage also of many philosophers, the word God connotes, among other attributes, personality. And on the personality of God depend most of the other attributes commonly ascribed to him. An impersonal being could be omnipotent, indeed, and could . "work for righteousness." It could also be rational, in the sense that its nature was such as to present an harmonious and coherent whole to the reason of the observer. But an impersonal being could not be wise or good. It could not love men. Nor could the emotions of acquiescence and admiration with which men might regard it be sufficiently like the emotions of one man towards another to merit the name of love. Certainly they would be very different emotions from those with which the believers in a personal God regard him.

For the ordinary conception of God, then, the attribute of personality seems of paramount importance. And so, when we are considering Hegel's system, the question "Does God exist?" may be fairly turned into the question "Is God a person?" Unquestionably Hegel regards God as infinite, as a unity, as spirit, as making for reason and righteousness. If we add personality to these qualities we have the ordinary conception of God. On the other hand, if we deny the personality, we get the conception of a being to whom, in ordinary language, the name of God would not be applied.

But what exactly is meant by personality? I may know, though it is difficult to define, what I mean when I say that I am a person. But it is clear that the nature of an infinite and perfect being must be very different from mine. And within what limits must this difference be confined, if that infinite and perfect being is to be called a person?

The characteristic which determines personality seems, on the whole, to be generally placed in the " I "—the synthetic unity of apperception. When a being distinguishes itself from . its content—when, in other words, it finds in that content an element which is never absent, though never present in isolation, which is always the same, and whose presence determines the content to be the content of that particular being, then we call that being personal. I know that I can say "I am." I know that a College cannot say "I am." If we conceive that it is consistent with God's nature to say " I am," we shall hold that God is a person, but not otherwise.

62. Is Hegel's God a person? The word God is so closely connected in ordinary usage with personality, that the question put in this way, has an unjustifiable suggestion in its terms of an affirmative answer. And as Hegel has another name for ultimate reality—the Absolute—it will be less confusing if we use it in future, remembering that the Absolute and God are for Hegel identical, and that if, for Hegel, a personal God exists at all, he must be the Absolute. It is, I think, best to use neuter pronouns in referring, during this discussion, to the Absolute, or to Hegel's God. The use of masculine pronouns would prejudge the question of the personality of the Absolute in the affirmative, while the more general neuter pronouns do not prejudge it so much in the negative. Moreover the view which I shall endeavour to defend is that the Absolute, as demonstrated by Hegel, must not be considered as personal, and is more appropriately called " it " than " he."

63. Hegel regards the Absolute as a unity. He regards it, not as an external and mechanical unity, not even as an organic unity, but as the deepest unity possible—one in which the parts have no meaning but their unity, while that unity, again, has no meaning but its differentiations. And this unity is unquestionably, according to Hegel, spirit. We may go further. There is no reason to think that Hegel held it possible for spirit to exist, except in the form of persons, while there is every reason to think that he regarded persons as the highest form of spirit[1].

It does not follow from this, however, that the Absolute is a person. It might be said of a College, with as much truth as it has been said of the Absolute, that it is a unity, that it is a unity of spirit, and that none of that spirit exists except as personal. Yet the College is not a person. It is a unity of persons, but it is not a person itself. And, in the same way, it is possible that the Absolute may be a unity of persons, without being a person. Of course the Absolute is a far more perfect unity than a College. The bearing of this on the question of its personality will be discussed later on[2].

---

[1] Cp. Chap. II.   [2] Sections 79—83.

I believe that Hegel did not himself regard the Absolute as personal. It seems clear from the Philosophy of Religion that the truth of God's nature, according to Hegel, is to be found in the Kingdom of the Holy Ghost (which must be distinguished from the idea of the Holy Ghost in the Kingdom of the Father). And the Kingdom of the Holy Ghost appears to be not a person but a community. But Hegel's own opinion on this subject will be discussed more conveniently in a later chapter[1]. In this chapter I wish to consider, not Hegel's own opinions on the personality of the Absolute, but the conclusions on the subject which ought logically to be deduced from his conception of the Absolute as determined in the Logic.

64. What light does the dialectic itself throw on our problem ? We saw in the last chapter that we must conceive the Absolute as differentiated into individuals, and that we must conceive the unity as being in each of these individuals. We saw, further, that we could only conceive this as happening if the unity was *for* each of its individuals. And we saw that the only way in which we could imagine a unity to be for each of its individuals was for each of those individuals to be conscious of the unity[2].

The unity is for each of the individuals. Are we also entitled to say that each of the individuals is for the unity ? Such a relation, indeed, would not justify us in concluding that the Absolute was a person, any more than the relation already established justified us, by itself, in concluding that the individuals in the Absolute were persons. We do not know, and cannot imagine, any way in which A can be for B, except by B's consciousness of A. But other ways may exist, and so, in proving that A must be for B, we do not actually prove that B must be conscious. Such a result, however, would render the consciousness of B probable, and might be the basis of a more definite proof.

When we consider how strictly reciprocal is the dependence

---

[1] Sections 216—218.

[2] Sections 64—67 are taken, with some alterations and transpositions, from the paper on Hegel's Treatment of the Categories of the Idea, already quoted. (*Mind*, 1900, p. 145.)

which exists between the unity and the individuals, it might seem probable that the individuals are for the unity. I believe, however, that this view is mistaken, and that, while the unity is for the individuals, the individuals are not for the unity. In more concrete language, the Logic does not suggest to us to consider the Absolute as a whole to be conscious, and therefore a person. I shall endeavour to show further on that the Logic cannot by itself *forbid* us to think of the Absolute as a person.

In the first place, there is no necessity of thought which compels us to regard the individuals as existing for the unity. We were driven to regard the unity as existing for the individuals, because we found it necessary that the unity should exist in each individual. Now in the ordinary sense of inclusion it was clearly impossible for the unity to be in each of the individuals which are parts of it, and the only alternative was that it should be in each of them in the sense of being for each of them.

It is as necessary, no doubt, to regard the individuals as being in the unity, as to regard the unity as being in each of the individuals. But then there is no difficulty in regarding the individuals as being in the unity in the ordinary sense of inclusion. So far from this being difficult, it is part of the definition of a unity of individuals that it includes them. And therefore we have no right to say that the individuals are for the unity. They are in it—that is proved. But the further step—that they can only be in it by being for it—is wanting.

65. And I think we may go further than this, and say that it is impossible that the individuals should be for the unity, in the sense in which we held it to be necessary that the unity should be for the individuals. For the whole significance of one being for the other was that there was some difference between them. If there was no difference, the one would *be* the other, and the whole conception, as we have got it here, of one being *for* the other would collapse. All the meaning we gave to the expression that A was for B was that the content of the one was also the content of the other. If A and B are different, this means something. But if A and B are identical

THE PERSONALITY OF THE ABSOLUTE

then it would only mean that a thing's content was its content—
which is not a new conception, but a useless tautology.

Let us apply this. The unity and the individuals are
identical—the unity has no nature except to be the individuals,
and the individuals have no nature except to be the unity.
This Hegel demonstrates in the category of Teleology. But
the unity is something different from *each* of the individuals,
and, therefore, if the content of the unity is found in each of
the individuals, there is a meaning in saying that it is for each
of the individuals. On the other hand, the unity is not
different from all the individuals together. (It is, of course,
not equivalent to a mere sum or aggregate of the individuals,
because it is their real unity. But then they exist as a real
unity, and not as a mere sum or aggregate, so that the unity
is identical with the individuals as they really are.) If therefore the content of the unity is identical with that of the
individuals, this merely means that the content is identical
with itself—not that it is identical with the contents of
anything else. And so the conception of the individuals being
for the unity becomes unmeaning.

66. The correctness of such a view may be challenged on
the ground of its atomism. If each of the many individuals
has this quality which is denied to the single unity, we have,
it may be said, reduced the unity to a comparative unreality.
All the reality is transferred to the separate individuals, who
are each centres for which all reality exists, and the unity falls
back into the position of a mere aggregate, or, at the most, of
a mechanically determined whole.

If this were the case, we should certainly have gone wrong.
Hegel has shown in the categories of Teleology and Life that
the unity must be as real as the individuals. And, so far from
dropping this in the final categories of the Logic, we saw in the
last chapter that the reason why we pressed on to the category
of Cognition was that in no other way could the full reality of
the unity be made compatible with the full reality of the
individuals.

If, therefore, the denial that the individuals existed for the
unity, subordinated the unity to the individuals, and involved

an atomistic view, the position would have to be changed somehow. But I believe that it does nothing of the sort, and that, on the contrary, it is the objection to it which implies an atomistic theory, and is therefore invalid.

A system of individuals of which each is conscious of the other (to go back to a concrete example of the notion before us) is of course differentiated. Each of the conscious beings is an individual, and stands out, by that, separate from the others. But they are just as much united as they are separated. For A can only be conscious of B in so far as they are united, and it is only, in such a system, by being conscious of B that A is an individual, or, indeed, exists at all. Common sense, however, clings by preference to the categories of Essence, and is consequently atomistic. To common sense, therefore, such a system is more thoroughly differentiated than it is united. But the dialectic has proved this to be a mistake. It has shown that in such a system the unity is as real as the differentiation, and it is only to an objector who ignores this that a system bound together by the mutual knowledge of its parts can be accused of atomism.

To think that the unity of the system would be greater if the individuals were for that unity is a mistake. It is true that each individual is also, in one sense of the word, a unity, and that the unity of the system is for each individual. But the sense in which an individual, which gets all differentiation from without, is a unity, is entirely different from the unity of the system. This has nothing outside to which it can be related, and it gets all its differentiations from within—from the individuals composing it. Such a difference in the nature of the two unities prevents us from arguing that they ought to unify their differentiations in the same way.

Indeed, if the system unified its internal differentiations in the same way that the individual unifies its external differentiations—by having them *for* itself—it seems difficult to deny that it would be an individual too. And if it was an individual, it would stand side by side with the other individuals, and could not be their unity—which is just what we set out by declaring that it was. And this supports our previous conclusion—that the two relations, though equally real, are not similar, and that, while the unity is for each individual, they are not for the unity.

67. Since, then, the individuals cannot be for the unity, the dialectic gives us no reason to suppose that the unity either is a conscious being, or possesses any qualities analogous to consciousness. In that case it gives us no reason to suppose that the Absolute, as a whole, is personal. But the dialectic does not give us by this any reason to *deny* personality to the Absolute. To suppose that it did would be to confound unjustifiably the category of pure thought, which Hegel calls Cognition, with the concrete fact after which it is named. To avoid such confusion altogether is very difficult. Hegel himself did not always succeed in doing so—for example in the category of Chemism, and in the details of the Subjective Notion and of Life. And this constitutes the chief objection to his practice of naming categories after the concrete subject-matter which best illustrates them. Such a plan is no doubt very convenient for an author whose penetration had discovered many more stages of thought than could be described by existing terminology. And it was also stimulating to the learner, assisting him to call up a vivid picture of the category, and suggesting its practical application and importance. But these advantages are more than counterbalanced by the dangers of such a nomenclature.

One of these concerns the dialectic itself. Any concrete state contains many abstract ideas as its moments, and if we call one of the abstract ideas by the name of the concrete state, we shall run considerable risk of mixing it up with the others, and of supposing that we have deduced by pure thought more than we really have deduced.

And there is another danger, arising from a question which is logically prior to the last difficulty. Is the abstract idea, which is named after the concrete state, really an essential element of that state at all ? This is a question which cannot be settled by the dialectic process, which only deals with such abstract ideas as can be reached by pure thought, and cannot discuss the question whether a particular pure thought can be

found by analysis in a particular empirical fact. By giving
such a name to the category, the dialectic assumes that the
answer to the question is in the affirmative, but does not prove
it. Should the assumption be mistaken, the only injury done
to the dialectic itself will be that the category has acquired an
inappropriate name, which may be misleading. But if, in the
application of the dialectic, we assume that such a category is
always true of the part of experience after which it is named,
we may go hopelessly wrong.

In the case before us, it is clear, as I have endeavoured to
show above, that, *according to Hegel's category of Cognition*,
nothing can cognize unless it has something outside itself to
be cognized, and that consequently it is impossible that the
unity, which has nothing outside itself, should cognize anything. But it by no means follows from this that we can
deny cognition or consciousness to that unity. For such a
step would imply that Hegel's category of Cognition was the
essential characteristic of what is ordinarily called thought,
and, whether this is true or false, it is certainly not proved.
All the thought, indeed, of which we are immediately conscious
is of this sort, for we know no thought directly but our own,
and we are finite beings. But supposing that Lotze was right
in asserting that an all-embracing reality could be conscious of
itself, then we should have to admit that it was not an essential
characteristic of thought to be for the thinker in the way in
which the unity is for the individual—and in which the
individual is not for the unity—in Hegel's category. Of course
this would not involve any inaccuracy in the dialectic. The
dialectic asserts that the individuals are not for the unity in a
specified sense. There is nothing incompatible with this in the
assertion that the unity is nevertheless conscious.

68. Lotze's views on this point are of peculiar interest to
us. He did not, indeed, accept Hegel's view of the Absolute
without important modifications. But he agreed with him in
identifying God with the Absolute—in making God not only
the supreme but the sole reality. And this God he asserted to
be personal, and defended his conclusion by arguments some
of which, if valid, would equally apply to the Absolute as

conceived by Hegel. Under these circumstances it may be profitable to consider these arguments in some detail. They will be found in the Microcosmus, Book IX. Chap. IV. The Outlines of the Philosophy of Religion prove that the subsequent development of his philosophy did not change his views on this subject.

In the first place, Lotze holds it to be "an immediate certainty that what is greatest, most beautiful, most worthy, is not a mere thought, but must be a reality, because it would be intolerable to believe of our ideal that it is an idea produced by the action of thought, but having no existence, no power, and no validity in the world of reality[1]." This argument we shall consider later[2]. His other two arguments he sums up as follows—"Self-hood, the essence of all personality, does not depend upon any opposition that either has happened or is happening of the Ego to a Non-Ego, but it consists in an immediate self-existence which constitutes the basis of the possibility of that contrast whenever it appears. Self-consciousness is the elucidation of this self-existence which is brought about by means of knowledge, and even this is by no means necessarily bound up with the distinction of the Ego from a Non-Ego which is substantially opposed to it.

"In the nature of the finite mind as such is to be found the reason why the development of its personal consciousness can take place only through the influences of the cosmic whole which the finite being itself is not, that is, through stimulation coming from the Non-Ego, not because it needs the contrast with something *alien* in order to have self-existence, but because in this respect, as in every other, it does not contain in itself the conditions of its existence. We do not find this limitation in the being of the Infinite; hence for it alone is there possible a self-existence, which needs neither to be initiated nor to be continuously developed by something not itself, but which maintains itself within itself with spontaneous action that is eternal and had no beginning.

"Perfect Personality is in God only; to all finite minds

---

[1] *op. cit.* Bk IX. Chap. IV (iii. 560, trans. ii. 670).
[2] Sections 73—78.

there is allotted but a pale copy thereof; the finiteness of the
finite is not a producing condition of this Personality, but a
limit and a hindrance of its development[1]."

69. Taking the first of these contentions we must remark
that the term Non-Ego is rather ambiguous, when the relation
of an Ego to a Non-Ego is spoken of. It may mean something
that is not an Ego at all, or it may only mean something that
is not the Ego which forms the other term of the relation. In
this sense two Egos might each be the other's Non-Ego. It is
in this wider sense that we must take it if we are to consider
any relation which on Hegelian principles can be regarded as
essential to the Ego. For Hegel certainly thinks that nothing
is real but spirit, and we saw reason in the last chapter to
believe that all spirit must be taken as selves. It follows that
no Ego could come into relation with anything but another
Ego, which would, as far as that relation went, be the Non-Ego
of the first.

We may, no doubt, unreservedly accept Lotze's statement
that "no being in the nature of which self-existence was not
given as primary and underived could be endowed with self-
hood by any mechanism of favouring circumstances however
wonderful[2]." This completely harmonises with the conclusion
reached in the last chapter, that it was impracticable to regard
a self as anything but a fundamental differentiation of the
Absolute. But the question still remains whether it is not an
essential part of the eternal, primary and underived nature of
each self that it should be related to some reality outside it.

Lotze further remarks that the "Ego and Non-Ego cannot
be two notions of which each owes its whole content only to its
contrast with the other; if this were so they would both remain
without content....Hence every being which is destined to take
the part of the Ego when the contrast has arisen must have
the ground of its determination in that nature which it had
previous to the contrast[3]" and, therefore, independent of the
contrast.

[1] *op. cit.* Bk IX. Chap. iv (iii. 580, trans. ii. 688).
[2] *op. cit.* Bk IX. Chap. iv (iii. 572, trans. ii. 680).
[3] *op. cit.* Bk IX. Chap. iv (iii. 570, trans. ii. 678).

Now it is quite true that if we tried to explain the Ego *exclusively* from the reality outside to which it is in relation, we should have fallen into a vicious circle, since that reality could only be explained with reference to the Ego. But it by no means follows from the impossibility of explaining the isolated Ego by the isolated Non-Ego, that the Ego can be explained without its Non-Ego, or is conceivable without it. There is a third alternative—that the isolated Ego cannot be explained at all, being an unreal abstraction which shows its unreality by its inexplicability, and that Ego and Non-Ego can only be explained when they are taken together as mutually explaining each other. The idea of the Ego is certainly *more* than the mere fact that it is related to the Non-Ego, but this does not prevent the relation to the Non-Ego being essential to the nature of the Ego. If, to take a parallel case, we tried to explain the idea of a parent merely in terms of the idea of a child, we should have fallen into a vicious circle, since we should find that the idea of a child could not be explained except in relation to the idea of a parent. But it would not be correct to argue from this that a parent could exist, or be conceived, without a child. They are certainly not " two notions of which one owes its whole content to its contrast with the other," but that does not prevent each of them from being meaningless without the other.

70. The Ego, therefore, would not necessarily become inexplicable, even if it could not be conceived except in relation to the Non-Ego. Can it be conceived otherwise? Lotze answers this question in the affirmative, so far as the Infinite Being is concerned. It, he says, " does not need—as we sometimes, with a strange perversion of the right point of view, think—that its life shall be called forth by external stimuli, but from the beginning its concept is without the deficiency which seems to make such stimuli necessary for the finite being, and its active efficacy thinkable[1]." Undoubtedly the Infinite Being can exist without stimulation from the outside. For as there is no outside, the only other alternative would be

---

[1] *op. cit.* Bk IX. Chap. IV (iii. 575, trans. ii. 683).

that the Absolute—that is, all reality—should be non-existent. But does it exist as a person?

Lotze says that "every feeling of pleasure or dislike, every kind of self-enjoyment (Selbstgenuss) does in our view contain the primary basis of personality, that immediate self-existence which all later developments of self-consciousness may indeed make plainer to thought by contrasts and comparisons, thus also intensifying its value, but which is not in the first place produced by them[1]." And we may so far agree with this, as to admit that personality consists in saying "I," not in saying "Smith," "table," or any other names which may be applied to the Non-Ego. But the question remains whether it is possible for the Absolute to say "I," since it can name no Smith, and no table, distinct from itself. The consciousness of the Non-Ego is not personality. But is it not an essential condition of personality?

Each of us is a finite person. And each of us finds that, for him, the consciousness of the Non-Ego is an essential condition of his personality. Each of us infers that he is surrounded by various other finite persons. And of each of them we have reason to infer that a consciousness of some Non-Ego is essential to his personality. Such a consciousness the Absolute cannot possess. For there is nothing outside it, from which it can distinguish itself.

It is true that the Absolute is by no means a blank unity. It is differentiated, and the differentiations are as essential as the unity. If it were merely its own aspect of unity, then it would have something to distinguish itself from—namely its differentiations. But then the Absolute is not merely the aspect of unity. If it were, it would not be all reality in its true and ultimate form. It would only be one aspect of that reality—an abstraction, and, therefore, taken by itself, false. This is not what Hegel and Lotze mean by the Absolute. The Absolute is the full reality—the differentiated unity, or the unified differentiations. And there is nothing which is in any way outside this, or which can in any way be distinguished from this.

[1] *op. cit.* Bk IX. Chap. IV (iii. 571, trans. ii. 679).

It is true, again, that the Absolute is something very different from any one of its differentiations, or from the sum, or from the mechanical aggregate, of all its differentiations. But this will not provide the Absolute with anything different from itself. For the differentiations do not exist as isolated, and do not exist as a sum, or as a mechanical aggregate. They only exist as they are unified in the Absolute. And, therefore, as they really exist, they have no existence distinguishable from the Absolute.

71. The Absolute, then, has not a characteristic which is admitted to be essential to all finite personality, which is all the personality of which we have any experience. Is this characteristic essential to personality, or only to finite personality? We know of no personality without a Non-Ego. Nor can we imagine what such a personality would be like. For *we* certainly can never say "I" without raising the idea of the Non-Ego, and so we can never form any idea of the way in which the Absolute would say "I." We cannot, indeed, say with complete certainty that it could not be done. It is abstractly possible that in some way utterly inexplicable to us the Absolute may be personal. But this is the barest and most worthless abstraction of possibility. To say that something which is utterly unimaginable may be true, because some unimaginable way may exist of bringing it about, is, by itself, merely trivial. On the same principle we could say that the Absolute might be scarlet. It is true that we do not know, and cannot imagine, scarlet except as spatially extended, and the Absolute is not spatially extended. But this may perhaps be only a peculiarity of finite scarlet. Infinite scarlet may be able to exist out of space.

But although all such arguments from bare possibility are merely trivial when taken by themselves, yet they may have a very different aspect when conjoined with some positive argument. If any line of reasoning leads us to the conclusion that the Absolute *must* somehow be personal, then the possibility that it *can* be personal, even if it has to be in some quite unimaginable way, becomes of real value.

72. Before considering, however, what positive arguments

there may be for the personality of the Absolute, we must note
that they will all have the disadvantage that the personality
which they support is of a kind which is beyond both our experience and our imagination. In this respect a criticism which
Lotze makes recoils on himself. He complains that those who
deny the personality of the Absolute separate spirit from personality in an unjustifiable manner, since they are never separated
in our experience[1]. To this we may reply that one theory, at
least, which denies personality to the Absolute, does not do this.
For it admits that all spirit is differentiated into persons, but
denies that the unity of persons need itself be personal. And
experience gives us examples of this in every body corporate.
On the other hand Lotze himself, when he speaks of a personal
Absolute, commits the very fault which he deprecates. For
personality without a Non-Ego is just as alien to our experience
as spirit without personality. A conclusion is not, of course,
proved to be false, because neither our knowledge nor our
imagination enables us to see *how* it can be true. But whatever amount of doubt is thrown on a conclusion by such an
inability on our part, belongs, in this controversy, not to the
denial of the personality of the Absolute, but to its affirmation.

73. To supplement his arguments for the possibility of the
personality of the Absolute, Lotze gives, as we have seen, two
positive arguments to prove that the personality is real. The
first is that we are immediately certain that the most perfect
must be real. The second is that the points in which the
Absolute differs from a finite being are points which make it
more truly personal than any finite being can be.

It is only as suggesting the immediate certainty of the
reality of the most perfect that Lotze allows any validity to the
Ontological Argument. As a formal demonstration it cannot
survive Kant's criticism. The Cosmological Argument does not
profess to prove a personal God, and the Physico-Theological
Argument, if it proved anything, could only prove, at the most, an
external creator of the part of reality which we know. It could
never prove that all reality formed a whole which was a person.

---

[1] *Outlines of the Philosophy of Religion*, Section 24.

" It is an immediate certainty," says Lotze, " that what is greatest, most beautiful, most worthy, is not a mere thought, but must be a reality, because it would be intolerable to believe of our ideal that it is an idea produced by the action of thought but having no existence, no power, and no validity in the world of reality. We do not from the perfection of that which is perfect immediately deduce its reality as a logical consequence ; but without the circumlocution of a deduction we directly feel the impossibility of its non-existence, and all semblance of syllogistic proof only serves to make more clear the directness of this certainty. If what is greatest did not *exist*, then what is *greatest* would not be, and it is impossible that that which is the greatest of all conceivable things should *not* be. Many other attempts may be made to exhibit the internal necessity of this conviction as logically demonstrable ; but all of them must fail." Nor can we, he continues, " prove from any general logical truth our right to ascribe to that which has such worth its claim to reality ; on the contrary, the certainty of this claim belongs to those inner experiences to which, as to the given object of its labour, the mediating, inferring, and limiting activity of cognition refers[1].

74. If we take this strictly, we can merely note the fact that Lotze had this immediate certainty as a biographical incident of more or less interest. Nothing that he has said can be of any force in determining the opinion of others. If *A* has this immediate certainty, he believes that the greatest must be real, but he believes it, not because Lotze has this certainty, or because he himself ought to have it, but because he has it. This immediate certainty can neither be confirmed nor shaken by any external considerations. For if it were affected by reasons, it would be a logical conclusion, which is just what it is not. But if, on the other hand, *B* has not got this immediate certainty—and it is beyond doubt that many people have not got it—then that concludes the controversy so far as he is concerned. We must not argue that he is wrong not to have it, because it is a reasonable belief, or because most

---

[1] *Microcosmus*, Bk IX. Chap. IV (iii. 561, trans. ii. 670).

people have it, or because the people who have it are cleverer or better than those who do not. Whether these statements are true or not, they are completely irrelevant. For, if they were relevant, then the conclusion would not rest on the fact that it is believed, but on the fact that it ought to be believed— that is, that there are reasons why we should believe it. Now the whole contention was that it was not believed for reasons.

When a man asserts that he has an immediate certainty of a truth, he doubtless deprives other people of the right to argue with him. But he also—though this he sometimes forgets—deprives himself of the right to argue with other people. Even the statement of his immediate certainty can only be justified if it is put forward as a reason for declining controversy, or as a contribution to psychological statistics, or to his own biography. To volunteer it as a contribution to the study of the subject to which the certainty refers is—in at least one sense of the word—impertinent. Nothing can be more important to me, in respect of any branch of knowledge, than my own immediate certainties about it. Nothing can be less important than the immediate certainties of other people.

75. But if the assertion that the most perfect must be real took up a less lofty position, and presented itself as a proposition which reason directed us to believe, what could then be said of it? If it is put forward as the basis on which to found a system of metaphysics, it must clearly, I think, be condemned as worthless. The most that could be said against the denial of it would be that, if that denial was true, the world would be a wicked and miserable place. And what right have we to take this as a *reductio ad absurdum*? How do we know that the world is not a wicked and miserable place? It is all very well for our aspirations after virtue and happiness to say that they must live. But what if the universe replies that it does not see the necessity? It can scarcely be denied that it has the power to act on its convictions.

76. The question takes a very different form, however, if we regard an idealist system of metaphysics as being already demonstrated. For if the universe is proved to be rational, and we can further prove that it could not be rational unless a certain proposition be true, it will, of course, be perfectly logical to conclude that the proposition must be true. Now Hegel unquestionably holds the Absolute to be an harmonious whole. And we saw reason to believe, in the last Chapter, that the fundamental differentiations of the Absolute were all persons, and that the whole nature of the Absolute is adequately expressed in the conscious relations between persons. If, therefore, it can be proved that the consciousness of the personality of the Absolute is essential to harmonious conscious relations between the persons who compose it, we should have a good ground for believing in the personality of the Absolute[1]. Now sin and misery are incompatible with the harmony of conscious beings. If they are to be harmonious they must be virtuous and happy—or else in some higher state which transcends and includes virtue and happiness. And so if the consciousness of the personality of the Absolute was shown to be essential to the virtue and happiness of finite persons, we could, on the basis of Hegel's philosophy, legitimately conclude that the Absolute was a person.

But how can the consciousness of the personality of the Absolute be shown to be essential to the virtue and happiness of finite persons? It would not suffice if it were shown to be essential for the virtue and happiness of every human being who is now living, or who has lived since the beginning of history. For what must be shown is that, without the belief in a personal Absolute, finite persons *could* not be perfectly virtuous and happy. And the fact that no person has been so yet, if it were a fact, would prove nothing of the sort. We are very far as yet from perfection. And so we continually make demands on reality which are so far from being conditions of perfect and harmonious existence, that, if realised, they would utterly destroy all harmony. In our ignorance we suppose our happiness to lie in what could only lead to our misery, we seek as a help what would prove a hindrance. That this is so in many cases is one of the common-places

---

[1] If the consciousness of the personality were necessary, the personality would be necessary, for a mistaken belief in the personality would be an intellectual error, incompatible with harmony.

of moralists. Now, even if the belief in the personality of the Absolute was invariably requisite, as far as our experience reached, to happiness or virtue, how can we tell that this is not one of those cases ? How can we tell that wiser men would not find greater happiness elsewhere, that better men would not rise without its aid to loftier virtue ? We may not be able to say positively that they would, but that is not sufficient. If we are to be able to deduce, in this way, the personality of the Absolute, we must be able to say positively that they would not.

77. It is superfluous to point out, moreover, that mankind has by no means been unanimous in demanding a personal God. Neither Brahmanism nor Buddhism makes the Supreme Being personal, but each of them holds that it is possible for men to reach a state of perfect blessedness. And, in the western world, many wise men have been both virtuous and happy, who denied the personality of God. It is sufficient to mention Spinoza and Hume. I am far from suggesting that we have any reason, on such inductions as these facts would open to us, to conclude that the denial of God's personality tends to greater virtue or happiness than its assertion. But I think that they are conclusive against any attempt to prove that the assertion always leads to greater virtue or happiness than the denial.

78. The only way in which we could hope to prove that the consciousness of the personality of the Absolute was essential either to perfect virtue or to perfect happiness would be by an argument *à priori*. For we are still too far removed from perfect virtue and happiness, for any inductions from our present condition to have the least value. If, however, we could by an *à priori* argument so determine the nature of a perfect finite being as to include, as a necessary element in its perfection, the consciousness of a personal Absolute, we should then know that the personality of the Absolute was an essential characteristic of a perfect universe, and therefore, on the basis of Hegel's idealism, might be accepted as true.

But, so far as I know, no attempt has been made to do this. And it is not easy to see on what ground such a demonstration could be based. Of course, if the Absolute *were* personal, no

finite being could be perfect without perceiving it, since otherwise the limitation of his knowledge, or its erroneous character,
would destroy the harmony of his nature. But, if the Absolute
were not personal, I can conceive nothing in the recognition of
that fact which need mar the harmony of the person who
recognizes it. He will know the other finite persons in the
universe. He will feel that his relations with them are consistent with his own deepest and most fundamental nature.
Why should he be dissatisfied because the unity in which those
relations bind him and them is not itself a person ?

79. We now pass to Lotze's second positive argument. He
asserts that " of the full personality which is possible only for
the Infinite a feeble reflection is given also to the finite ; for the
characteristics peculiar to the finite are not producing conditions of self-existence, but obstacles to its unconditioned
development, although we are accustomed, unjustifiably, to
deduce from these characteristics its capacity of personal
existence. The finite being always works with powers with
which it did not endow itself, and according to laws which
it did not establish—that is, it works by means of a mental
organization which is realised not only in it, but also in
innumerable similar beings. Hence in reflecting on self it may
easily seem to it as though there were in itself some obscure
and unknown substance—something which is in the Ego though
it is not the Ego itself, and to which, as to its subject, the
whole personal development is attached. And hence there arise
the questions—never to be quite silenced—What are we ourselves ? What is our soul ? What is our self—that obscure
being, incomprehensible to ourselves, that stirs in our feelings
and our passions, and never rises into complete self-consciousness ? The fact that these questions can arise shows how
far personality is from being developed in us to the extent
which its notion admits and requires. It can be perfect only in
the Infinite Being which, in surveying all its conditions or
actions, never finds any content of that which it suffers, or any
law of its working, the meaning and origin of which are not
transparently plain to it, and capable of being explained by
reference to its own nature. Further the position of the finite

mind, which attaches it as a constituent of the whole to some definite place in the cosmic order, requires that its inner life should be awakened by successive stimuli from without, and that its course should proceed according to the laws of a psychical mechanism, in obedience to which individual ideas, feelings, and efforts press upon and supplant one another. Hence the whole self can never be brought together at any one moment, our self-consciousness never presents to us a complete and perfect picture of our Ego—not even of its nature at any moment, and much less of the unity of its development in time. ...In point of fact we have little ground for speaking of the personality of finite beings; it is an ideal, which, like all that is ideal, belongs unconditionally only to the Infinite, but like all that is good appertains to us only conditionally and hence imperfectly[1]."

80. It may be freely admitted that a perfect personality is a self-determined whole, not hampered and thwarted from the outside, and that the Absolute is such a whole. It must also be granted that every finite self is in relation to, and determined by, its surroundings. But it does not follow from these admissions, either that the finite person is not a perfect realisation of personality, or that the Absolute is a person at all. For determination from outside is compatible with complete self-determination, and thus the finite person may be a self-determined whole. And, on the other hand, not every self-determined whole is a person, and the Absolute may therefore be self-determined without being personal.

Every self-determined whole is a unity. And every unity must, as Hegel teaches us, have a multiplicity connected with it. But there are two ways in which this may happen. The multiplicity may be simply inside the unity which it differentiates. Or it may be outside that unity. It can never be *merely* outside it, for in that case it would not affect it at all. But, in this case, it is in the unity, only because, and in so far as, it is also outside it. We may say of these different relations to multiplicity that in the first case the unity is a *system* of differentiations, in the second it is a *centre* of differentiations. One unity is as real as the other, but they differ, and the difference is important.

The Absolute has the first sort of unity. Its multiplicity is necessarily due to differentiations inside it, since nothing exists outside it. On the other hand the finite self has the second sort of unity. Its multiplicity is in one sense inside it, since nothing can differentiate consciousness which is not in consciousness. But, on the other hand, the multiplicity is equally outside the self. All knowledge, all volition, all emotions involve a reference to some reality other than the self which knows, wills, and feels. Suppose the self to exist alone, all other reality being destroyed, and all the content of the self goes, and the self with it.

It is difficult to illustrate this distinction by other examples, because it is found in perfection nowhere else. There is nothing but the Absolute which has no external relations. There is, I think, nothing but a finite person which has no completely internal relations. But we may perhaps make the point clearer by comparing the nature of a state with that of a citizen (taking him merely as a citizen, not in any of his other aspects). The state and the citizen are equally unities. They are equally dependent on multiplicity. But the state has a multiplicity within itself, and can be conceived without reference to anything external. As, in fact, it has reality outside it, it has relations to external objects. But if it were the only thing in the universe, it would not fail for want of multiplicity, since it has differentiations outside itself. The position of a citizen is quite different. His existence as a citizen depends on the existence of other human beings. For, although a man might be able to exist in a world which, beside himself, contained only the lower animals and inorganic matter, it is clear that he could not be a citizen. Withdraw the relations to his fellow-citizens, and the citizen ceases to exist as such.

(It may be remarked that when these two sorts of unities are considered by an atomistic system of metaphysics, the failure to recognize their reality leads to a different fallacy in each case. In the case of a unity of system, atomism concludes that, since it has no particular existence separate from its parts, it is a mere aggregate of those parts, and has no qualities except the resultant of the qualities which such parts would have when isolated.   In the case of a unity of centre, atomism denies that it has any reality at all, since it has no reality in isolation from other things.   Thus in such a system as Hume's, the universe becomes a mere aggregate, but the soul is rejected altogether. The comparative favour extended to the unity of system is to be ascribed to the belief that units can be added together without altering them.   If atomism realised that any sort of combination must affect internally the combined units, it would be forced to reject the universe as utterly as it rejects the self.)

81.   There is no doubt to which of these two species of unities the finite person belongs.   His existence obviously depends on his external relations.   Indeed, as was said above, there is no other example, except the finite self, which completely realises this type.   But it does not follow that the finite person is, therefore, imperfect as a person.   A perfect person must, certainly, be self-determined.   But then there is nothing to prevent the finite person from being self-determined.

Hegel has shown in the Logic, when treating of Quality, that determination by another involves determination by self. But the self-determination which is considered in such an early stage of the dialectic, is, of course, a comparatively abstract and unreal notion.   If a person is to be considered as self-determined, a fuller and deeper self-determination must be meant.   It is characteristic of a person that he has an ideal, to which his actual existence may or may not conform.   There would be no meaning in saying that a stone ought to have a different shape from that which it actually has—unless we were considering some external relation which the stone bore to conscious beings.   It has no ideal of existence, which would enable us to say that, in itself, it was less perfect than it ought to be.   But there is a very intelligible meaning when it is said of a drunkard or a fool—either by himself or by others—that he is not what he should be, and this without reference to his effect upon any other person.

When an individual proposes an end to himself, as every person does, we cannot call such an individual self-determined unless that ideal is realised in his actual condition. And, if it is so realised, we call him completely self-determined—with some reservation in the case of an ideal which we conceive to be imperfect, and therefore transitory. Now there is no reason whatever why a finite person should be incapable of realising his ideal nature. He can only do so, no doubt, by his relations to others. But why should he be unable to do it perfectly in this way? The finite persons that we know have no aspect of their nature which does not come under knowledge, volition, or emotion. If all these were realised in their perfection—whether that perfection lay in themselves, or in some higher unity to which they all led—we could conceive nothing more wanting to the perfect development of the person. Now so far from knowledge, volition, and emotion being hampered, or restrained from perfection, by the relation to outside reality of the person who experiences them, we find that they actually consist in his relations to outside reality.

82. We may notice, too, that as our personality becomes more self-determined, its relations with outside. reality become more vivid, intimate, and complex. A man of clear thought, firm will, and intense feelings, living under favourable circumstances in a community of civilized men, is surely a more perfect person, and more completely self-determined than an idiot, or a baby. But such a man certainly realises more vividly than an idiot or a baby the distinction between himself and the surrounding reality, and is more fully conscious of the way in which his relations to that reality permeate and determine his whole nature.

There can be only one meaning in calling a thing imperfect without qualification—that it does not realise the ideal inherent in its nature. Now what necessary imperfection in the realisation of my nature is brought about by the mere fact that I am not the universe? What postulate or aspiration is involved in personality which is incompatible with external relations on the part of the person? Lotze mentions none, nor can I conceive what they would be.

Of course, if the relations of the person with the rest of reality are such as to cramp and thwart the development of his ideal nature, then the personality will be rendered more or less imperfect. But then the imperfection—which is never quite absent, no doubt, in the world we live in—is not the result of the finitude. It is not because we are in relation to other reality that we are imperfect, but because we are in the wrong relations.

Relation to something external does not in itself destroy the harmony of the related object. No doubt it does so in any being which does not accept and acquiesce in the relation. For then there would be conflict and not harmony. Nothing could be less harmonious than the state of a finite being who was trying to realise an ideal of isolation. But if the ideal which he posited was one of life as a part of a vitally connected whole—and such an ideal does not seem repugnant to our nature—what want of harmony would be introduced by the fact that he was a member of such a whole?

83. There is thus no reason to hold that a finite person is necessarily an imperfect person. And, even if this were so, it would give us no reason to believe that the Absolute was a person. It is true that the Absolute is not finite, and is not related to anything outside itself. And therefore it has a quality which, *if it were a person,* would make it the only perfect person, on this theory of what constitutes the perfection of personality. But, even if it were *essential* to a perfect person to have nothing outside him, it would not follow that to be the whole of reality was *sufficient* to constitute a perfect person, or even to constitute a person at all. Personality, Lotze has told us, consists in self-enjoyment, in "direct sense of self[1]," and, even if we admit his contention that only the Infinite could have this perfectly, it does not follow that the Infinite has it at all. (I am using Infinite here in the more ordinary sense of the word. By Hegel's usage a "finite" person who was not the whole reality but was completely harmonious with himself would be as infinite as the Absolute.)

---

[1] *op. cit.* Bk IX. Chap. IV (iii. 571, trans. ii. 679).

84. Thus Lotze's argument has two defects. He has not shown that the finitude of finite persons makes them imperfect, and he has not shown that the perfect self-determination of the Absolute is the self-determination of a person. In leaving the consideration of Lotze's treatment of the subject, it is to be noticed that our objections to it do not challenge Lotze's right to consider the Absolute as personal. For he regarded the Absolute as not exhausted by its manifestations, and those manifestations as to a certain extent, from an ethical point of view, outside the Absolute. And this obviously introduces fresh considerations. We have only dealt with those of his arguments for the personality of the Absolute which are also· applicable to the Absolute as Hegel has conceived it.

85. These criticisms of Lotze may suggest to us a more direct and independent argument. The finite person is dependent, for the element of differentiation and multiplicity, on its relations with outside reality. And, while that element is, in one sense, inside the person, in another sense it is outside him. For the person distinguishes himself from every element of his content. There is no part of that content which he cannot make into an object, and so put over against himself as the subject.

There must, therefore, be some element in the person other than the differentiation or multiplicity—some element which is not only inside the person in the sense in which the multiplicity is inside, but which is also inside in the sense in which the multiplicity is outside. For unless something remains inside, in this sense, it would be impossible to say that anything was outside. This element can have no differentiation or multiplicity in it. For all multiplicity belongs to the content which can be distinguished from the self, and which can therefore be said, in this sense, to fall outside the person. It follows that the element in question must be absolutely simple and indivisible—a pure unit.

Here again we must be on our guard against a class of objections to such conclusions as this, which, while professing to be objections to atomism, are really based upon it. To deny that an element in a whole can have a nature, which it would be impossible for the whole itself to have, is an atomistic fallacy. For it tacitly assumes that a complex whole is built up out of its elements, and that those elements could exist, or at any rate be imagined, outside of the whole. In that case they would themselves be wholes, and could have no characteristics incom-. patible with this. But we shall avoid this error, if we remember that a self-subsistent whole can be analysed into elements which are not self-subsistent, and which cannot ever be imagined in isolation.

In the present case we must admit that such a simple and indivisible unity, if taken for a separate being, would not only be utterly insignificant, but could not exist at all. The only category under which we could bring it would be Pure Being, and it does not require much speculative subtlety to see, in this case, that Pure Being is equivalent to Nothing. But then we do not assert that such an indivisible element does exist by itself. On the contrary, it only exists in connection with the element of multiplicity, and cannot exist, or be conceived, without it.

It is also evident that no such person could exist, or be conceived as existing, apart from all other reality. For the element of the not-self in each person is obviously dependent on the existence of outside reality. And the only other element in the person—the indivisible unity to which the element of the not-self stands in relation—cannot exist except as combined with the element of the not-self. It follows, certainly, that an isolated self is impossible. But this was not denied, nor is it incompatible with any of the conclusions which we have previously reached. We found reason, indeed, in the last chapter, to consider finite selves as fundamentally real. But they were not real as isolated, or as externally connected. They were only real as connected in a unity which was as close and vital as its differentiations. Indeed, it was the very closeness of the unity which made us conclude that its fundamental differentiations could only be selves.

86. We are thus entitled to adhere to our conclusion that, in every finite person, a simple and indivisible unity exists as an element. This element is, of course, no more essential to the personality than the other element of multiplicity. But, although not more essential, it may perhaps be called a more positive element of personality, for reasons somewhat analogous to those for which the Thesis of a triad is a more positive element in the Synthesis than the Antithesis is. The element of the unity in the person belongs exclusively to him, while the element of the multiplicity, though it belongs to him, belongs also to the outside reality, with which he is in connection. And, while the element of multiplicity is an element in his nature, it is only part of his nature by the fact that he distinguishes himself from it, separates himself from it, and excludes it from himself in one sense, while he includes it in another. The element of the unity, on the other hand, is in no sense distinguishable from the person.

The unity of the Absolute is as real as its differentiations, and as real as the unity of a perfect finite self—while it is much more real than the unity of a finite self as it manifests itself imperfectly in this imperfect world. But the Absolute is a unity of system, and not a unity of centre, and the element of unity in it cannot be a simple and indivisible point, like that of the finite self. For if the unity is of this sort, then, by virtue of its simplicity and indivisibility, it excludes its differentiations from itself in one sense, while including them in another. But the Absolute cannot exclude its differentiations from itself in any sense. A finite person can exclude his differentiations, for they have somewhere to exist in, in so far as they are excluded from his self—namely, the rest of reality, to which in fact they belong as much as they do to him. But there is nothing outside the Absolute. And it would therefore be impossible for it to exclude its differentiations from itself in any sense. For in as far as they are not in it, they are absolutely wrong.

Now it seems to me that it is just the presence of this element of indivisible unity which forms for us that "direct sense of self" in which Lotze rightly places the positive essence of personality. The unity, indeed, cannot exist without the multiplicity. But then it is true of the sense of self, also, that it is never found alone. We are never conscious of self without being conscious of something else as well. If, for us, the sense

6—2

of self is not in this element of indivisible unity, I cannot tell where it is.

87. The Absolute, as we have seen, cannot have this element of indivisible unity. And, therefore, it cannot have the personality that we have. "But," it will perhaps be answered, "it can have some other sort of personality. No one ever supposed the Absolute to be exactly the same sort of person as we are, and how can we tell that it cannot be a person in some different way?"

This, however, is unjustifiable. The position is no longer the same as when we were discussing Lotze's arguments for the possibility of a sense of self without a Non-Ego. There we admitted that the consciousness of the Non-Ego was *not* the direct sense of self, and that we could distinguish in thought the one from the other. We knew of no case in which the sense of self was found without the consciousness of the Non-Ego; there was nothing in experience which suggested that they could exist apart; nor could we even imagine in what way a direct sense of self could exist without the consciousness of the Non-Ego, how it would supply the place of that consciousness, or what difference the change would make to itself. Still, the sense of self *is* not the consciousness of the Non-Ego. And thus there is an abstract probability, though a valueless one, that the sense of self may exist where there is no Non-Ego, and consequently no consciousness of it.

But here the case is different. The sense of self *is* the indivisible unity in consciousness. The Absolute has not the indivisible unity, and therefore it has no sense of self. Therefore it is not a person. There is no room left for any further possibilities. If the argument has any validity whatever, all such possibilities are excluded. The argument is no longer that the qualities of the Absolute are inconsistent with an accompaniment without which we cannot imagine personality. It is that the qualities of the Absolute are inconsistent with the essence of personality itself.

88. Our conclusion then is that personality cannot be an attribute of a unity which has no indivisible centre of reference, and which is from all points of view (as the personalities we know

are from one point of view) all in every part. The impossibility
of this may become more obvious if we consider that the differentiations, of which the Absolute is the unity, are themselves persons. If the Absolute had a consciousness of self,
that consciousness could not fall outside the finite persons.
For then those persons would not fully manifest the Absolute,
and the relation would be one of those expressed by the
categories of Essence—which certainly cannot be an adequate
expression of the nature of the Hegelian Absolute. And the
self-consciousness of the Absolute, again, cannot be in each
differentiation separately, for then it would be identical with
the self-consciousness of each finite person, and the Absolute,
as a unity, would have no self-consciousness at all. But the
only remaining alternative is that the self-consciousness of the
Absolute is in the unity of its differentiations. Can we attach
any meaning to the statement that one self-conscious being
should consist of a multiplicity of self-conscious beings, in
such a way that it had no reality apart from them? Or
that one self-conscious being should be part of another in
such a way that it had no reality apart from it? And yet
these statements must be accepted if the Absolute is to be
self-conscious. If it is more than its differentiations, we fall
into the contradictions of Essence. If it is not more than
its differentiations it cannot distinguish itself from them
without distinguishing them from itself, and so annihilating
them.

89. Of course we might, if we thought it worth while,
apply the term personality to all spiritual unities (or to all
spiritual unities where the unity was as vital as the differentiations) and not merely to those which have a direct sense of
self resembling that which we each know in ourselves. And
so we should gain the right—whatever that may be worth—to
speak of the Absolute as personal. But this rather empty
gain would be balanced by several serious inconveniences.
There are two different views about the Supreme Being—one
that it is a spiritual unity, and one that it has a sense of self
like our own. The first of these is not always accompanied by
the second, and it is convenient to have a separate name for

each. At present we can call the first Idealism, and the second
Theism. But if we call Idealism by the name of Theism, we
shall have no name left to distinguish those Theists who do,
and those Theists who do not, take the spiritual unity in
question to have a sense of self with some conceivable resemblance to our own. And the distinction, which is thus
ignored, is of great importance for metaphysics, and still more
for religion.

Moreover, if the Absolute is to be called a person because
it is a spiritual unity, then every College, every goose-club,
every gang of thieves, must also be called a person. For they
are all spiritual unities. They all consist exclusively of human
beings, and they all unite their members in some sort of unity.
Their unities are indeed much less perfect than the unity of
the Absolute. But if an imperfect unity is not to be called an
imperfect person, then the name of person must be denied to
ourselves as manifested here and now. For assuredly none
of us at present have reached that perfect and harmonious self-
determination which is essential to a perfect person. Now we
call ourselves persons, but no one, I believe, has ever proposed
to call a football team a person. But if we now called the
Absolute a person, we should have no defence for refusing the
name to the football team. For it shares its imperfection
with human beings, and its want of a direct sense of self with
the Absolute. It can only, therefore, be confusing to call the
Absolute a person because it is a spiritual unity.

It might be suggested that the word person should be
applied to the Absolute and to ourselves, to the exclusion of
other spiritual unities, on the ground that they alone are
completely adequate expressions of reality. The Absolute, of
course, is so, and finite persons are its fundamental differentiations. And thus they deserve—even when manifested
imperfectly—a title which is properly refused to unities which,
in perfection, are not perfected but transcended. But this
change in the meaning of personality would also be confusing.
For it would compel us to say of such philosophies as Lotze's
and Mr Bradley's, which do not accept the finite self as an
adequate expression of reality, that they denied human person-

ality, which would be a considerable departure from the ordinary meaning of words.

Thus considerable inconvenience would be caused by extending the meaning of personality to include an Absolute without a direct sense of self. Nor does it appear what advantage would be gained by keeping a name when the old meaning has been surrendered.

90. It has often been suggested that the Absolute, if not a person, may be something higher than a person. And this view has often been gladly adopted by those to whom the only other alternative seemed to be that it should be something lower. But from what has been said about the nature of the Absolute, it will follow that the whole question is unmeaning. The unity of the Absolute is not more or less perfect than that unity of each of its differentiations which we call personality. Each has an entirely different ideal of perfection—the Absolute to be the unity of its differentiations, the perfect differentiation to be the unity of all the surrounding differentiations. Neither of these ideals is higher than the other. Each is indispensable to the other. The differentiations cannot exist except in the Absolute, nor could the Absolute exist unless each of its differentiations was a person.

To ask which of the two is the higher is as unmeaning as to ask whether the state or the citizen[1] is higher. The state and the citizen have each their own excellencies. And these cannot be compared, since they have different ideals of excellence. The perfection of the citizen is not to be like a state, nor the perfection of a state to be like a citizen. And neither of them has any worth except in its difference from the other, for, except for that difference, neither could exist. A state cannot exist without citizens, nor citizens without a state.

The general unwillingness to regard the Absolute as impersonal is, I think, largely due to a failure to recognize

---

[1] That is, *as* citizen. It is quite possible to maintain that the man, who is the citizen, is an eternal and adequate expression of reality, while the state is a transitory and imperfect expression of it. But then the man, in so far as he is such an eternal and adequate expression, and therefore superior to the state, is not only a citizen.

this complementary character of the two unities. It is supposed that, if the Absolute is not personal, it must be higher or lower than persons. To suppose it to be lower might perhaps be maintained to be contradictory, and would certainly be cheerless. But if we make the Absolute to be higher than personality, it must surpass and transcend it, and it is thus natural to say that the Absolute is personal and more.

91. I have now explained, as far as I am able, the grounds on which I think that personality ought not to be ascribed to the Absolute, if we accept Hegel's account of the Absolute as correct. It remains for us to consider what effect, on our conduct and our feelings, would be produced by the general adoption of such a belief—a belief which is, of course, equivalent to a rejection of the notion of a personal God. I have endeavoured to show above[1] that the nature of these effects is irrelevant to the truth of the belief. But it is nevertheless a matter of interest.

Let us begin with the effects of such a belief on conduct. Would it, in the first place, render virtue less binding, less imperative, than before? Surely not. Different philosophers have given very differing accounts of the nature of moral obligation, but I doubt if any of them have so bound it up with the notion of God's personality that the disproof of that personality would efface the distinction between virtue and vice. Some moralists, indeed, have asserted that any satis- factory morality rests entirely on the belief that God will ensure that the righteous shall be happier than the wicked. And it has also been asserted that it.would be absurd to act virtuously unless we believed that virtue would win in the long run. But these two theories, while they certainly require that the Absolute should work for righteousness, do not require a personal Absolute. If, on the other hand, we hold it not impossible to pursue the good, irrespective of our personal happiness, and without the certainty of eventual victory, the obligation, whatever it may be, to virtuous action will remain unaffected by whatever theory we may hold as to the nature of the Absolute.

[1] Sections 75—78.

Nor would our views on the personality of the Absolute affect our power of determining particular actions to be virtuous or vicious. Some systems assert that good and evil depend on the arbitrary will of God. But this is only a theory of the genesis of distinctions which are admitted to exist. Indeed, it is only from the existence of the distinctions that the will of God in the matter is inferred. If a personal God were rejected, these systems would require a fresh theory of the causes which make benevolence right and cowardice wrong. But the rejection could have no tendency to make us suppose that benevolence was wrong and·cowardice right.

92. So much is very generally admitted. It is seldom asserted at the present day that, without a belief in a personal God, we should have no obligation to be virtuous, or no means of ascertaining what virtue is. But it is sometimes maintained that, without a belief in a personal God, our motives for doing right would be so diminished in strength that we should become perceptibly less moral.

The point is important, but I do not see how it is to be settled. For, since we are not now discovering what we ought to do under the circumstances, but what we should do, it cannot be decided by abstract reasoning. It is a matter for empirical observation and induction. And there seems to be no experience which is relevant.

On the one hand, we can draw no inference from the fact that many people who do believe in a personal God use that belief as an incentive in well-doing. It does not follow that, if it was withdrawn, they would do less well. Many convalescents continue to use sticks which they would find, if they tried, they could dispense with. And the abandonment of a belief is never entirely a negative process. It must produce positive changes in the beliefs which remain, and may itself be caused by a new positive belief. In the present case we only found reason to reject the idea of a personal God because it was incompatible with a very positive notion of the Absolute. And the new positive beliefs whose arrival is the correlative of the disappearance of the old one may have the same effects on action as their predecessors had.

On the other hand it is unfair to infer from the cases of men of illustrious virtue who have rejected the doctrine of a personal God, that the general rejection of that doctrine would not injure morality. For all men are swayed by public opinion and by tradition; and it is impossible to demonstrate the falsity of the suggestion that the virtues of Atheists may depend in part on the Theism of their neighbours and parents.

There are countries, indeed, in which religions have flourished for many years which involve, at any rate for their educated adherents, the denial of a personal *supreme* God. And the fact that educated Brahmanists and Buddhists are about as virtuous as other men sufficiently disproves all danger of a complete moral collapse as a consequence of the disbelief in God's personality. But then it is impossible to prove that the standard of virtue in India and China would not be rather higher if more of their inhabitants had adopted Theistic religions, or that the standard of virtue in England would not slightly fall with the abandonment of such religions.

93.   The question seems insoluble except by an experiment conducted on a large scale for several centuries, and such an experiment mankind seems in no hurry to make. We may, however, observe that there is an argument commonly used on such subjects, which, whether true or not, is irrelevant here. It endeavours to show that, without the belief that all things work together for good, and, in particular, without the belief in immortality, men, or at any rate most men, would not have sufficient energy and enthusiasm to attain a high standard of virtue, though the obligation to be virtuous would not be diminished. Even if this were so, it would not prove that the adoption of the theory supported in this chapter would have any bad effect on morality. For our theory is compatible with—is even directly connected with—the belief in immortality which is expounded in the last chapter, and the Absolute, although not personal, is nevertheless spiritual, and cannot, therefore, be out of harmony with the most fundamental desires of our own spirits.

Again, if nothing but the influence of tradition and surroundings keeps morality from deteriorating when the belief

in a personal God is rejected, it might surely be expected that
some trace of moral deterioration might be found at those times
and places when this belief is most often questioned. And
I doubt if an impartial study of history would discover anything
of the sort.

Whether the belief in a personal God is now more or less
universal than it has been in the centuries which have passed
since the Renaissance cannot, of course, be determined with
any exactness. But such slight evidence as we have seems to
point to the conclusion that those who deny it were never so
numerous as at present. And those who do hold it, hold it,
it can scarcely be doubted, with far less confidence. There was
a time when this belief was held capable of demonstration with
evidence equal to the evidence of mathematics—a time when
the safest basis for our moral duties was held to be a demonstration that they could be deduced from the existence of God.
But at the present time we find that the belief in a personal
God is, with many men who are counted as believing it, not
much more than a hope, entertained with more or less confidence,
that a doctrine, the truth of which appears to them so eminently
desirable, may in fact be true. Even when arguments from
probability are accepted, the old ideas of mathematical certainty
are seldom to be found. And when attempts are made, at the
present time, to show that the personality of God is logically
connected with morality, it is the personality of God, and not
morality, which is thought to be supported by the conjunction.

All this might be expected to produce some change for the
worse in our morality, if our morality really was dependent on
the belief in a personal God. But is such a deterioration to
be detected ? Our moral ideals change, no doubt, but in their
changes they seem to become more, not less, comprehensive.
And there is nothing to suggest that we realise those ideals
to a smaller extent than our ancestors realised their own.

94. The effect which the abandonment of the belief in
the personality of God would have on the satisfaction of our
emotions is perhaps even more interesting than its effect on
morality. But it is even more difficult to determine. Some
people find all love for finite persons inadequate, and are

unsatisfied if they cannot also regard the infinite and eternal with that love which can only be felt for a person. Others, again, would say that our love for finite persons was only inadequate in so far as it fell below its own ideal, and that, if perfect, it would afford such an utterly complete realisation of our whole nature, that nothing else would be desirable or possible. It would be superfluous to add the love of God to a love which, not in metaphor, but as a statement of metaphysical truth, must be called God, and the whole of God.

Which of these is the higher? Is it the first class, because they demand more objects of love than the second? Or is it the second, because they find more in one sort of love than the first? I do not see how this is to be answered. Or rather, I do not see how the answer which each of us will give can be of interest except to himself and his friends. For there are no arguments by which one side might convince the other.

95. But even if the belief that there was no personal God were disadvantageous to our morality and our feelings, would the belief that the Absolute was personal be any better? I think it very improbable. For if there is any reason to regard the belief in a personal God as essential in these respects, it can only be the belief in a personal God as it has hitherto prevailed among mankind. And this belief certainly does not refer to a personal Absolute, but to a being who is not the only reality, though he is the supreme reality. It regards us as the creatures of whom God is the creator, as the subjects of whom he is the king, as the children of whom he is the father, but emphatically not as the parts of which he is the whole, or as the differentiations within his unity. Royalty and fatherhood are, indeed, only metaphors, and admittedly not perfectly adequate. But then the fact that neither of the related beings is part of the other does not seem to be a point in which the metaphor is considered as inadequate. On the contrary, it seems rather one of the points in the metaphor on which popular religion insists. However much the dependence of the human being may be emphasised, there never seems any tendency to include him in the deity. (Such tendencies indeed appear from time to time among mystical thinkers, but they are no more evidence of the general needs of mankind than the other systems which do without a personal God at all.) And this is confirmed by the fact that the common metaphors all agree on this point. Such relations as that of a cell to an organism, or of a citizen to the state, have never been found to be appropriate expressions of the ordinary religious emotions. It seems to follow that, if the conception of a personal God had shown itself indispensable to our practical life, we should find no satisfaction in such an Absolute as Hegel's, even if we had contrived to regard it as personal.

96. One question remains. Is it appropriate to call the Absolute by the name of God, if we deny it personality ? There is eminent authority in philosophy—especially that of Spinoza and of Hegel himself—for giving this name to the true reality, whatever that may be. But this seems wasteful. We have three distinct conceptions, (a) the true reality whatever it may be, (b) a spiritual unity, (c) a spiritual unity which is a person. We have only two names to serve for all three—the Absolute and God—and, if we use them as synonymous, we wilfully throw away a chance of combining clearness and brevity.

Then there is no doubt that God is not used in that sense in popular phraseology. In popular phraseology God is only used of a spiritual unity which is a person. In such a matter as this, I submit, philosophy ought to conform its terminology to that of popular usage. It is impossible to keep philosophical terms exclusively for the use of philosophical students. Whenever the subject is one of general interest—and the existence of a God is certainly one of these—the opinions of great philosophers will be reported at second hand to the world at large. And if the world at large hears Spinoza described as a "God-intoxicated man," or as more truly an Acosmist than an Atheist, or if it finds that Hegel's Logic is one long attempt to determine the nature of God, it will be very apt to conceive that Spinoza and Hegel believed in God as a person. Now it is universally admitted that Spinoza did nothing of the kind, and I shall try to prove, in Chapter VIII, that Hegel did not do so either. At any rate it is clear that his use of the word God proves, when we consider his definition of it, nothing at all as to his belief in a personal God.

If the philosophical and the popular usage ought to be made identical, it is clear that it is philosophy that ought to give way. The terminology of a special branch of study may be changed by the common àction of a moderate number of writers on philosophy. But to change the popular meaning of the word God, and its equivalents in the other European languages, in the mouths of the millions of people who use them, would be impossible, even if it were desirable. Besides, the popular terminology has no word by which it can replace God, while philosophy has already a synonym for God in the wider sense—namely the Absolute. And, finally, philosophers are by no means unanimous in agreeing with the usage of Spinoza and Hegel. Kant himself uses God in the narrower sense.

I think, therefore, that it will be best to depart from Hegel's own usage, and to express our result by saying that the Absolute is not God, and, in consequence, that there is no God. This corollary implies that the word God signifies not only a personal, but also a supreme being, and that no finite differentiation of the Absolute, whatever his power and wisdom, would be entitled to the name. It may be objected that this would cause the theory of the dialectic to be classed, under the name of Atheism, with very different systems—such as deny the unity of all reality to be spiritual, or deny it to be more vital than a mere aggregate. But all negative names must be more or less miscellaneous in their denotation. It is much more important to preserve a definite meaning for Theism than for Atheism, and this can only be done if Theism is uniformly used to include a belief in the personality of God.

CHAPTER IV.

THE SUPREME GOOD AND THE MORAL CRITERION.

97. WHAT may we conclude, on Hegelian principles, about the Supreme Good? The Logic has given us the Absolute Idea, which stands to knowledge in the same relation as the idea of the Supreme Good, if there is one, stands to action. In examining the Absolute Idea, we find it involves the existence of a unity of individuals, each of whom, perfectly individual through his perfect unity with all the rest, places before himself an end and finds the whole of the universe in complete harmony with that end.

If we have been justified in taking the Absolute Idea as only expressible in a unity of individuals, the rest of this description clearly follows. The individuals must be in harmony, and how can a conscious individual be in harmony with another, except by proposing an end to which that other is a means, though not, of course, a mere means? Besides this, if we look at the final stages of the Logic, we shall find that the idea of End, once introduced at the close of the Objective Notion, is never again lost. It is identical with the category of Life: in Cognition (which includes Volition) the only change is that the End has become conscious; while the transition to the Absolute Idea only alters the manner in which the harmony is held to be produced.

This is the supreme reality—the only reality *sub specie aeternitatis*, the goal of the process of the universe *sub specie temporis*. It will be very desirable if we can identify the supreme reality with the supreme good.

It is not the supreme good simply because it is the supreme reality. This is scarcely more than a truism. But it always wants repetition, and never more than at present. It is often asserted that ideals are real because they are good, and from this it follows by formal logic that, if they were not real, they would not be good. Against this we must protest for the sake both of truth and of goodness. The idea of the good comes from that paradoxical power which is possessed by every conscious member of the universe—the power to judge and condemn part or all of that very system of reality of which he himself is a part. If the whole constitution of the whole universe led, by the clearest development of its essential nature, to our universal damnation or our resolution into aggregates of material atoms, the complete and inevitable reality of these results would not give even the first step towards proving them good.

98. But although the supremely real, as such, is not the supremely good, we may admit, I think, that if the supreme reality be such as Hegel has described it to be, then it will coincide with the supreme good. For, in the reality so defined, every conscious being—and there are no other beings—will express all his individuality in one end, which will truly and adequately express it. The fulfilment of such an end as this would give satisfaction, not partial and temporary, but complete and eternal. And since each individual finds the whole universe in harmony with his end, it will necessarily follow that the end is fulfilled. Here is a supreme good ready to our hands.

99. Hegel has thus helped us to the conception of the supreme good, firstly by suggesting it, and secondly by proving that it contains no contradictory elements. Such a supreme good, we notice, is not purely hedonistic. It contains pleasure, no doubt, for the fulfilment of the ends of conscious beings must always involve that. But the pleasure is only one element of the perfect state. The supreme good is not pleasure as such, but this particular pleasant state.

100. It does not follow, however, that, because we have determined the supreme good, we have therefore determined the criterion of morality. They can be identical, no doubt, but they need not be so. The object of a criterion is merely practical—to guide our actions towards good. For this purpose we require something which shall be a sure sign of the good. But a thing may have many marks besides its essence, and one of these may often be the more convenient test. A stock is not made safe by a stock-broker's belief in it. But an ordinary investor will find the opinion of a good stock-broker a much surer test of the safety of a stock than could be furnished by his own efforts to estimate the forces, which will be the real causes of safety or danger.

We must remember, also, that for a satisfactory criterion of morality we do not require a sure test of all good, but only a sure test of such good as can possibly be secured by our voluntary efforts to secure it. If we find a criterion which will tell us this, it will be unnecessary to reject it because it is not also a satisfactory test of some other element of good, which we may enjoy when we get it, but cannot get by our own action.

101. But is a moral criterion wanted at all? It might be maintained that it was not. It would only be wanted, it might be said, if we decided our actions by general rules, which we do not. Our moral action depends on particular judgments that A is better than B, which we recognize with comparative immediacy, in the same way that we recognize that one plate is hotter than another, or one picture more beautiful than another. It is on these particular intuitive judgments of value, and not on general rules, that our moral action is based.

This seems to me to be a dangerous exaggeration of an important truth. It is quite true that, if we did not begin with such judgments, we should have neither morality nor ethics. But it is equally true that we should have neither morality nor ethics if we stopped, where we must begin, with these judgments, and treated them as decisive and closing discussion. For our moral judgments are hopelessly contradictory of one another. Of two intelligent and conscientious men, A often judges to be right what B judges to be wrong. Or A, at forty, judges that to be wrong, which at twenty he judged to be right.

Now these judgments are contradictory. For every moral judgment claims to be objective, and demands assent from all men. If *A* asserts that he likes sugar in his tea, and *B* asserts that, for his part, he does not, both statements may be true. But if *A* asserts that to be right which *B* asserts to be wrong one of them must be in error, since they are making contrary statements about the same thing.

It is therefore impossible to treat all particular judgments of value as valid. We must do with them as we do with the particular judgments of existence—that is to say, treat them as the materials in which truth may be discovered, but not as themselves all true. We must reject some, and accept others. Now I do not see how this is to be done except by discovering some common quality which the valid judgments, and they alone, possess. And, if we test the particular judgments by means of this quality we have a moral criterion. Even if we confine ourselves to saying that the judgments of the best, or of the wisest, men are to be followed, there will be a criterion. For we cannot recognize the best, or the wisest in ethical matters, without a general idea of the good. To make the recognition itself depend on one of the particular intuitive judgments to be tested would be a vicious circle.

102. A criterion is therefore necessary. Before considering its nature, we must consider an ambiguity as to the matter which it is to judge. The ethical significance of the content of any moment of time is double. It may be considered in itself. In that case its moral significance will depend on the closeness with which it resembles the content which would realise the supreme good. Or·it may be considered as a means towards a future end. In that case its moral significance will depend on the degree in which it tends to advance or to retard the eventual complete realisation of the supreme good.

It would be desirable, no doubt, if these two standards always coincided—if every action which was immediately good hastened the coming of the supreme good, and every action which was immediately bad retarded it. But we have no reason to believe that this is so in any particular case, and we have many reasons to believe that it is not so always. We know that good often comes out of evil, and evil out of good. This is a matter of every-day observation. And Hegel has shown us that good never comes, except out of conquered evil, and that evil must arise before it can be conquered[1]. To bring our conduct to-day as close as possible to the supreme good may be to help or to hinder the coming of the supreme good in all its perfection.

This does not, however, introduce any conflict into our moral life. For of the two possible standards by which omniscience might judge a proposed action only one is practicable for us. We can see, to some extent, what conduct embodies the supreme good least imperfectly. But we have no material whatever for deciding what conduct will tend to bring about the complete realisation of the supreme good. That lies so far in the future, and involves so much of which we are completely ignorant, that we are quite unable to predict the road which will lead to it. What we do know, if we follow Hegel, is this—that the road we do take will lead to it, because the supreme good is also the supreme reality, and is therefore the inevitable goal of all temporal process.

It follows that the criterion of moral action which we require is not one which will determine what actions will most conduce to the eventual establishment of absolute perfection. It is one which will tell us what actions will bring about, immediately, or in the comparatively near future which we can predict with reasonable certainty, the state which conforms as closely as possible to that perfection.

The points I wish to prove in this chapter are (1) that the idea of perfection cannot give us any criterion of moral action ; (2) that the hedonic computation of pleasures and pains does give us a definite criterion, right or wrong ; (3) that the use of this latter criterion is not incompatible with the recognition of perfection as the supreme good, and would give us, if not unerring guidance, still guidance less erroneous than would be afforded by any other applicable criterion. .

103. Let us consider the first point. When two courses are presented to a man who wishes to act rightly, and he is in

---

[1] Cp. Chap. vi.

doubt which of them he shall adopt, will he be assisted by reflecting on the nature of the supreme reality, which we have decided to be also the supreme good ? It is clear, to begin with, that if either of the courses would result in the immediate realisation of the supreme good, it would be the course to take. But it is equally clear that this cannot ever take place, in the present state of ourselves and our experience. The reality contemplated by Hegel in his Absolute Idea is absolutely spiritual, absolutely timeless, absolutely perfect. Now none of us ever get a chance of performing an action the result of which would satisfy these three conditions. The result of any actions possible to us now would be a state in which spirit was still encompassed with matter, in which change still took place, and in which perfection, if rather nearer than before, was still obviously not attained.

It is useless then to test our actions by enquiring if they will realise the supreme good. None of them will do that, and we are reduced to considering which of them will enable us to reach rather nearer to supreme good than we were before.

104. This question has not, I think, been faced quite fairly by the school who assert the idea of perfection to be an adequate criterion. They generally take a case in which some form of the desire for good as good—some form of specifically moral feeling—is opposed to something desired regardless of, or in opposition to, morality. They have then comparatively little difficulty in asserting, with some probability, that the idea of perfection would be a sufficient guide to direct us to the first rather than to the second. For perfection clearly includes a positing of the supreme good by each person as his end ; and this positing would only differ from desire in excluding all thought of the possibility of non-fulfilment. Surely, then, the good will must raise any state, of which it is a moment, above all other states which do not participate in it.

But even if this criterion is true, it is almost always useless. It is of some use if there is a question of another will besides that of the agent. For then there would be some meaning in saying that A's duty to B was to endeavour to make B do that which B himself thought morally right. Here the will to be made good is not the agent's own will, and so there is no tautology.

But we have other duties besides our duty to influence the wills of our neighbours. And the attempt to use the criterion more generally, by applying it to the agent's will, breaks down. If A demands which of two courses the ideal of perfection prescribes for him here and now, all the reply that can be made is that it will be best for him to take the course which he takes believing it to be the best. Now he certainly will take the course which he believes to be morally the best. For, if not, he would not have sought guidance in an ethical criterion. Such a criterion can never give a reason why the morally good should be desired. All it can do is to tell us what things are morally good.

If A has not decided to act morally, the criterion will be ineffective, for, if he has not decided to act rightly, why should he refrain from an action because it is wrong ? If, on the other hand, he has decided to act morally, and appeals to the criterion to tell him what course he should take, it is clear that each course claims to be the morally right one, and he is undecided. In that case to tell him that he will be right, if he pursues the course which he judges to be right, is to tell him nothing, for what he wants is to be helped in judging which of them is right.

105. The practical use of ethics—and it is this we are considering—can only occur, then, when a man has resolved to act in conformity with duty, and is not certain what course duty prescribes. Two courses of action may each be in itself morally desirable, and may be incompatible, so that we are in doubt which to pursue.

Two courses of conduct, let us suppose, are presented to us. By taking a we shall further the end a, by taking b the end β. Both a and β are good, but a and b are incompatible. Can the principle of perfection tell us whether a or β is, under the circumstances, to be preferred? It seems to me that it is impossible in most cases, if not in all. It is clear that neither a nor β can be expected to be realised unchanged in the supreme good. For any end which can be attained by an action in our present state would still be an element in an imperfect and incomplete world, would still be tainted with imperfection, and could not therefore, as such, form part of absolute perfection. On the other hand every end which a man could represent to himself as a moral ideal has some real good in it. It would therefore form an element, however transcended and altered, of the supreme good. Thus we should only be able to say, of both a and β, that they were imperfect goods. Which is the least imperfect? That could only be settled by comparing each of them with the supreme good—a comparison which it is scarcely ever possible to carry out so as to assign a preference to either alternative.

106. Let us take an example. Most people think that the institution of marriage, as it at present exists in civilized countries, is on the whole a good thing. But others think it a mistake. They hold that all unions between man and woman should be terminable at any moment by the simple desire of the parties, who should then each of them be free to form a fresh union. And this they put forward as a moral advance. Can the contemplation of the supreme good help us to decide this question? It is clear, at any rate, that we cannot solve the difficulty by simply copying the pattern which the supreme good lays down for us. For there the difficulty could not arise at all. In a world of pure spirit there could be no sexual desire, and in a world which was timeless there could be no propagation of children—two elements which have considerable importance when we are dealing with marriage. And in such a state all relations would be permanent together, so that the question could never be raised whether outside relations ought to change in harmony with internal changes.

Whichever course we take, therefore, we shall not be able to model ourselves completely on the supreme good. Which course will lead us to the result least removed from the supreme good? We find ourselves in a hopeless antinomy—hopeless, not from the actual want of a solution, but because the solution requires a knowledge of detail far beyond our power.

The conservative side may assert, and with perfect truth,

that in perfection all relations are absolutely constant. But if they infer from this that a minimum of change in the relationships between particular men and particular women is most consonant to the supreme good, the innovators may reply, with equal truth, that in perfection all relations will be the free expression of the inner nature of the individual, and draw from this—with equal right—the contrary conclusion —that every relation between a man and a woman should cease with the cessation of the feelings which led them into it. If it is answered to this—as it certainly may be—that true freedom, as we find it in perfection, is not capricious but manifests itself in objective uniformities, it may with equal force be retorted that true constancy does not lie in clinging to external arrangements which have become unfit expressions of the internal nature of the persons concerned, but in the continuous readjustment of the external to the developing nature of the internal. If there is a rejoinder that true development does not consist in yielding to caprice, there may be a rebutter that true order does not lie in blindly accepting experience, but in moulding it. And so on, and so on, until the stock of edifying truths runs out, if it ever does. We can never get forward. One side can always prove that there is some good in α, and some imperfection in β. The other side can prove the converse propositions. But to know which is best, we should have to discover whether we should be nearer to perfection if at the present moment we emphasised freedom, even at the price of caprice, or emphasised order, even at the price of constraint. And how are we to discover this?

And yet the particular problem we have been discussing is one on which most people in the world, and most of the independent thinkers of the world, have come to the same conclusion. But that, I fancy, is because they take a more practical criterion. If we estimate the gain or loss of happiness which would follow from the abolition of marriage, we may perhaps find excellent reasons for declining to make the change. But we shall not have been helped in our decision by the idea of the supreme good.

Innumerable similar cases could be found. Public schools

knock a great deal of pretence out of boys, and knock a certain amount of Philistinism into them. In heaven we shall be neither shams nor Philistines. But are we nearer to heaven, if at this moment we buy genuineness with Philistinism, or buy culture with Schwärmerei? The man who answers that question would need to be deep in the secrets of the universe.

107. But although the supreme good is useless as a help in a real investigation of an ethical question, it is a dangerously efficient ally in a barren and unfair polemic. For α is always partly good, β never quite good. Ignore the corresponding propositions, that β is also good, and α also imperfect, and we have an admirable argument for anything. For this purpose the words "true" and "higher" are useful. Thus the opponent of marriage, if confronted with the goodness of order, may reply that the true, or the higher, order is freedom. But then the supporter of marriage may enter on the same sophistry, by representing that the true, or the higher, freedom is order. Both propositions are quite true. In the supreme good, order and freedom are so transcended, that they are compatible—indeed, identical. It is true that the perfect forms of each are identical, and that the perfect form of either would always include and surpass the other's imperfect form. The sophistry lies in making this the ground for preferring the imperfect form of the one to the imperfect form of the other. When we consider how short and simple such a device is, as compared with a laborious empirical calculation of consequences, and that it can be applied on any side of any dispute, we may expect that it will in the future furnish as convenient a shelter for prejudices and indolence as innate moral ideas, or the healthy instincts of the human mind.

108. Another class of difficulties occurs in which the ends are not in themselves incompatible, but in which the inadequacy of the means renders it necessary to sacrifice one—at any rate partially. We have continually to divide our energy, our time, and our money, between several objects, each of which has admittedly a claim to some, and which could absorb between them, with good results, more than the total amount we have to divide. Ethical problems arise here to which the answers must be quantitative, and I fail to see what hope there is of settling them by means of the idea of the supreme good.

A man with some leisure may admit—and will generally be wise if he does—that he should devote some of it to work of public utility, and some to direct self-improvement. But how much to each ? He could very probably use all his leisure for either purpose with good results. At any rate, he will—in the great majority of cases—often find an hour which he could use for either. Which shall he sacrifice ? Shall he attend a committee meeting, or spend the evening studying metaphysics ? These difficulties come to all of us. The contemplation of the supreme good will tell us, it may be granted, that both metaphysics and social work have an element of good in them. But our contemplation cannot tell us which to prefer to the other, for the supreme good chooses neither, but, transcending both, enjoys both in their full perfection simultaneously, which is just what, in the present imperfect state of things, we cannot do. And it is no good telling us to neglect neither, or to make a division of our time. For a division cannot be made in the abstract. We must make it at a particular point, and assign the marginal hour of which we have been speaking either to philanthropy or to metaphysics.

The distribution of wealth presents us continually with similar questions. A man with a thousand a year would probably feel that he ought to give something to relieve distress, and also to give his children a better education than the average child gets at present. But this abstract conviction will not divide his income for him. Shall he send his sons to a second-rate school, and pension his old nurse, or shall he send them to a first-rate school, and let her go to the workhouse ? Problems like these are the real ethical difficulties of life, and they are not to be solved by generalities—nor even by contemplating the idea of the supreme good, in which there are neither school-bills nor workhouses, and whose perfections are in consequence irrelevant to the situation.

109. It may be said that it is not within the province of ethics to deal with individual cases such as this. And in one sense this is true. A system of ethics is not bound to lay down

beforehand the precise action a man ought to take in every conceivable contingency. This would, to begin with, be impossible,
owing to the number of possible contingencies. And, even if
possible, it would be undesirable. In applying rules to a given
set of circumstances we require not so much philosophical
insight as common sense and special knowledge of those circumstances. The philosopher is not likely, perhaps, to have more
common sense than the man whose action is being considered.
And the latter is much more likely to understand his own
circumstances for himself than the philosopher is to understand
them for him. The particular problems of conduct,-therefore,
are best solved at the place and time when they actually occur.
But it is, none the less, the duty of ethics to provide the
general principles upon which *any* doubtful point of conduct
ought to be settled. It would plainly be absurd to assert that
any one distribution of our time and wealth among good objects
would be as good as any other distribution. It would be still
more absurd to assert that a man who desired to act rightly
would not care whether he made the best possible distribution.
Surely the only alternative is to look to ethics for the principle
on which we must make the distribution. And it is just this
in which the idea of the supreme good fails to help us.

110. It has been suggested that a suitable formula for
ethics may be found in " my station and its duties." Each of
us finds himself in a particular place in the world. The particular characteristics of the situation suggest certain duties.
Do these, and in this way the supreme good will be most
advantaged.

As an analysis of morality this theory has many recommen-
dations, and it was not, if I understand rightly, originally put
forward as a moral criterion. But, for the sake of completeness,
it will be well to point out that it is not available as a criterion.
In the first place, it fails to tell us how we are to judge those
persons who have endeavoured to advance the good by going
beyond, or contrary to, the duties of the station in which they
then were, and so transforming their society and their own
station in it. The number of these may be comparatively small.
But the effect of their action is so important for everyone that

it is essential for a moral criterion to be able to determine when such innovations should be accepted and when rejected.

These cases can be brought within the scope of the formula, if it is only taken as an analysis of morality.   For there is no contradiction in saying that my duty in a certain station—*e.g.* that of a slave-holder, or of a slave—may be to destroy that station.   But such cases are clearly fatal to any attempt to use the formula as a criterion.   Some fresh criterion would be wanted to tell me whether my duty in my station did or did not involve an attempt to fundamentally alter its nature.

Again,. even in the ordinary routine of life, such a principle would give but little real guidance.   It lays down, indeed, the wide boundaries within which I must act, but it does not say precisely how I shall act within these boundaries, and so leaves a vast mass of true ethical questions unsettled.   My station may include among its duties that I should seek a seat in Parliament.   If I get one, my station will demand that I should vote for some bills and against others.   But which ?   Shall I vote for or against a Sunday Closing Bill, for example ?   Such questions can in the long run only be answered by reference to an ethical ideal.   And the ideal of my station and its duties will not help us.   For while the ideal M.P. will certainly vote for the bills he thinks ought to pass, and against those he thinks ought not to pass, there is nothing in the conception of a perfect member of parliament which can tell us in which of these classes he will place a Sunday Closing Bill.

Or my station may be that of a schoolmaster.   This defines my duties within certain limits.   But it cannot tell me whether in a particular case it is worth while to make a boy obedient at the cost of making him sulky.

Thus the principle, if taken as a criterion, is not only inadequate, but it proclaims its own inadequacy.   For the duty of an M.P. or a schoolmaster is not only to vote on bills, or to act on boys, regardless of the manner, but to vote rightly on bills, or to act rightly on boys.   And, since the right way in each particular case can never be got out of the mere idea of the station, the formula itself shows that some other criterion is needed for the adequate guidance of our action.

111. I now proceed to the next branch of my subject—namely that the calculation of pleasures and pains does give a definite criterion of action. (Calculation is, I think, a better word than calculus, which, as a technical term of mathematics, seems to imply a precision unattainable, on any theory, in ethics.) I am not now maintaining that it is a correct criterion —that it will enable us to distinguish right from wrong, but merely that it is sufficiently definite to be applied to actions in an intelligible way. The question of its correctness from an ethical point of view must be postponed for the present.

112. The elements at any rate of such a calculation are clear. We do know what a pleasure is, and what a pain is, and we can distinguish a greater pleasure or pain from a lesser one. I do not mean, of course, that the distinction is always easy to make in practice. There are some states of consciousness of which we can hardly tell whether they give us pleasure or pain. And there are many cases in which we should find it impossible to decide which of two pleasures, or of two pains, was the greater.

This, however, while it no doubt introduces some uncertainty into our calculations, does not entirely vitiate them. For when we can see no difference, as to amount of pleasure or pain between two mental states, we may safely conclude that the difference existing is smaller than any perceptible one. And, in the same way, if we are unable to tell whether a particular state is more pleasurable than painful, we may safely conclude that the excess of one feeling over the other must be small. Thus the margin of vagueness which is left is itself limited. This is quite different from the far more dangerous vagueness which we found in considering perfection. When we were unable to tell whether the maintenance or the abolition of marriage would bring us nearer to the supreme good, this uncertainty by no means gave us the right to infer that it made little difference which happened. The choice might make a very great difference. The uncertainty came from our ignorance, and not from the close equality of the two alternatives. But if we are doubtful whether a plate of turtle or a bunch of asparagus would give us most pleasure, or whether the pleasure of a long walk outweighs the pain of it, we may at least be certain that we shall not lose very much pleasure, whichever alternative we finally select.

113. It has been objected to hedonistic systems that pleasure is a mere abstraction, that no one could experience pleasure as such, but only this or that species of pleasure, and that therefore pleasure is an impossible criterion. It is true that we experience only particular pleasant states which are partially heterogeneous with one another. But this is no reason why we should be unable to classify them by the amount of a particular abstract element which is in all of them. No ship contains abstract wealth as a cargo. Some have tea, some have butter, some have machinery. But we are quite justified in arranging those ships, should we find it convenient, in an order determined by the extent to which their concrete cargoes possess the abstract attribute of being exchangeable for a number of sovereigns.

114. Another objection which is often made to hedonism lies in the fact that pleasures vanish in the act of enjoyment, and that to keep up any good that might be based on pleasure, there must be a continuous series of fresh pleasures. This is directed against the possibility of a sum of pleasures being the supreme good. As we are here only looking for a criterion, we might pass it by. But it may be well to remark in passing that it seems unfounded. For so long as we exist in time, the supreme good, whatever it is—perfection, self-realisation, the good will—will have to manifest itself in a series of states of consciousness. It will never be fulfilled at any one moment. If it be said that all these states have the common element of perfection or the good will running through them, the hedonist might reply that in his ideal condition all the states of consciousness will have the common element of pleasure running through them. Pleasure, it may be objected, is a mere abstraction. Certainly it is, and the element of a pure identity which runs through a differentiated whole must always be to some extent an abstraction, because it abstracts from the differentiation. In the same way, perfection or good will, if conceived as timeless elements of a consciousness existing in time, are just as much abstract, since abstraction is thus made of the circumstances under which alone they can be conceived as real and concrete.

So long, therefore, as our consciousness is in time, it can be no reason of special reproach to pleasure that it can only be realised in a continuous succession. And if our consciousness should ever free itself of the form of succession, there is no reason why pleasure should not be realised, like all the other elements of consciousness, in an eternal form. Indeed pleasure seems better adapted for the transition than the other elements of consciousness. A timeless feeling is no doubt an obscure conception. But we can, I think, form a better idea of what is meant by it than we can of the meaning of timeless cognition or of timeless volition.

115. We now come, however, to a more serious difficulty. Hedonic calculations require, not only that we should compare the magnitudes of pleasures, but that we should add and subtract them. The actions which we propose to ourselves will not each result in a single pleasure or pain. Each will have a variety of results, and, as a rule, some of them will be pleasures, and some pains. To compare two projected actions, therefore, it will be necessary in each case to take the sum of the pleasures, subtract from it the sum of the pains, and then enquire which of the two remainders is the larger positive, or the smaller negative, quantity.

Now pleasures and pains are intensive, not extensive, quantities. And it is sometimes argued that this renders it impossible for them to be added or subtracted. The difference between two pleasures or two temperatures is not itself, it is said, pleasant or hot. The possibility of adding or subtracting intensive quantities depends, it is maintained, on the fact that the difference between two of them is a third quantity of the same kind—that the difference between two lengths is itself a length, and the difference between two durations is itself a duration. And, since this characteristic is wanting in intensive quantities, it is concluded that it is impossible to deal with them arithmetically.

The question is one of great importance, and the answer

affects more than the hedonic criterion of moral action. It will, I believe, be found on further consideration that, reasonably or unreasonably, we are continually making calculations of pleasures and pains, that they have an indispensable place in every system of morality, and that any system which substitutes perfection for pleasure as a criterion of moral action also involves the addition and subtraction of other intensive quantities. If such a process is unjustifiable, it is not hedonism only, but all ethics, which will become unmeaning.

116. Introspection, I think, will convince us that we are continually adding and subtracting pleasures and pains, or imagining that we do so, and acting on what we suppose to be the result of our calculations. Whether we do it as a moral criterion or not, we are continually doing it in cases in which we do not bring morality into the matter. Suppose a man to be presented with two bills of fare for two equally expensive and equally wholesome dinners, and to be invited to choose which he shall take. Few of us, I fancy, would either find ourselves unable to decide the question, or admit that our answer was purely capricious and unmeaning. Yet how can such an answer be given except by adding pleasures ? Even the most artistic composition can scarcely give such unity to a dinner as to admit of the pleasures we derive from it being regarded as anything but a succession of pleasures from each dish—not to say each mouthful. And, if we still prefer one dinner to the other, does not this involve the addition of pleasures ?

Such cases make up a great part of our lives. For even when distinctively moral considerations come in, they very often leave us a choice of equivalent means, which can be settled only by our own pleasure. My duty may demand that I shall be at my office at a certain hour, but it is only my pleasure which can give me a motive for walking there on one side of the street rather than on the other. My duty may demand that I shall read a certain book, but there may be no motive but pleasure to settle whether I shall use a light copy with bad print, or a heavy copy with good print. And almost all such decisions, if made with any meaning at all,

require that pleasures and pains should be added and subtracted. It is only in this way that we can decide, whenever
several pleasures and pains of each course have to be taken
into consideration, and whenever a pleasure has to be balanced
against a pain. Moreover, even if a single pleasure or pain
from one has to be balanced against a single pleasure or
pain from another, we still require addition if each of these
feelings is to be looked on as an aggregate of several smaller
ones. And they must be looked at in that way, at any rate,
in the very common case in which the greater keenness of one
feeling is balanced against the greater length of the other.

117. This calculation of pleasures is not only requisite
for life, but it fills an indispensable, though subordinate, place
in even non-hedonist morality. If, with two courses a and b
before me, I can find no perceptible difference either to the
welfare of others, or to my own perfection, while at the same
time a is pleasanter than b, is it morally indifferent which
course I shall take? Surely it cannot be held to be indifferent,
unless we deny that pleasure is better than pain—an outrage
on common sense of which the great majority of non-hedonist
moralists cannot be accused. If pleasure *is* better than pain,
then, *caeteris paribus*, it is our duty to choose it—a duty which
may not require very constant preaching, but the neglect of
which is none the less morally evil.

But, even if we leave this out, it can scarcely be denied
that there are cases when it is our duty to give pleasure,
simply as pleasure, to others. Even Kant admits this. And
if we have to do this we must either confess our actions to
be utterly absurd, or else base them on a calculation of
pleasures. Whenever either course produces a succession of
pleasures or pains, whenever pleasures and pains have to be
balanced against one another, whenever the intensity of one
feeling has to be balanced against the length of another, or
the intensity of one man's feeling against a plurality of weaker
feelings in many men—in all these cases we must either add
pleasures and pains, or work absolutely in the dark.

118. I have, I think, said enough to show that the rejection
of all calculations about pleasure is not a simple question, and

that it would necessarily lead to a good deal of doubt—almost amounting to positive denial—of the possibility of our acting rationally at all. But we may carry this line of argument further. The only reason which we have found for doubting the legitimacy of such calculations is that they involved the addition of intensive quantities. Now if it should be the case that the opposed theory of ethics, which would have us take perfection as a criterion, also requires the addition of intensive quantities, we should have got, at the least, an effective argument *ad hominem* against our chief opponents.

We should, however, have got more than this. For every ethical theory accepts either perfection or pleasure as a criterion, except the theory which holds that the good is shown us by immediate intuitive judgments, which, as we have seen above[1], rejects all criteria whatever. Even that other form of Intuitionism, which maintains that we are immediately conscious of the validity of certain general moral laws, requires one or both of these criteria. For some of the moral laws are always represented as laws of imperfect obligation. We are to be as good as possible, or to do as much good as possible. And such laws always involve either perfection or pleasure as a standard.

The only criteria offered are perfection and pleasure. Pleasure as a criterion admittedly involves the addition of intensive quantities. If perfection as a criterion does the same, we shall be reduced to a dilemma. Either we must find room within ethics for the addition of intensive quantities, or we must surrender all hope of directing our conduct by an ethical principle.

119. Is it then the case that the criterion of perfection does require the addition of intensive quantities? I do not see how this can be avoided. Absolute perfection—the supreme good—is not quantitative. But we shall not reach absolute perfection by any action which we shall have a chance of taking to-day or to-morrow. And of the degrees of perfection it is impossible to speak except quantitatively. If we can say— and we must be able to say something of the sort, if perfection is to be our criterion—that a man who stays away from the

[1] Section 101.

poll acts more perfectly than a man who votes against his conscience for a bribe, and that a man who votes according to his conscience acts more perfectly than one who stays away —then we are either talking about quantities or about nothing. And these quantities are clearly intensive. The difference between one perfection and another cannot be a third perfection.

The incomplete stages of perfection, which, on this theory, must be the immediate ends between which we have to choose, are quantities then, and intensive quantities. Does the regulation of our conduct require that they should be added and subtracted ? Again I do not see how this can be denied.

120. A boy is to be sent to one of two schools. At A he will get better manners, and a purer Latin style, than he would at B. But at B he will acquire habits of greater industry, and greater bodily vigour, than he would at A. How is the question to be decided, with perfection as the criterion ? I have already tried to show in the preceding part of this chapter that it cannot be decided at all on such principles, since we have absolutely no data to enable us to guess whether a particular English boy, in 1901, will be nearer to the supreme good with industry and bad manners, or with good manners and indolence. But supposing this obstacle got over, the success of the method would then depend entirely on our being able to add intensive quantities. For here you have two elements of perfection—manners and Latin style—on the one hand, and two more elements—industry and bodily vigour—on the other. And unless the perfections attained at A have a sum which can be compared with the sum of the perfections attained at B, your action will be absolutely unreasonable, on whichever school you may decide.

Nor would it be fair to attempt to evade this by saying that perfections of character cannot be taken as units which can be aggregated or opposed, but should be considered as forming a unity. No doubt this is true of absolute perfection. All moments which form part of the supreme good are not only compatible, but essentially and indissolubly connected in the supreme good. In the supreme good whatever elements correspond to those imperfect goods which we call manners, and

Latin style, and industry, and bodily vigour, will imply and determine one another.   But not even a public school can land us straight in heaven.   And in this imperfect world these four qualities must be considered as four separable goods, for every one of the sixteen combinations which their presence and absence could produce is notoriously possible.   We must consider the problem before us as one in which two separate goods are gained at the expense of two others.   And how we are to come to any opinion on this point, unless we add the goodness of the goods together, I fail to conceive.

Or again, with a limited sum to spend on education, shall we educate a few people thoroughly, or many less thoroughly? Let us assume—and it seems at least as reasonable as any other view—that a slightly educated person is nearer to perfection than one completely uneducated, and that a thoroughly educated person is still nearer to perfection.   How are we to decide between the greater improvement in each one of a few people, and the smaller improvement in each one of many people, except by estimating the sum of the perfections gained by each course?   Or the difficulty may arise about oneself.   Two foreign tours may each offer several quite heterogeneous goods.   If I go to Italy, I may study pictures and improve my knowledge of Roman antiquities.   If I go to Germany, I may hear Wagner and investigate German socialism.   If we are to use perfection as a criterion here, must we not begin by summing the good which would result from each course?

121.   And thus it would seem that ethical criteria in general must share the fate of the hedonic criterion.   For the only serious charge that has been brought against the latter is that it involves the addition and subtraction of intensive quantities.   And we have now seen that the only other criterion which has been suggested is equally impotent to act, in most cases, except by the addition and subtraction of intensive quantities.

This would destroy all ethical systems except those which made our particular moral judgments immediate and ultimate. And this position, as I have endeavoured to show above[1], is as

---

[1] Section 101.

destructive to ethics in another way, since it destroys all possibility of saying that any moral judgment is wrong.

And not only ethics, but all regulation of conduct with regard to consequences, seems equally involved. For what consequence of action, which we can regard as valuable, has not intensive quantity? And how can we act rationally with regard to consequences, unless the different intensive quantities in different sets of consequences can be compared?

122. Let us now consider whether the arguments which lead to such a negative result are really valid. I do not think that they are. If we have two pleasures of different intensities, it is true, no doubt, that the excess of A over B is not *a* pleasure. For we cannot imagine that part of the intensity of A existing by itself. Its meaning depends on its being in combination with the rest of A's intensity. It would be meaningless to ask what the heat of an average June day would be like after the heat of an average December day had been subtracted from it. The remainder would cease to be what it had been, as soon as it was separated from the other part.

But although the excess of A's intensity over B is not *a* pleasure, I submit that it is, nevertheless, pleasure. Whatever has quantity must be homogeneous in respect of some quality, and is only quantitative in respect of that homogeneous quality. If therefore pleasure has an intensive quantity, then each part of that quantity must be pleasure, including that part by which it is greater than another.

If then the excess of intensity of A over B is pleasure, and a quantity, it must be capable of being brought into numerical relations with other quantities of pleasure. And thus, while it is true that we cannot imagine that excess as a separate pleasure, we can imagine a separate pleasure which shall be equal to that excess. If this is called C, then we shall be able to say that the pleasure in A is equal to the pleasure in B and C. And this is all that is wanted for the hedonic criterion.

I must confess that I find no difficulty in making such judgments, and that they seem to me to have a perfectly

definite meaning. I feel no hesitation in affirming that the
pleasure I get from a plate of turtle-soup is more than twice the
pleasure I get from a plate of pea-soup, or that the pleasure
I get from reading a new novel, together with the pain of a hot
walk to get it, leaves a balance of pleasure greater than the
pleasure from reading an old novel off my shelves. Of course
I may make mistakes over these judgments. But mistakes can
be made about extensive quantities also. I may judge A to be
six feet high, when he is really an inch less. But this does not
prevent his height from having a real and definite relation to
the length of a yard-measure.

123. The certainty of any particular judgment as to an
intensive quantity, and the minuteness to which such judgments
can be carried, is far less, certainly, than is the case with judgments as to space, or as to anything which can be measured by
means of spatial standards. It would be impossible to say with
any confidence that one pleasure was 3·77 times as great as
another, or even *exactly* twice as great. This has sometimes
been taken as a proof of the impossibility of the hedonic criterion. But it is unfair to argue from the impossibility of
absolute certainty or exactitude in any class of judgments that
the judgments are without any meaning, and that there is no
objective truth to which the judgments approximate. This
would render *all* judgments of quantity invalid. When we
pronounce a yard-measure to be equal to the standard yard at
Westminster, that is only an approximation, dependent on the
accuracy of our instruments, which may be great but is never
perfect. The approximation in the measurement of pleasure is
no doubt much rougher, but there is only a difference of degree,
and if the uncertainty does not completely invalidate the judgment in one case, it cannot do so in the other.

It may be objected that the uncertainty of this criterion,
while not destroying its theoretical validity, deprives it of all
practical use. Even if this were the case, it would be no worse
off than any other criterion. For, as was pointed out above,
the value of an action cannot be judged by the standard of
perfection without the addition and subtraction of intensive
quantities. The only difference is one which is to the advantage

of hedonism, for no one ever mistakes intense pain for intense pleasure, while ideals of perfection have been so different and incompatible that, whoever is right, many people must have mistaken great defects for great excellencies.

But there seems no reason for supposing that our estimates of pleasures and pains are so inaccurate as to be useless. We all make these estimates many times daily—even those of us who do not accept them as moral criteria. Can it be asserted that they have no worth whatever, and that everyone would on the whole be just as happy if he always took the course which seemed to him in anticipation to be less pleasant? Supposing that, on the next Bank Holiday, every person who should think that he would enjoy Epping Forest more than Hampstead Heath, should nevertheless go to Hampstead, is there any doubt that there would be a net loss of pleasure? Much uncertainty and error there certainly is in our estimates. But the only fair consequence to draw from this is that the conduct of human life is often a doubtful and difficult matter. And this conclusion is neither novel nor absurd.

124. We now pass on to the third division of the subject. Even if pleasure gives us a criterion which is applicable, does it give us one which is correct?

The supreme good, as defined at the beginning of this chapter, may be analysed into two moments. On the one hand each individual has a nature, whose satisfaction he postulates. On the other hand, the relation of each individual with others is such that it satisfies the natures of all of them. This analysis of the supreme reality, which is also the supreme good, is not the only one which is possible. Indeed it may be said that it is not a perfectly adequate analysis, since it gives a primacy to the nature of the individual over the nature of the whole which misrepresents the perfectly equal and reciprocal relation indicated in the Absolute Idea. But it is, I think, the most adequate analysis of absolute reality which is possible for Ethics. Ethics is based on the idea of Volition—an idea which the Logic shows us is transcended by the Absolute Idea—and cannot rise above the view of reality under the category of Volition, the peculiarity of which is exactly this over-emphasis on the nature of the individual as compared with the nature of the whole[1].

The imperfection by which we fall short of the supreme good is two-fold. On the one hand the ideals of which we postulate the fulfilment are not absolutely the same ideals which would be found in a state of perfection. On the other hand the ideals which we have are not completely satisfied. The two sides are closely connected. Nothing but perfect ideals could ever be perfectly satisfied, nor could an unsatisfied ideal be quite perfect. For all things react on one another, and the perfection of any part of the universe is only possible on condition that the rest is perfect too. At the same time, the two sides are sufficiently distinct for progress in the one to co-exist, for a time at least, with retrogression in the other. A man may become less in harmony with his surroundings as his ideal rises, and may become more in harmony with them by lowering his ideal.

125. Other things being equal, a man is happier in proportion as he is in harmony with his environment. In so far, therefore, as our efforts are devoted to the increase of happiness, they will tend to produce a greater amount of harmony between individuals and their environment, and so will be directed to the increase of one moment of the supreme good.

So far, then, the hedonic criterion would be a trustworthy guide. But there is the other element in the supreme good to be considered. Our ideals must be developed more fully as well as more completely satisfied. And to this element the criterion of happiness has no necessary or uniform relation.

Very often, indeed, a man is led by desire for his own happiness to actions which develop his ideals towards perfection. A man with a certain taste for music, for example, may be desirous of the intense happiness which music gives to those whose taste is more developed, and may consequently give such time and attention to it, as will make his taste purer and more subtle than before. Or, again, without any desire for a higher

---

[1] Cp. Sections 276—279.

musical ideal, he may give his attention to music simply to satisfy the desire which he already has for it, and may, through the knowledge and experience thus gained, find that his appreciation of music has become more discriminating and more intense.

Very often, again, a man develops his own ideals by his desire for the happiness of others. If he educates himself in order that he may support his parents, or serve his country, he will probably find that one effect of his education has been to develop his ideals of knowledge and beauty. Again, benevolence is a disposition which increases by being indulged, and one result of acting for the happiness of others is often to desire that happiness more keenly than before.

There are also the cases where the agent's action is directed to improving the ideals of another person on the ground that this will conduce to the happiness either of the person improved, or of a third person. Much of the moral education of children falls under this head. In some cases, no doubt, a quality is inculcated because it is thought desirable *per se*, but very frequently the reason is to be found in a consideration of the future happiness of the child, or of the people with whom it will associate in after life.

126. But there are cases in which the hedonic criterion would by no means lead us to the development of what we should regard as a higher ideal. It is true that, if we accept Hegel's principles, and if we see reason to include among them the immortality of the individual, we should be bound to hold that every heightening of the ideal would eventually mean increased happiness. For happiness depends for its amount, not merely on the completeness with which the environment answers to our ideals, but also on the vividness and completeness of those ideals. The more numerous and the more earnest are our wishes, the happier we shall be in their satisfaction, if they are satisfied. The more completely we are self-conscious individuals, the greater will be the happiness and the misery of which we are capable. Since the end of the time-process will be absolute harmony, we may safely assert that anything which makes our ideals more perfect will in the long run be the cause of greater happiness, since it will increase the intensity of our demands, and so of their eventual satisfaction.

But although the complete development of our ideals might be known *à priori* to involve the greatest happiness, it does not follow that the hedonic criterion would lead us in the direction of the complete development of our ideals. For this coincidence of development and happiness is only known to be certain in the indefinitely remote future, a future far too remote to be known by any empirical calculations. We may be certain that complete development will mean complete happiness. But it by no means follows that, if we aim at the greatest happiness which we can perceive to be attainable by our present action, we shall be aiming in the direction of complete development.

127. And there are many cases in which we should judge that the development of our ideals would indicate a course which would rather diminish than increase happiness. A man is generally admitted to be nearer to perfection in proportion as his love of truth, or his concern for the happiness of others, increases. And yet the love of truth may force us to change very comforting beliefs for very depressing ones. And in so imperfect a state as the present increased sympathy for the happiness or misery of others often produces more misery than happiness for the sympathiser.

Of course the hedonic criterion does not take account of the pleasure of the agent only, but of all people who are affected by the action. This makes a considerable difference, for it not infrequently happens that a development which makes a person more miserable makes him also more useful. But there are cases where the opposite happens. To lose a false, but inspiriting, belief may diminish a man's utility as well as his happiness. And, if my chances of helping others are few, an increase of benevolence on my part may deprive me of much more happiness than it enables me to bestow upon others.

There are circumstances in which an exclusive regard for happiness would lead us not only to shrink from development, but actually to endeavour to fall back in the scale. It would be generally admitted that a man who was chronically under the influence of drugs had fallen, so far as his ideals went, below the level of a man who kept his intellect and will unclouded. And there are men whose physical and mental sufferings are so great that they would be happier—or at least less unhappy—if they were kept continually drugged with opiates. This might increase not only their own happiness, but happiness in general, for a man who is in great and constant pain is not likely to cause much pleasure to anyone, while his condition will certainly cause pain to his friends.

There are thus cases in which the hedonic criterion would direct us to a goal which, as far as we can see, is, in respect of the other moment of the supreme good, something lower, and not higher than the starting-point. Under such circumstances ought we to follow the hedonic criterion, or to reject it ?

128. The question is not put fairly if it is represented as a choice between happiness and perfection. For the happiness is also an element of perfection. The supreme good consists in a complete development of our ideals, and a complete satisfaction of them when developed. We are more perfect in proportion as either of these takes place, and less perfect in proportion as it is wanting. Happiness is not by itself the supreme good, but any happiness, so far as it goes, is good, and any absence of happiness bad.

This comes out more clearly if we take examples in which the happiness at stake is not that of the agent. For so much sin comes from attaching excessive weight to the happiness of the sinner, and morality has to check self-interest so much oftener than to encourage it, that we are apt to fall into the delusion that happiness should not be measured against development. But if we ask whether I ought always to choose to slightly elevate another person's ideals, at the cost of great suffering to him, or if I ought always to choose to slightly elevate my own ideals, at the cost of great suffering to some one else, it becomes clear that happiness and development are ethically commensurable, and that we have no right to treat a loss of either as ethically indifferent.

Thus the conflict is between two elements of the good. Now we saw above that it was impossible to compare such elements with any hope of discovering which was the most desirable. And in this case the difficulty is greater than in any other, because we are comparing the two primary elements, which exhibit the greatest heterogeneity to be found in the content of the good. How miserable would civilized men have to be, before it would be better for them to change their state for that of happy savages? How much more misery would make it worth their while to accept the passivity of oysters?

129. Common Sense generally deals with this class of questions by judging that a great change for the good in one element will counterbalance a moderate change for the bad in the other. It would approve of a man who sought refuge from extreme physical pain in drugs which left his mind slightly less clear, but not of one who paid this price to avoid a slight discomfort. It would count a keen insight into fallacies as good, although life was thereby made somewhat more dreary, but not if the result was to destroy entirely the happiness of the thinker, and to injure the happiness of his friends.

130. But such a position as this is theoretically indefensible. It implies that we have some means of knowing, within very broad limits, how much happiness will be more worth having than a given degree of development. And it is impossible to settle this. On the other hand the position is so vague that it has very little practical value. For, in most of the cases which present themselves, the gains and losses are not so extreme in proportion to one another as to allow Common Sense to give an opinion at all.

The matter can often be settled, no doubt, by adhering strictly to the hedonic criterion on the ground that we are much more certain of the happiness or the misery than we are of the advance towards, or the retreat from, the goal of a perfectly developed ideal. But this is not always true. It sometimes happens that the retrogression in development, which accompanies the increased happiness, seems beyond all doubt.

131. To sum up—we have seen that a moral criterion is necessary, if any sincere ethical judgment is to be pronounced either right or wrong—that is, if morality is to have any objectivity at all. We have seen that the possible criteria appear to be confined to pleasure and perfection. We have seen that perfection breaks down, if we attempt to use it in this way. Pleasure, on the other hand, does seem to be a possible criterion—difficult, indeed, to apply, but offering no greater difficulties than those which appear to be inherent in ethics. But when we enquire if it is a correct criterion of the good, we find that it only measures one of the two elements into which the good may be analysed.

There are four possible cases. In the first, the action to which the hedonic criterion would guide us, involves in our judgment a greater development of ideals. In this case it is clear that we should take this course, since both elements of the good are increased.

In the second case, our action, whichever way we act, will as far as we can see make no difference to the development of ideals. Here too we can safely abide by the hedonic criterion, since that measures the only element of the good which our decision can be seen to affect.

In the third case, our action may make a considerable difference to the development of our ideals, but we are unable to tell whether the difference will be for good or for evil. Once more we shall do well to follow the hedonic criterion. For then, at any rate, we shall gain in respect of one element of the good. We *may* indeed lose much more in respect of development. But then we *may* gain in respect of that element also. Since the effect on development is unknown, the only rational course, if we must act, is to be guided by the effect on happiness, which is known.

But in the fourth case the course to which the hedonic criterion would guide us has in our judgment an unfavourable effect on the development of ideals, as compared with the alternative course. In this case there seems no reasonable solution. For we cannot estimate the quantity of loss to development, and, if we could, we are ignorant of the common standard by which this could be compared with the gain in pleasure.

132. In considering how much uncertainty this brings into ethics, we must remember once more that the question is not limited to the pleasure and the development of the agent but includes the consideration of the pleasure and development of all people affected by the action. This diminishes the number of cases of the fourth class, for the happiness a man gives is generally more closely proportioned to the development of his ideals than is the happiness he enjoys.

And, again, we must remember that the object of a moral criterion is strictly practical. Its object is to guide our action. It follows from this that it is comparatively unimportant if it fails to indicate which of two events would be the better, in those cases in which our action cannot bring about or hinder either alternative. It is no doubt convenient to know what would be gain and what loss, but the real need to know arrives only when our knowledge can help us to bring about the gain or avoid the loss.

Now the development of our ideals is, in many cases, entirely out of our power, to help or hinder. It is possible that a man might get more pleasure if he could retain his childish taste for sweetmeats, and avoid the growth of a taste for claret. At any rate he could satisfy himself at less expense. But no efforts, on his own part or that of his teachers, will prevent the relative places of sweetmeats and claret in the scale of pleasures being different for the average man from what they were for the average boy.

It is possible, again, that the general religious attitude of the twelfth century gave a greater balance of pleasure than was given by the general religious attitude of the nineteenth century. But if the majority had known this beforehand, and had acted on the most rigidly Utilitarian principles, could their united efforts have averted the Renaissance, the Reformation, or the Illumination?

Our desires have a dialectic of their own, and no finite ideal can satisfy us indefinitely. Some we transcend as soon as we have attained them. For others a period of enjoyment is necessary before they pall. In other cases, again, the mere desire for an unattained ideal seems to be sufficient to demonstrate, after a time, its inadequacy. Our volition has, no doubt, a certain influence on this process. But there are many cases in which it would proceed in spite of all our efforts to restrain it. And even if in these cases, the process should diminish happiness, we should do but little harm if we directed our action by the hedonic criterion. For, while such action would be mistaken, it would be also ineffective.

133. But after all these deductions it remains true that there are cases of the fourth class in which our decisions will have a decisive effect on the result, and that ethics offers us no principle upon which to make the decisions. There is thus no possibility of moral action in deciding them.

This is a less revolutionary conclusion than it appears at first sight. It does not deny that one of the two alternatives is always objectively better than the other[1]. One of the two finite and incompatible goods—the particular gain in pleasure, or the particular gain in development of ideals—would raise us nearer to the supreme good than the other. This is the one to be accepted. But, since they have no common standard but the supreme good, we could only compare them if we knew the exact relation of each of them to the supreme good, and this we do not know.

134. The impossibility of decision arises, then, not from the facts of the case, but from our ignorance about them. Now every system of ethics, with the exception of those which believe in an immediate and unerring intuition for every particular choice, must hold that there are some cases where it is impossible to see what the best course is. If we take the hedonic criterion, there are cases in which the alternative actions seem to present such equal balances of pleasure that it is impossible to see which is the greater. If we take perfection, two incompatible goods may seem so equally good that no reason can be found for choice. Indeed an ethical system which denied that the best and wisest men were

---

[1] There is of course the abstract possibility of the good produced by each alternative being *exactly* equal. But the chance of this is too small to be worth considering. And, if it did occur, it is obvious that we could not go wrong, whatever we did, which would not be an unsatisfactory conclusion.

sometimes compelled to act utterly in the dark would be in glaring contradiction to the facts of life.

There is only one difference between the difficulties I have described above as arising on my theory and these others which exist on any theory. The latter are merely quantitative. They arise from the complexity, or the equality, of data whose nature is not incompatible with a reasoned choice, and which admit of such choice when the instance is simpler or less evenly balanced. In the cases of the fourth class, which I described in Section 131, on the other hand, the problem is one to which the only methods of decision possible to us, in our present imperfect state, do not apply at all.

My theory does thus involve rather more ethical scepticism than the others. But this is of no importance in practice. For in practice the important point is not to know the reason why some moral problems are insoluble. Practice is only concerned to enquire how many, and how serious, are the insoluble problems.

135. And, fortunately, the attainment of the good does not ultimately depend upon action. If it did, it might be rather alarming to think that there were certain cases in which we did not know how to act. But, after all, if it did depend on action, things would be so bad on any theory of ethics that minor differences would be unimportant. If the nature of reality was hostile or indifferent to the good, nothing but the most meagre and transitory gains could ever be made by creatures so weak and insignificant as we should be in such a universe. But if, as Hegel teaches us, that which we recognize as the supreme good is also the supreme reality, then it must inevitably realise itself in the temporal process, and no mistakes of ours can hinder the advance and the eventual attainment.

136. There is therefore nothing in this occasional failure of the only available criterion which should make us think more meanly of reality, or more hopelessly of the good. And we should count it a gain, and not a loss, if it emphasises the inadequacy both of the practice of morality, and of the science of ethics. For this is one of the most profound and important consequences of all metaphysical idealism. Virtue, and the science which deals with it, imply the possibility of sin, they imply action, and they imply time. And they share, therefore, the inadequacy of matter and of the physical sciences. The conception of virtue is, indeed, more adequate than such conceptions as matter and notion. But, like them, it reveals its own imperfection, and, like them, it must be transcended and absorbed before we can reach either the absolutely real or the absolutely good.

CHAPTER V.

PUNISHMENT.

137. WE may define punishment as the infliction of pain on a person because he has done wrong. That it must be painful, and that it must be inflicted on a person who has done, or is thought to have done, wrong, will be generally admitted. But we must also remember that it is essential that it should be inflicted *because* of the wrong-doing. In the children's books of an earlier generation, the boy who went out without his mother's leave was struck by lightning. This cannot, unless theology is introduced, be considered as a punishment. For the lightning would have struck with equal readiness any boy on the same spot, although provided with the most ample parental authority. And more modern and pretentious works, while less amusing, are not more accurate. They speak of the rewards and punishments which Nature herself distributes among us. But Nature—the Nature of science and common sense—though she often destroys, never punishes. For the moral value of an action makes no difference to her. She takes no account of intention or purpose. She destroys, with a magnificent indifference, alike the man who has injured his body by self-indulgence, and the man who has injured his body in his work for others. Her bacteria are shed abroad equally on the man who let the drains go wrong, on the man who is trying to put them right, and on the child who was not consulted in the matter. Some people assert Nature to be above morality, but, whether above or below, she

is certainly indifferent to it.   And so, to get a proper use of
the idea of punishment we must go beyond her.

138.   Punishment, then, is pain, and to inflict pain on any
person obviously needs a justification.   There are four ways
in which punishment is usually justified—not by any means
incompatible.   One punishment might be defended under all
of them.   The first is the theory of vindictive punishment.
It asserts that, if a man has done wrong it is right and just
that he should suffer for it, even if the pain does no good,
either to himself or to others.   The punishment is looked on
as a satisfaction of abstract justice, and he is said to deserve
it.   The second way in which a punishment may be defended
is that it is deterrent.   It is desirable to suppress wrong-doing.
And so we try to attach to a fault a punishment so certain,
and so severe, that the remembrance of it will prevent the
offender from offending again, while the fear of a similar
punishment will deter others from a similar crime.

We must mark here an important distinction.   In these
two cases the object which justified our action could only be
obtained by punishment.   In the first, abstract justice was
supposed to require that the man should be made unhappy.
In the second case, it is clear that you can only deter—that
is, frighten—men from crime by making its consequences
painful.   But now we come to two other uses of punishment
which do not depend on its being painful, but on other
qualities which the particular punishment happens to possess.
The first of these is that it may deprive the criminal under
punishment of the chance of committing fresh crimes.   A man
cannot steal while he is in prison, nor commit murder—in this
life—after he has been hanged.   But this effect does not come
because the man has been punished.   If he welcomed imprison-
ment or death gladly, they would cease to be punishments, but
they would be equally preventive of crime.

The second of these further advantages of punishment is
the reformation of the criminal.   This does not mean that the
punishment frightens him from offending again.   That is the
deterrent effect, of which we spoke before.   But a punishment
may sometimes really cure a man of his vicious tendencies.

The solitude which it gives him for reflection, or the religious influences which may be brought to bear on him in prison, or the instruction which he may receive there, may give him a horror of vice or a love of virtue which he had not before. But if his punishment does this, it is not *as* a punishment. If his character is, by such means, changed for the better, that change is not made because he was unhappy. Thus, for reformation, as well as for prevention, punishment may be a useful means, but only incidentally; while it is only by means of punishment that we can avenge a crime, or deter men from repeating it.

139. Of late years we have almost given up the theory of vindictive punishment, both in law and education, though it is still retained in theology by those who accept the doctrine that punishment may be eternal. The ordinary view of the use of punishment in law is, I take it, that its main object is deterrent—to prevent crime by making the possible criminal afraid of the punishment which would follow. Its preventive use—of checking crime by restraining or removing persons who have already proved themselves criminals—is also considered important, but in a lesser degree. Finally, if the state *can* reform the criminal while punishing him, it considers itself bound to try; but the primary object of criminal justice is held to be the protection of the innocent rather than the improvement of the guilty, and therefore the discouragement of crime is taken as of more importance than the reform of the criminal.

Capital punishment, indeed, is still sometimes defended on the ground of vindictive justice, but more often as being deterrent of crime on the part of others, and a safeguard against its repetition by the particular criminal executed. And in other cases vindictive punishment has dropped out of law, and, perhaps, still more out of education.

There is no tendency to the contrary in Sir James Stephen's ingenious defence of the vindictive pleasure that men feel in punishing atrocious criminals. He defends that pleasure on the ground that it renders their punishment more certain. But he does not recommend that a man should be punished merely because he has done wrong. He only says that, in cases where punishment is desirable for the good of society, it is advisable to cultivate any feelings which will lead people to exert themselves to bring that punishment about.

140. We have now seen what the ordinary view of punishment is. My object is to consider what relation to this view is held by Hegel's theory of punishment, as expressed in his Philosophy of Law. It has often been said that he supports vindictive punishment. And, at first sight, it looks as if he did. For he expressly says that it is superficial to regard punishment as protective to society, or as deterring or improving the criminal. Now in so far as it is not protective or deterring, we must give up the theories which we have called the preventive and the deterrent. In so far as it is not improving, we must give up the reformatory theory. Hegel does not deny that punishment may deter, prevent, or improve, and he does not deny that this will be an additional advantage. But he says that none of these are the chief object of punishment, and none of these express its real nature. It would seem, therefore, that he must intend to advocate vindictive punishment. And this is confirmed by the fact that he expressly says the object of punishment is not to do "this or that" good.

Nevertheless, I believe that Hegel had not the slightest intention of advocating what we have called vindictive punishment. For he says, beyond the possibility of doubt, that in punishment the criminal is to be treated as a moral being— that is, one who is potentially moral, however immoral he may be in fact, and one in whom this potential morality must be called into actual existence. He complains that by the deterrent theory we treat a man like a dog to whom his master shows a whip, and not as a free being. He says that the criminal has a right to be punished, which indicates that the punishment is in a sense for his sake. And, still more emphatically, "in punishment the offender is honoured as a rational being, since the punishment is looked on as his right[1]."

---

[1] *Philosophy of Law*, Sections 99 and 100.

Now this is incompatible with the view that Hegel is here approving of vindictive punishment. For he says that a man is only to be punished because he is a moral being, and that it would be an injury to him not to punish him. The vindictive theory knows nothing of all this. It inflicts pain on a man, not for his ultimate good, but because, as it says, he has deserved to suffer pain. And, on Hegel's theory, punishment depends on the recognition of the criminal's rational and moral nature, so that, in his phrase, it is an honour as well as a disgrace. Nothing of the sort exists for vindictive punishment. It does not care whether the sinner can or will be good in the future. It punishes him because he has done wrong in the past. If we look at the doctrine of hell—which is a pure case of vindictive punishment—we see that it is possible to conceive punishment of this sort when the element of a potential moral character has entirely disappeared, for I suppose that the supporters of this doctrine would deny the possibility of repentance in hell, since they deny the possibility of pardon.

141. What, then, is Hegel's theory? It is, I think, briefly this. In sin, man rejects and defies the moral law. Punishment is pain inflicted on him because he has done this, and in order that he may, by the fact of his punishment, be forced into recognizing as valid the law which he rejected in sinning, and so repent of his sin—really repent, and not merely be frightened out of doing it again.

Thus the object of punishment is that the criminal should repent of his crime and by so doing realise the moral character, which has been temporarily obscured by his wrong action, but which is, as Hegel asserts, really his truest and deepest nature. At first sight this looks very much like the reformatory theory of punishment which Hegel has rejected. But there is a great deal of difference between them. The reformatory theory says that we ought to reform our criminals *while* we are punishing them. Hegel says that punishment, as such, tends to reform them. The reformatory theory wishes to pain criminals as little as possible, and to improve them as much as possible. Hegel's theory says that it is the pain which will improve them, and therefore, although it looks on pain in itself as an evil, is by no means anxious to spare it.

When Hegel says, then, as we saw above, that the object of punishment is not to effect "this or that good," we must not, I think, take him to mean that we do not look for a good result from punishment. We must rather interpret him to mean that it is not in consequence of some *accidental* good result that punishment is to be defended, but that, for the criminal, punishment is inherently good. The use of "this or that" to express an accidental or contingent good seems in accordance with Hegel's usual terminology. And we must also remember that Hegel, who hated many things, hated nothing more bitterly than sentimental humanitarianism, and that he was in consequence more inclined to emphasise his divergence from a reformatory theory of punishment than his agreement with it.

We have thus reached a theory quite different from any of the four which we started this chapter by considering. It is not impossible that the world has been acting on the Hegelian view for many ages, but as an explicit theory it has found little support. We all recognize that a man can be frightened into or out of a course of action by punishment. We all recognize that a man can sometimes be reformed by influences applied while he is being punished. But can he ever be reformed simply by punishment? Repentance and reform involve either that he should see that something was wrong which before he thought was right, or else that the intensity of his moral feelings should be so strengthened that he is enabled to resist a temptation, to which before he yielded. And why should punishment help him to do either of these things?

142. There are certain people who look on all punishment as essentially degrading. They do not, in their saner moods, deny that there may be cases in which it is necessary. But they think that, if any one requires punishment, he proves himself to be uninfluenced by moral motives, and only to be governed by fear. (It is curious, by the way, that this school generally accepts the idea that government by rewards is legitimate. It does not appear why it is less degrading to be bribed into virtue than to be frightened away from vice.) They look on all punishment as implying deep degradation in some one,—if it is justified, the offender must be little better than a brute; if it is not justified, the brutality is in the person who inflicts it.

This reasoning appears to travel in a circle. Punishment, they say, is degrading, therefore it can work no moral improvement. But this begs the question. For if punishment could work a moral improvement, it would not degrade but elevate. The humanitarian argument alternately proves that punishment can only intimidate because it is brutalizing, and that it is brutalizing because it can only intimidate. The real reason, apparently, of the foregone conviction which tries to justify itself by this argument is an unreasoning horror of the infliction of pain. That pain is an evil cannot be denied. But, even if it were the ultimate evil, we could not assert that it was always wrong to inflict it. For that would be equivalent to a declaration that a dentist was as criminal as a wife-beater. No one can deny that the infliction of pain may in the long run increase happiness—as in the extraction of an aching tooth. If pain, in spite of its being evil *per se,* can thus be desirable as a means, the general objection to pain as a moral agent would seem to disappear also.

143. Of course, there is nothing in simple pain, as such, which can lead to repentance. If I get into a particular train, and break my leg in a collision, that cannot make me repent my action in going by the train, though it will very possibly make me regret it. For the pain in this case was not a punishment. It came, indeed, because I had got into the train, but not because I had done wrong in getting into the train.

Hegel's theory is that punishment, that is, pain inflicted because the sufferer had previously done wrong, may lead to repentance for the crime which caused the punishment. We have now to consider whether this is true. The thesis is not that it always produces repentance—which, of course, is not the case—but that there is something in its nature which tends to produce repentance. And this, as we have seen, is not a common theory of punishment. " Men do not become penitent and learn to abhor themselves by having their backs cut open

with the lash; rather, they learn to abhor the lash[1]." That
the principle expressed here is one which often operates cannot
be denied. Can we so far limit its application that Hegel's
theory shall also be valid?

We have so far defined punishment as pain inflicted because
the sufferer has done wrong. But, looking at it more closely,
we should have to alter this definition, which is too narrow,
and does not include cases of mistaken punishment. To bring
these in we must say that it is pain inflicted because the person
who inflicts it thinks that the person who suffers it has done
wrong. Repentance, again, is the realisation by the criminal,
with sufficient vividness to govern future action, that he has
done wrong. Now is there anything in the nature of punishment to cause the conviction in the mind of the judge to be
reproduced in the mind of the culprit? If so, punishment will
tend to produce repentance.

144. I submit that this is the case under certain conditions.
When the culprit recognizes the punishing authority as one
which embodies the moral law, and which has a right to enforce
it, then punishment may lead to repentance, but not otherwise.

Let us examine this more closely. A person who suffers
punishment may conceive the authority which inflicts it to be
distinctly immoral in its tendencies. In this case, of course,
he will not be moved to repent of his action. The punishment
will appear to him unjust, to incur it will be considered as a duty,
and he will consider himself not as a criminal, but as a martyr.
On the other hand, if the punishment causes him to change his
line of action, it will be due, not to repentance, but to cowardice.

Or, again, he may not regard it as distinctly immoral—as
punishing him for what it is his duty to do. But he may regard
it as non-moral—as punishing him for what he had a right,
though not a duty, to do. In this case, too, punishment will
not lead to repentance. He will not regard himself as a
martyr, but he will be justified in regarding himself as a very
badly-treated person. If the punishment does cause him to
abstain from such action in future, it will not be the result of

---

[1] George Eliot, *Felix Holt*, Chap. XLI.

repentance, but of prudence. He will not have come to think it wrong, but he may think that it is not worth the pain it will bring on him.

If, however, he regards the authority which punishes him as one which expresses, and which has a right to express, the moral law, his attitude will be very different. He will no longer regard his punishment either as a martyrdom or as an injury. On the contrary he will feel that it is the proper consequence of his fault. And to feel this, and to be able to accept it as such, is surely repentance.

145. But it may be objected that this leads us to a dilemma. The punishment cannot have this moral effect on us, unless it comes from an authority which we recognize as expressing the moral law, and, therefore, as valid for us. But if we recognize this, how did we ever come to commit the sin, which consists in a defiance of the moral law? Does not the existence of the sin itself prove that we are not in that submissive position to the moral law, and to the power which is enforcing it, which alone can make the punishment a purification?

I do not think that this is the case. It is, in the first place, quite possible for a recognition of the moral law to exist which is not sufficiently strong to prevent our violating it at the suggestion of our passions or our impulses, but which is yet strong enough, when the punishment follows, to make us recognize the justice of the sentence. After all, most cases of wrong-doing, which can be treated as criminal, are cases of this description, in which a man defies a moral law which he knows to be binding, because the temptations to violate it are at that moment too strong for his desire to do what he knows to be right. In these cases the moral law is, indeed, recognized—for the offender knows he is doing wrong—but not recognized with sufficient strength; for, if it was, he would abstain from doing wrong. And, therefore, the moral consciousness is strong enough to accept the punishment as justly incurred, though it was not strong enough to prevent the offender from incurring it. In this case, the significance of the punishment is that it tends to produce that vividness in the recognition of the moral law, which the occurrence of the offence shows to have been previously wanting. The pain and coercion involved in punishment present the law with much greater impressiveness than can, for the mass of people, be gained from a mere admission that the law is binding. On the other hand, the fact that the pain coincides with that intellectual recognition, on the part of the offender, that the law is binding, prevents the punishment having a merely intimidating effect, and makes it a possible stage in a moral advance.

146. Besides these cases of conscious violation of a moral law, there are others where men sincerely believe in a certain principle, and yet systematically fail to see that it applies in certain cases, not because they really think that those cases are exceptions, but because indolence or prejudice has prevented them from ever applying their general principle to those particular instances. Thus there have been nations which conscientiously believed murder to be sinful, and yet fought duels with a good conscience. If pressed, they would have admitted a duel to be an attempt to murder. But no one ever did press them, and they never pressed themselves. As soon as a set of reformers arose, who did press the question, duels were found to be indefensible, and disappeared. So for many years the United States solemnly affirmed the right of all men to liberty, while slavery was legally recognized. Yet they would not have denied that slaves were men.

When such cases occur with a single individual, punishment might here, also, tend to repentance. For it was only possible to accept the general law, and reject the particular application, by ignoring the unanswerable question, Why do not you in this case practise what you preach ? Now you *can* ignore a question, but you cannot ignore a punishment, if it is severe enough. You cannot put it on one side: you must either assert that it is unjust, or admit that it is just. And in the class of cases we have now been considering, we have seen that when the question is once asked, it must condemn the previous line of action. Here, therefore, punishment may lead to repentance.

147. A third case is that in which the authority is recognized, but to which it is not known beforehand that it disapproved of the act for which the punishment is awarded. Here, therefore, there is no difficulty in seeing that recognition of the authority is compatible with transgression of the law, because the law is not known till after it has been transgressed. It may, perhaps, be doubted whether it is strictly correct to say in this case that punishment may lead to repentance, since there is no wilful fault to repent, as the law was, by the hypothesis, not known at the time it was broken. The question is, however, merely verbal. There is no doubt that in such cases the punishment, coming from an authority accepted as moral, may lead a man to see that he has done wrong, though not intentionally, may lead him to regret it, and to avoid it in future. Thus, at any rate, a moral advance comes from the punishment, and it is of no great importance whether we grant or deny it the name of repentance.

148. It may be objected, however, that punishment in the last two cases would be totally unjust. We ought to punish, it may be said, only those acts which were known by their perpetrators, at the time they did them, to be wrong. And therefore we have no right to punish a man for any offence, which he did not know to be an offence, whether because he did not know of the existence of the law, or because he did not apply it to the particular case.

I do not think, however, that we can fairly limit the proper application of punishment to cases of conscious wrong-doing, plausible as such a restriction may appear at first sight. We must remember, in the first place, that ignorance of a moral law may be a sign of a worse moral state than that which would be implied in its conscious violation. If a man really believed that he was morally justified in treating the lower animals without any consideration, he would not be consciously doing wrong by torturing them. But we should, I think, regard him as in a lower moral state than a man who was conscious of his duty to animals, though he sometimes disregarded it in moments of passion. Yet the latter in these moments would be consciously doing wrong. A man who could see nothing wrong in cowardice would surely be more degraded than one who recognized the duty of courage, though he sometimes failed to carry it out. Thus, I submit, even if punishment were limited to cases of desert, there would be no reason to limit it to cases of conscious wrong-doing, since the absence of the consciousness of wrong-doing may itself be a mark of moral defect.

But we may, I think, go further. There seems no reason why we should enquire about any punishment whether the criminal deserved it. For such a question really brings us back, if we press it far enough, to the old theory of vindictive punishment, which few of those who ask the question would be prepared to advocate. On any other theory a man is to be punished, not to avenge the past evil, but to secure some future good. Of course, a punishment is only to be inflicted for a wrong action, for the effect of all punishment is to discourage the repetition of the action punished, and that would not be desirable unless the action were wrong. But to enquire how far the criminal is to be blamed for his action seems irrelevant. If he has done wrong, and if the punishment will cure him, he has, as Hegel expresses it, a right to his punishment. If a dentist is asked to take out an aching tooth, he does not refuse to do so, on the ground that the patient did not deliberately cause the toothache, and that therefore it would be unjust to subject him to the pain of the extraction. And to refuse a man the chance of a moral advance, when the punishment appears to afford one, seems equally unreasonable.

Indeed, any attempt to measure punishment by desert gets us into hopeless difficulties. If we suppose that every man is equally responsible for every action which is not done under physical compulsion, we ignore the effect of inherited character, of difference of education, of difference of temptation, and, in fact, of most of the important circumstances. Punishments measured out on such a system may, perhaps, be defended on the ground of utility, but certainly not on the ground of desert. Again, if we did attempt, in fixing desert, to allow for different circumstances, desert would vanish altogether. On a determinist theory every act is the inevitable result of conditions existing before the birth of the agent. If we admit free will, any responsibility for the past becomes unintelligible.

The only alternative seems to be the admission that we punish, not to avenge evil, but to restore or produce good, whether for society or the criminal. And on this principle we very often explicitly act. For example, we do not punish high treason because we blame the traitors, who are often moved by sincere, though perhaps mistaken, patriotism. We punish it because we believe that they would in fact, though with the best intentions, do harm to the state. Nor do parents, I suppose, punish young children for disobedience, on the ground that it is their own fault that they were not born with the habit of obedience developed. They do it, I should imagine, because punishment is the most effective way of teaching them obedience, and because it is desirable that they should learn it.

149. We must now return to the cases in which punishment can possibly produce repentance, from which we have been diverted by the question of the justice of the punishment inflicted in the second and third cases. There is a fourth and last case. In this the authority which inflicts the punishment was, before its infliction, recognized faintly and vaguely as embodying the moral law, and therefore as being a valid authority. But the recognition was so faint and vague that it was not sufficient to prevent disobedience to the authority's commands. This, it will be seen, is rather analogous to the second case. There the law was held so vaguely that the logical applications of it were never made. Here the authority is recognized, but not actively enough to influence conduct. It is scarcely so much that the criminal recognizes it, as that he is not prepared to deny it.

Here the effect of punishment may again be repentance. For punishment renders it impossible any longer to ignore the authority, and it is, by the hypothesis, only by ignoring it that it can be disobeyed. The punishment clearly proves that the authority is in possession of the power. If it is pressed far enough, there are only two alternatives—definitely to rebel and declare the punishment to be unjust, or definitely to submit and acknowledge it to be righteous. The first is impossible here, for the criminal is not prepared definitely to reject the authority. There remains therefore only the second.

Perhaps the best example of this state of things may be found in the attitude of the lower boys of a public school towards the authority of the masters. Their conviction that this is a lawful and valid authority does not influence them to so great an extent as to produce spontaneous and invariable obedience. But it is, I think, sufficient to prevent them from considering the enforcement of obedience by punishment as unjust, except in the cases where their own code of morality comes explicitly in conflict with the official code—cases which are not very frequent. In fact, almost all English school systems would break down completely, if they trusted to their punishments being severe enough to produce obedience by fear. Their continued existence seems important evidence that punishment can produce other effects than intimidation, unless, indeed, any ingenious person should suggest that they could get on without punishment altogether.

150. We have now seen that when punishment is able to fulfil the office which Hegel declares to be its highest function—that of producing repentance—it does so by emphasising some moral tie which the offender was all along prepared to admit, although it was too faint or incomplete to prevent the fault. Thus it essentially works on him as, at any rate potentially, a moral agent, and thus, as Hegel expresses it, does him honour. It is no contradiction of this, though it may appear so at first sight, to say that a punishment has such an effect only by the element of disgrace which all deserved punishment contains. The deterrent effect is different. A punishment deters from the repetition of the offence, not because it is a punishment, but because it is painful. An unpleasant consequence which followed the act, not as the result of moral condemnation, but as a merely natural effect, would have the same deterrent result. A man is equally frightened by pain, whether he recognizes it as just or not. And so a punishment may deter from crime quite as effectually when it is not recognized as just, and consequently produces no feeling of disgrace. But a punishment cannot lead to repentance unless it is recognized as the fitting consequence of a moral fault, and it is this recognition which makes a punishment appear disgraceful.

151. It is sometimes maintained that it is undesirable to attempt to emphasise the element of disgrace in punishment, especially in the education of children. We are recommended to trust principally to rewards, and if we should unhappily be forced to inflict pain, we must represent it rather as an inconvenience which it would be well to avoid for the future, than as a punishment for an offence which deserved it. And for this reason all punishments, which proclaim themselves to be such, are to be avoided.

It seems to me that to trust to the influence of the pleasures of rewards, and of the pain of punishments, implies that the person to be influenced is governed by his pleasure and pain. On the other hand, to trust to the fact that his punishment will appear a disgrace to him implies that he is, to some degree, influenced by a desire to do right; for otherwise he would feel no disgrace in a punishment for doing wrong. And this second view of human nature is, at any rate, the more cheerful of the two.

It is necessary to distinguish between degradation and disgrace. A man is degraded by anything which lowers his moral nature. A punishment which does this would of course be so far undesirable. But he is disgraced by being made conscious of a moral defect. And to become conscious of a defect is not to incur a new one. It is rather the most hopeful chance of escaping from the old one. It can scarcely be seriously maintained that, if a fault has been committed, the offender is further degraded by becoming ashamed of it.

This confusion seems to be at the root of the controversy as to whether the corporal punishment of children is degrading. There is no doubt that it expresses, more unmistakeably and emphatically than any substitute that has been proposed for it, the fact that it is a punishment. It follows that, unless the offender is entirely regardless of the opinions of the authority above him, it is more calculated than other punishments to cause a feeling of disgrace. But, supposing it to be inflicted on the right occasions, this is surely an advantage in a punishment. That it produces any degradation is entirely a separate assertion, which demands a separate proof—a demand which it would be difficult to gratify.

152. But although a punishment must, to fulfil its highest end, be disgraceful, it does not follow that we can safely trust to the disgrace involved in the offence itself as a punishment—a course which is sometimes recommended. The aim of punishment is rather to produce repentance, and, as a means to it, disgrace. If we contented ourselves with using as a punishment whatever feeling of disgrace arose independently in the culprit's mind, the result would be that we should only affect those who were already conscious of their fault, and so required punishment least, while those who were impenitent, and so required it most, would escape altogether. We require, therefore, a punishment which will produce disgrace where it is not, not merely utilize it where it is. Otherwise we should not only distribute our punishments precisely in the wrong fashion, but we should also offer a premium on callousness and impenitence. As a matter of prudence it is as well to make sure that the offender, if he refuses to allow his punishment to be profitable to him, shall at any rate find it painful.

And in this connection we must also remember that the feeling of disgrace which ensues on punishment need be nothing more introspective or morbid than a simple recognition that the punishment was deserved. On the other hand, an attempt to influence any one—especially children—by causing them to reflect on the disgrace involved in the fault itself, must lead to an habitual self-contemplation, the results of which are not unlikely to be both unwholesome to the penitents, and offensive to their friends.

153. I have thus endeavoured to show that there are certain conditions under which punishment can perform the work which Hegel assigns to it. The question then arises, When are these conditions realised? We find the question of punishment prominent in jurisprudence and in education. It is found also in theology, in so far as the course of the world is believed to be so ordered as to punish sin. Now it seems to me that Hegel's view of punishment cannot properly be applied in jurisprudence, and that his chief mistake regarding it lay in supposing that it could.

In the first place, the paramount object of punishment from the point of view of the state ought, I conceive, to be the prevention of crime, and not the reformation of the criminal. The interests of the innocent are to be preferred to those of the guilty—for there are more of them. And the deterrent effect of punishment is far more certain than its purifying effect. (I use the word purifying to describe the effect of which Hegel treats. It is, I fear, rather stilted, but the word reformatory, which would be more suitable, has by common consent been appropriated to a different theory.) We cannot, indeed, eradicate crime, but experience has shown that by severe and judicious punishment we can diminish it to an enormous extent. On the other hand, punishment can only purify by appealing to the moral nature of the culprit. This may be always latent, but is sometimes far too latent for us to succeed in arousing it. Moreover the deterrent effect of a punishment acts not only on the criminal who suffers it, but on all who realise that they will suffer it if they commit a similar offence. The purifying influence can act only on those who suffer the punishment. From these reasons it would appear that if the state allows its attention to be distracted in the humble task of frightening criminals from crime, by the higher ambition of converting them to virtue, it is likely to fail in both, and so in its fundamental object of diminishing crime.

154. And in addition there seems grave reason to doubt whether, in a modern state, the crimes dealt with and the attitude of the criminal to the community are such that punishment can be expected to lead to repentance. The crimes with which a state has to deal may be divided into two classes. The first and smaller class is that in which the state, for its own welfare, endeavours to suppress by punishment conduct which is actuated by conscientious convictions of duty—as is often the case with high treason. Now in these cases the criminal has deliberately adopted a different view of his duty to that entertained by the state. He is not likely, therefore, to be induced to repent of his act by a punishment which can teach him nothing, except that he and the state disagree in their views of his duty—which he knew before. His punishment may be resented by him as unjust persecution, or may be accepted as the inevitable result of difference of opinion, but can never be admitted by him as justly deserved by his action, and cannot therefore change the way in which he regards that action.

155. In the second, and much larger, class of criminal offences, the same result happens, though from very different reasons. The average criminal convicted of theft or violence is, no doubt, like all of us, in his essential nature, a distinctly moral being. And, even in action, the vast majority of such criminals are far from being totally depraved. But by the time a man has become subject to the criminal law for any offence, he has generally become so far callous, with regard to that particular crime, that his punishment will not bring about his repentance. The average burglar may clearly learn from his sentence that the state objects to burglary. He might even, if pressed, admit that the state was, from an objective point of view, more likely to be right than he was. But, although he may have a sincere objection to murder, he is probably in a condition where the state's disapproval of his offences with regard to property will rouse no moral remorse in him. In such a case repentance is not possible. Punishment can, under the circumstances I have mentioned above, convince us that we have done wrong. But it cannot inspire us with the desire to do right. The existence of this is assumed when we punish with a view to the purification of the offender, and it is for this reason that the punishment, as Hegel says, honours him. Where the desire to do right is, at any rate as regards one field of action, hopelessly dormant, punishment must fall back on its lower office of intimidation. And this would happen with a large proportion of those offences which are dealt with by the criminal law.

156. Many offences, no doubt—especially those committed in a moment of passion, or by persons till then innocent—are not of this sort, but do co-exist with a general desire to do right, which has been overpowered by a particular temptation. Yet I doubt if, at the present day, repentance in such cases would often result from punishment by the state. If the criminal's independent moral will was sufficiently strong, he would, when the particular temptation was removed, repent without the aid of punishment. If it was not sufficiently strong, I doubt if the punishment would much aid it. The function in this respect of punishment was, as we have seen, to enforce on the offender the disapproval with which his action was considered by an authority, whom he regarded as expressing the moral law. But why should the modern citizen regard the state as expressing the moral law? He does not regard it as something above and superior to himself, as the ancient citizen regarded his city, as the child regards his parent, or the religious man his God. The development of individual conscience and responsibility has been too great for such an attitude. The state is now for him an aggregate of men like himself. He regards obedience to it, within certain limits, as a duty. But this is because matters which concern the whole community are matters on which the whole community is entitled to speak. It does not rest on any belief that the state can become the interpreter of the moral law for the individual, so that his moral duty lies in conforming his views to its precepts. Not only does he not feel bound, but he does not feel entitled, to surrender in this way his moral independence. He must determine for himself what he is himself to hold as right and wrong. The result of this is that, if he sees for himself that his action was wrong, he will repent without waiting for the state to tell him so, and, if he does not see it for himself, the opinion of the state will not convince him. I do not assert that there are no cases in which a man finds himself in the same childlike relation to the state as was possible in classical times, but they are too few to be of material importance. And except in such cases we cannot expect the punishments of jurisprudence to have a purifying effect.

157. Hegel's mistake, in applying his conception of punishment to criminal law, resulted from his high opinion of

the state as against the individual citizen.   The most significant
feature of all his writings on the metaphysics of society is the
low place that he gives to the conscience and opinions of the
individual.   He was irritated—not without cause—at the
follies of the writers who see nothing in morality but conscientious convictions, or "the good will."   But he did not
lay enough emphasis on the fact that, though the approval
of conscience does not carry us very far, by itself, towards a
satisfactory system of morality, yet *without* the approval of
the individual conscience no system of morality can now be
satisfactory.   It has become impossible for any adult man to
yield up his conscience into the hands of any other man or body
of men.   A child, in so far as it is young enough to be treated
entirely as a child, can and ought to find its morality in the
commands of others.   And those who believe in a divine
revelation will naturally endeavour to place themselves in an
attitude of entire submission to what appears to them to be
the divine will, whether manifested through books, or through
some specially favoured organization of men.   But a man is
not a child, and the state is not God.   A man may indeed
accept the direction of a teacher whom he has chosen—even
accept it implicitly.   But then this is by virtue of his own act
of choice.   We cannot now accept any purely outward authority
as having, of its own right, the power of deciding for us on
moral questions.

158.   Hegel points out, indeed, in the Phenomenology, that
the highest realisation of the state—that in which it is the
universal which completely sums up the individuals which
compose it—may be considered as being in the past or the
future, but not in the present.   But when he comes to deal
with the state in detail he seems to forget this.   Sometimes he
appears to think of the classical state as not yet passed away.
The ancient state did, indeed, endeavour to stand in the same
relation to its citizens as the father to the child, or even as God
to man, as is indicated by the very close connection which
existed in the ancient world between religion and patriotism.
But to attempt to bring this idea into the modern world is to
ignore the enormous development of the idea of individuality,

which accompanied, whether as cause or effect, the rise of Christianity, and was marked by the increasing prominence of the ideas of immortality and conscience. The individual began then to claim the right of relating himself directly to the highest realities of the universe—and, among others, to duty. He insisted on judging for himself. The state could be no longer the unquestioned judge of right and wrong; it could now itself be judged and condemned by the individual on moral grounds. It had still a claim to obedience, but not to unquestioning veneration. Nor is there anything inconsistent with this in the authority—perhaps as strong as that of the classical state—which the church exercised during the middle ages. For the church was regarded as a supernaturally commissioned authority. It could never have held its position if it had been looked on as an assembly of mere men. And in the course of years it became evident that even the church's claim to unquestioning veneration could not stand before the demand of the individual to have everything justified before the tribunal of his own spirit.

159. From another point of view, Hegel may be said to have supposed that the ideal state had already come, when it was still far in the future. Indeed we may go further, and say that, by the time the state had become ideal, it would have long ceased to be a state. No doubt Hegel looked forward, and by his philosophical system was justified in looking forward, to an ultimate ideal unity which should realise all, and far more than all, that the classical state had ever aimed at. He contemplated a universal so thoroughly realised in every individual that the most complete unity of the whole should be compatible with the most complete self-development of the parts. But before this last and highest development of reality could be reached, we should have to leave behind us altogether the world of matter and time, which would be incompatible with such a complete perfection of spirit. Still more would it be impossible in a stage of development in which external government and criminal justice still existed. And to encourage the actual state, as we see it in the world to-day, to assume functions justified only in the far past, or in the remote future, is disastrous both in theory and in practice.   No part of Hegel's teaching has been productive of more confusion than his persistent attempt to identify the kingdom of Prussia with the kingdom of Heaven.

160.   The result then, to which we have come, is as follows. Hegel's view of the operation of punishment is one which is correct under certain circumstances.   And when punishment has this function, it is fulfilling its highest end, since only in this manner does it succeed in really eradicating the fault which caused it.   But this function is one which it scarcely ever succeeds in performing at present, when administered in the course of criminal law, and which it is not more likely to succeed in performing in the future.

This does not, however, render it unimportant.   For, although it is disappearing in jurisprudence, it is persistent and important in education.   There is not the same need in education as in law that punishment shall be deterrent at all costs.   The ordinary offences of children are not very dangerous to the structure of society, and we can therefore turn our attention, without much risk, rather to curing them than suppressing them.   And, as a general rule, the decisions of the elder world are tacitly accepted by the younger as righteous.   In cases where the authority who inflicts the punishment, or the law upon which it is inflicted, are explicitly rejected as unjust by the offender, we cannot hope that punishment will be more than deterrent.   But such cases are infrequent, and there is good reason to suppose that they will remain so.   For it is a fact which, though often forgotten, cannot well be denied, that children are born young—a fact which has some significance.

CHAPTER VI.

SIN.

161. HEGEL'S doctrine of Sin is complicated, and cannot be found in any single place in his writings. It may, I believe, be accurately summed up as follows. Innocence, Sin, and Virtue are respectively the Thesis, Antithesis, and Synthesis of a triad. Sin, again, may be analysed into three subordinate terms, which also form a triad—Sin proper, Retribution, and Amendment. There is, therefore, if this theory is correct, something in the nature of Innocence which spontaneously produces Sin, in Sin, which produces Retribution, in Retribution which produces Amendment, and in Amendment which produces Virtue.

Sin, then, is the Thesis in a triad which forms the Antithesis of a larger triad. It is thus both positive and negative—positive within a limited sphere, but negative inasmuch as that whole sphere is negative. And this does justice to the double nature of sin. All sin is in one sense positive, for it is an affirmation of the sinner's nature. When I sin, I place my own will in a position of supremacy. This shall be so, because I will it to be so, regardless of the right. But this right, which my sin violates, is itself a far deeper and truer reality than my sinful will. Indeed it is the true reality of that will itself. The fact that I sin implies that I am amenable to the moral law. And that means that it is my nature to be virtuous. If I did not violate the deepest law of my own nature by sinning, it would not be sin. And thus my sin while from one point of view an affirmation of my

own nature, is from a more comprehensive standpoint a denial
of it. No theory of sin can account for all the facts unless it
allows for both these aspects.

162. Before we consider the theory in detail, let us enquire
of what species of proof it is susceptible. An *à priori* proof
is impossible. For the subject matter to be dealt with is not
exclusively *à priori*. It contains empirical elements. And
therefore the proof must itself be empirical.

We must not, then, demand for these triads a demonstration
of the same nature as the demonstrations of the triads of the
Logic. For there the terms were *à priori*, and so were the
demonstrations. Moreover the dialectic method, as Hegel uses
it in the Logic, could not bring out the results required here.
For the result of each of those demonstrations is to prove the
lower steps of the process to be inadequate representations of
the truth, and so to deprive them of any absolute validity
whatever, and reduce them to moments of the higher term
which transcends them.

Now Hegel's object is not to prove that Innocence and Sin
are inadequate expressions for a reality for which Virtue is an
adequate expression. He is here speaking of a process in time,
and his assertion is that Innocence produces Sin, and Sin
produces Virtue. Each of them is a separate phenomenon in
time, and, from that point of view, one is as real as the other.
All temporal processes, no doubt, are based for Hegel on a
non-temporal reality, but here he is confining himself to the
temporal process. And therefore the Synthesis, though it
proceeds from the lower terms, and has a greater significance
than they have, is not the sole reality of those terms, as is
the case in the transitions of the Logic, which, according to
Hegel, go deeper into the truth of things.

All that Hegel has demonstrated *à priori* is the general
nature of reality. His explanations of any empirical fact, such
as Sin, must depend on the degree in which they succeed in
accounting for the phenomena. We know that Innocence, Sin,
and Virtue exist. In some way or another they must spring
from the general nature of reality, as deduced in the Logic.
In so far as Hegel's theory of Sin agrees both with the

empirical facts, and with the conclusions of the Logic, we shall have reason to think it true.

It is clear that all the evidence which can support such an argument falls very far short of demonstration. But there is no reason to suppose that Hegel did not see this. As I have pointed out elsewhere[1] there is no trace of any belief on Hegel's part that the application which he made of his Logic shared the demonstrative certainty which he unquestionably attributed to the Logic itself. He may have been too sanguine as to the degree of certainty which could be attributed to his theories of ethics, of history, and of religion, but we find no assertion that their certainty is of the same nature as that which is possessed by the process of categories leading on to the Absolute Idea.

Before proceeding further, we must notice two points which will be discussed more fully later on. In the first place the triad of Innocence, Sin and Virtue is put forward by Hegel as the sufficient explanation of Sin, but not as the sufficient explanation of Virtue. Sin never occurs except as the Antithesis of such a triad, but Virtue, as we shall see, can occur in other circumstances, and not only as the Synthesis of Innocence and Sin. In the second place, Hegel does not commit himself to the statement that, wherever Innocence is found, the other terms must follow, but only says that there is something in the nature of each term which *tends* to bring on its successor. What is the precise meaning of such a tendency is a question which must be deferred.

163. The statement of the principal triad—of Innocence, Sin and Virtue—is to be found in the Philosophy of Religion. The third part of this deals with the Absolute Religion, and is divided into three sections, the second of which deals with the "Kingdom of the Son." This is again subdivided, the third division being entitled "Bestimmung des Menschen." It is in the first half of this division[2] that Hegel considers the question now before us.

The exposition is too condensed to admit of further

---

[1] *Studies in the Hegelian Dialectic*, Section 207.
[2] *op. cit.* ii. 257—282 (trans. iii. 45—72).

abbreviation, but the following passages strike the key-note:—
" The primary condition of Man, which is superficially represented as a state of innocence, is the state of nature, the
animal state. Man must (*soll*) be culpable; in so far as he
is good, he must not be good as any natural thing is good,
but his guilt, his will, must come into play, it must be possible
to impute moral acts to him. Guilt really means the possibility
of imputation.

" The good man is good along with and by means of his
will, and to that extent because of his guilt (*Schuld*). Innocence (*Unschuld*) implies the absence of will, the absence
of evil, and consequently the absence of goodness. Natural
things and the animals are all good, but this is a kind of
goodness which cannot be attributed to Man; in so far as he
is good, it must be by the action and consent of his will[1]."

" The animal, the stone, the plant is not evil; evil is first
present within the sphere of knowledge; it is the consciousness
of independent Being, or Being-for-self relatively to an Other,
but also relatively to an Object which is inherently universal
in the sense that it is the Notion, or rational will. It is only
by means of this separation that I exist independently, for
myself, and it is in this that evil lies. To be evil means,
in an abstract sense, to isolate myself; the isolation which
separates me from the Universal represents the element of
rationality, the laws, the essential characteristics of Spirit.
But it is along with this separation that Being-for-self originates, and it is only when it appears that we have the Spiritual
as something universal, as Law, what ought to be[2]."

" The deepest need of Spirit consists in the fact that the
opposition in the subject itself has attained its universal, *i.e.*
its most abstract extreme. This is the division, the sorrow,
referred to. That these two sides are not mutually exclusive,
but constitute this contradiction in one, is what directly proves
the subject to be an infinite force of unity; it can bear this
contradiction. This is the formal, abstract, but also infinite
energy of the unity which it possesses.

[1] *op. cit.* ii. 260 (trans. iii. 48).
[2] *op. cit.* ii. 264 (trans. iii. 53).

"That which satisfies this need is the consciousness of reconcilement, the consciousness of the abolition, of the nullity of the opposition, the consciousness that this opposition is not the truth, but that, on the contrary, the truth consists in reaching unity by the negation of this opposition, *i.e.*, the peace, the reconciliation which this need demands. Reconciliation is the demand of the subject's sense of need, and is inherent in it as being what is infinitely one, what is self-identical.

"This abolition of the opposition has two sides. The subject must come to be conscious that this opposition is not something implicit or essential, but that the truth, the inner reality (*das Innere*), implies the abolition and absorption of this opposition. Accordingly, just because it is implicitly, and from the point of truth, done away with in something higher, the subject as such in its Being-for-self can reach and arrive at the abolition of this opposition, that is to say, can attain to peace or reconciliation[1]"

164. Innocence, says Hegel, "implies the absence of will." This must be taken as a limit only. If Innocence is used as an attribute of conscious beings, it cannot involve the complete absence of will. To suppose that knowledge could exist entirely separated from will would be a mistake of a kind completely alien to Hegel's system. But Innocence, as it is used by Hegel, is clearly a matter of degree, and so we can say that, in proportion as a conscious being is innocent, he is devoid of will.

Now whatever is devoid of will is in harmony with the universe. It is only purposes which can be real, and yet out of harmony with all other reality. All facts (including, of course, the existence of purposes, regarded as mental events) must be compatible with one another. If two asserted facts would be incompatible, we are certain that one at least of them is unreal. Every fact therefore is compatible with every other, and so with the universe, which is the unity of which all these facts are differentiations. And there is no meaning

---

[1] *op. cit.* ii. 277 (trans. iii. 67).

in saying that two compatible facts are inharmonious, unless
one of them is, or includes, a purpose which the other prevents
it from realising.

Whatever is innocent, then, is in harmony with the universe.
But this involves, for Hegel, that it is good. For the universe as a whole is most emphatically good for Hegel. He
has told us that the real is rational, and the rational is real.
Thus he says that "natural things and the animals are all
good."

Yet he also says that innocence "implies the absence of
goodness." In this he refers no longer to natural things,
but to man. It is evident that a goodness which has nothing
to do with the will is not moral goodness. And a man is not
properly called good unless he is morally good. A stone or
a cabbage have no possibility of will, and it would be unreasonable to deny their harmony with the universe the name
of goodness, on the ground that they do not possess a good
will. But a man has a will, and so the possibility of moral
goodness. He is therefore to be judged by a more exacting
standard, and Hegel will not call him good if he only possesses that harmony which forms the goodness of beings
without will.

165. When a man is virtuous, he wills to follow certain
principles. These principles, according to Hegel's idealism,
are the same as those in conformity to which the universe
works. And, this being so, the virtuous man, like the innocent
being, is in harmony with the universe—but this time in a
deeper harmony. He is in harmony with it, not merely as
a part which cannot be out of harmony, but as an individual
who can propose to himself an end, and who has proposed
to himself an end which is good, and therefore, since the
universe is good, in harmony with the universe. The will
is, of course, part of the universe, but it need not be in
harmony with it. For that is the nature of will—it is a fact,
and causally determined by the world of reality, and yet it
may be so determined as to postulate what the world of
reality forbids, and to condemn what the world of reality
insists on. Where there is will, there can be discord. But

between a virtuous will and a righteous universe there is
harmony.

Innocence and Virtue agree, then, in the fact that the
nature of each of them is good. But Innocence is merely
blindly determined to good from the outside. Virtue, on the
other hand, freely determines itself to goodness. (It is scarcely
necessary to repeat that Hegel's use of the words Freedom and
Self-determination has nothing to do with what is generally
called Free-will, but refers simply to the unthwarted development of the internal nature of the agent.) The element which
Virtue has, and which Innocence lacks, is the individual and
his self-determination.

166. There can be no doubt, for a philosophy like Hegel's,
which finds all reality to be Spirit, that Virtue is higher than
Innocence. And, in that case, there will be *sub specie temporis*
a process from one to the other. In what manner may we
expect that this will happen?

We may reasonably hope that we shall be able to trace
in it a dialectic triad. We cannot, for reasons which I have
pointed out elsewhere[1], be certain that we shall be able to
do so. But it is at any rate worth trying. All process is,
if Hegel's philosophy is right, of a dialectic nature, and, in
spite of the complexity of all concrete phenomena, we may be
able to perceive it in this particular case.

The nature of Virtue suggests very strongly that it may
turn out to be a Synthesis of Innocence with some other term,
since it combines in its unity an element which Innocence
possesses, and one in which Innocence is deficient. In that
case the other term will emphasise the element in which
Innocence is deficient, while it will unduly ignore the element
which is specially characteristic of Innocence.

Even apart from the dialectic, this would not be an
improbable method of progress. Whether Hegel's Logic be
correct or not, we have only to look round us to see many
cases where progress can only be made by successively over-
estimating each of two complementary and partial truths.

[1] *Studies in the Hegelian Dialectic*, Chap. VII.

Not until the falsity of the first of these, taken in isolation, has driven us on to the second, and that also has proved unsatisfactory by itself, are we in a position to combine both in a really adequate manner.

167. Now if there is such a dialectic process to be traced in this case, the complementary extreme will be the self-determination of the individual regardless of the relation which that determination bears to the good. And thus we get Sin as the remaining term of the triad. For although this random self-determination may sometimes cause me to will something, which it is, more or less, desirable that I should will, the position would still be morally wrong. It is, indeed, the essence of all moral wrong, because it denies all difference between the wrong and the right. Not only do I do what I will—which is a tautology when we are dealing with voluntary action—but this ends the matter. There is no other criterion of action except that I will it. And since all my voluntary actions satisfy this test, all distinctions of good and evil are swept away.

This position is involved in all Sin. It is true that a man often acts sinfully with a perfectly clear intellectual conviction that there is a moral law, and that he is breaking it. But in committing the sin, he rejects the moral law practically, if not theoretically, and the question is one of practice. He decides that for him, at any rate at that minute, the will to do the action shall be its sufficient justification.

By saying that this is of the essence of Sin, we do not imply that nothing can be virtuous, unless it is done from the motive of being virtuous. It is quite possible to hold that actions from other motives are also virtuous. The position of Sin lies in the assertion—or rather in the practical adoption—of the maxim that my motives need no other justification than the fact that they are my motives.

It should be noted in passing that such self-determination as this can never issue in conduct exactly like that which would be the result of virtue. A sinful motive may result, no doubt, in action which resembles very closely the action which would be taken in similar circumstances by an agent

who was acting virtuously. A dishonest judge may condemn
for a bribe a man who really deserves condemnation. A
subscription to a charity, which was given to catch a title,
may be used for the effective relief of real misery. But
content and form are never without some influence on one
another. And an action inspired by a sinful motive will never
exactly resemble an action inspired by a virtuous motive,
though they may, of course, share some particular characteristic, which from some particular point of view may be the
only important one.

Sin, then, is the complementary moment to Innocence.
And it is clear that Innocence precedes Sin, and does not
follow it. Innocence is therefore the Thesis, and Sin the
Antithesis.

168. This stage is the most novel, and the most paradoxical, of the whole theory. The arguments for it, as was
remarked above, rely on the fact that it is consistent with the
general nature of reality, as demonstrated by Hegel in the
Logic, and that it is able to explain, on the basis of that
general nature, the existence of Sin. But we are now in a
position to notice that it is only able to explain the existence
of Sin on the assumption of the existence of Evil.

Evil is, of course, a much wider conception than Sin,
which implies a conscious acceptance of Evil. Whatever is
imperfect is evil. Innocence is therefore evil as much as Sin
is. Indeed, it is in one sense more evil, for it is further from
Virtue. Now Hegel's explanation of Sin is that it is the
inevitable transition from Innocence to Virtue. But this leaves
unexplained the necessity of any progress towards Virtue at
all. Why is the first step in the time-process anything so
imperfect, and therefore so evil, as Innocence? If Virtue is
the perfect state, why, in a rational universe, were we not all
virtuous all along? Why do we find ourselves in such a
position that we have to climb up to Virtue by means of Sin?
This is part of the general question of the origin of Evil.
Hegel's treatment of this subject does not fall within the
scope of this chapter[1].

---

[1] Cp. *Studies in the Hegelian Dialectic*, Chap. v.

169. It is clear from the sections of the Philosophy of Religion to which I have referred that Hegel regards the movement from Innocence to Sin as followed and completed by a movement from Sin to Virtue. But the details of this are not given by him here. When, however, he deals, in the Philosophy of Law, with the action of the state as regards crime, he does, as we have seen, give a triad, which in this special case leads from Sin to Virtue. We have, first, Sin. Then, as the Antithesis, comes Punishment. The result, in which both the assertion of self in Sin, and the suppression of self in Punishment, are contained, is Repentance[1].

The relation of Punishment and Repentance to Sin is not regarded by Hegel as invented by society for its own advantage, but as due to the inherent nature of Sin. It is not, I think, an unreasonable inference to conclude that an analogous process is to be found in the case of those other transitions from Sin to Virtue which are not due to the punishments deliberately inflicted by other human beings, acting as conscious guardians of right. Hegel, so far as I know, does not state this view anywhere. But his emphasis, in the Philosophy of Law, on the inevitability of the relation is so strong that I think we are justified in holding that he believed some such relation to exist in every case of Sin.

170. In every case of Sin, then, there would follow suffering consequent on it, and tending to repress the self-assertion in which the sin consisted. And when this had been effected, the agent would be in a condition in which he was freed from his sin. It would, however, be inconvenient to use in all cases the terms Punishment and Repentance. The common use of Punishment confines it to cases of suffering inflicted by a conscious being with the explicit motive of counteracting the sin in some way. And we do not usually speak of the effect of Punishment on a man except in cases where the suffering is realised by him to have been inflicted because of a belief that he had sinned. The effect of a penalty which was not recognized to be meant as a penalty would scarcely be called the effect of Punishment.

[1] Cp. Chap. v.

Now if we are speaking of suffering which always follows sin, we shall have to exclude these two elements. It may be true that it always does follow. But it certainly is not always inflicted by other men as a punishment for the sin, nor is it always recognized by the sinner as the consequence of his action. The word Punishment is therefore rather inappropriate, and, for this wider meaning, it might be more suitable to use Retribution.

In the same way, Repentance is not used except in cases where the sin is remembered, and explicitly regretted. In this sense Repentance cannot be an invariable step between Sin and Virtue, for there are many cases where our recovery from a past fault simply consists in the gradual development of a more healthy character, and where we cannot repent of the sin, because it is not remembered—perhaps, indeed, was never recognized as a sin at all. Here too, therefore, we shall require a fresh term. Now the word Amendment is not, I think, limited, like Repentance, to a process of whose ethical meaning the agent is conscious, and thus it will be suitable for our present purpose.

The sub-triad of Sin, then, will be made up of the following members, Sin proper, Retribution, and Amendment. And in this way, as I remarked at the beginning of the chapter, Hegel does justice both to the positive and the negative aspects of Sin. It is negative as against Innocence and Virtue. For it consists in opposition to that order of the universe which Innocence blindly obeys and Virtue freely accepts. But from another point of view Sin, as the assertion of the ultimate value of the particular individual in his particularity, is just the unbridled positive, which requires checking and moderating. Both these characteristics are accounted for by taking Sin as the Thesis in a triad which is itself an Antithesis.

171. But why, it may be asked, does Retribution follow, or at all events tend to follow, every act of Sin, independently of the conscious efforts of mankind to inflict Punishment? The answer is that the universe agrees with the ideals of morality. In so far, therefore, as any man seeks his good in ends which are incompatible with those ideals, he is placing his will in opposition to the principles which regulate the world as a whole, and which are the deeper truth of his own nature. And thus he must be baffled—either by external things, or, if that should not happen, by the internal discord which his action will produce in himself.

It is in this second form that the inevitability of Retribution, and its intrinsic connection with sin, are most clearly shown. The whole position of Sin is contradictory, in a way which Hegel's system brings out, perhaps, with greater clearness than any other. For Sin depends on the emphasis laid on the self. The attitude of the sinner is that what he wants is of supreme importance. And he is so far right, that every self is of supreme importance, and that its claim to be treated as an end is entirely justifiable. But, while the sinner is right in treating himself as of supreme importance, he is wrong in his conception of his nature. The true self of any man is not something which exists in particularity and isolation, and which finds its satisfaction in the gratification of desires arising from its particular and isolated nature. On the contrary it only exists in its individuality by reason of its necessary and vital unity with all other selves, and it can only find satisfaction in so far as it places its good in the realisation, by means of its individual nature, of that unity. The only true peace for the self is to be found in its free self-determination to carry out the purpose of the universe, since that purpose is its own deepest nature; and the purpose of the universe—the universe which has been demonstrated to be rational—is in accordance with the principles of Virtue.

Thus Sin is a contradiction, since it at once asserts the supreme value of the self, and seeks satisfaction in that which—just because the self *has* supreme value—can never satisfy. To commit sin is very like drinking sea-water to quench thirst. And, like the drinking of sea-water, it requires no external retribution, but brings about its own.

172. From Retribution follows Amendment. If what has been said above is correct, it follows that in the long run sin must always disgust the person who commits it. You have only got to go on sinning long enough to have it borne in on you with ever increasing force that it is not in this way that true self-satisfaction is to be found. With a pessimistic theory of the universe, indeed, it might be possible to condemn certain conduct as sinful, and yet to maintain that it yielded all the satisfaction which could be got in such a very imperfect world. Or again, another theory might hold that there was in this respect some fundamental and original difference between one man and another, so that some of them would find their true satisfaction in sin, and would never be deterred from it simply by experience of it. But neither of these views is possible for Hegel. The true nature of every self, he maintains, is such that it can only find satisfaction in its own free co-operation with the purpose of the universe. And so experience will bring home to it inevitably that it cannot find satisfaction in sin.

But is this conviction properly to be called Amendment? We took this term to designate a state analogous to Repentance and indicating a moral improvement. Can what we have reached be called a moral improvement, or is it simply the correction of a miscalculation? Is it anything more than a discovery that sin does not pay, and can that be called a moral advance?

There would, certainly, be no moral significance in a discovery that sin would fail to produce satisfaction because of some external circumstance which has been arbitrarily attached to it. But then this is not what happens. It is the sin itself which, in the process of Retribution, loses the charm which it had hitherto possessed. It had been committed because the agent imagined that he could find satisfaction in it. It is abandoned because he learns that he cannot—just because it is sin.

Now this *is* a moral change. The difference between a vicious man and a virtuous man is precisely that the former finds his satisfaction in sin, and the latter in virtue. It is impossible to eliminate so much reference to self as is implied in this. A man need not act for his own pleasure, but he must always act for his own satisfaction. And thus no more fundamental expression could be found for a moral change than the realisation that sin did not and could not satisfy the sinner. To stop sinning because some of the consequences of sin are unsatisfactory is simply prudence. But to stop sinning because sin itself has become unsatisfactory is to become virtuous.

To realise that sin cannot give satisfaction is, in itself, only a negative result. Taken by itself, it might teach us not to sin, but could scarcely teach us to do anything else. But then it is not taken by itself. It is only an incident in the development of a self which is implicitly moral all through, though it requires to be made explicitly so. In passing to Sin from 'Innocence a man is so far right—that he realises the supreme importance of himself. He has only mistaken what his self really is. And when that mistake is corrected, there remains the perception that the self has to be satisfied, coupled with the new perception that nothing will satisfy us that is not virtuous.

173. All this, it may be objected, is not very like the Repentance brought about by Punishment, of which Hegel speaks in the Philosophy of Law. For there the Punishment is not an inevitable and inherent consequence of the crime, but is something which is affixed to it by the decision of the law-givers. Their decision indeed is not arbitrary, but does not arise spontaneously out of the crime. And, besides, the Punishment is not the failure of the crime to produce the satisfaction sought for, but a distinct and independent evil annexed to it.

But we must remember that the effect of punishment, in the triad described in the last chapter, does not arise from the fact that it is something unpleasant which balances the satisfaction to be expected from the crime. For if this were the effective element, it is clear that the result could only be deterrent, and not that which I have called purifying. Now it is the purifying effect of which Hegel is speaking. And the work of Punishment in producing this result is simply to force on the attention of the criminal the fact that his crime is condemned by some moral authority which he is not prepared explicitly to reject. The work of Punishment is thus to crush the false independence of the subject, so as to give a chance to the true independence to manifest itself. And this is just what is done by the inherent collapse of Sin, which I have called Retribution. Their functions are thus analogous. It is only in so far as this analogy arises that Hegel is interested in Punishment at all—in so far, that is, as Punishment reveals to the criminal that the crime is not the outcome of his deepest nature. When the effect is preventive, or merely deterrent, or merely vindictive, Hegel finds no philosophical meaning in it.

174. From Amendment we now pass to Virtue. In the larger triad Virtue is the Synthesis of Innocence and Sin. That it is in its right place here will be seen from what has been already said. Innocence has the positive quality of being in harmony with the good. But it has the defect of not being a free self-determination of the individual. And thus it is not really in harmony with the good, because it is not in harmony with it in the way which is appropriate to a conscious being. A conscious being, who imitates the goodness of a stone, is not good, but bad. On the other hand Sin has the positive quality of being a self-determination. But then it is not in harmony with the good. And the good is the essential nature of every conscious being. And so Sin turns out not to be really an assertion, but a negation of the true individuality of the sinner.

Thus each of the two terms is found, by means of its defects, to involve a contradiction. Because Innocence is only good, it is not good but bad. Because Sin only asserts Individuality, it does not assert, but rather negates it. But Virtue transcends these imperfections, and therefore resolves these contradictions. It is really good, because it is really self-determination. It is really self-determination, because it is really good.

175. If we take into account the sub-triad of Sin, the immediate transition to Virtue will be from Amendment, which is the Synthesis of the sub-triad. The relation which exists between the Synthesis of one triad and the commencement of the next is expressed by Hegel in the formula that, in passing from the one to the other, the notion "collapses into immediacy."

It would be difficult perhaps to find a clearer example of such a collapse into immediacy than the transition from Amendment to Virtue. The phrase means, I think, that whereas in the Synthesis the result gained is looked at as the result of a process, as having overcome the contradictions which had been developed in the lower terms, in the new Thesis it is looked on as the starting-point of a new process, as something which leaves the old contradictions and its victories over them behind it, which asserts itself as the absolute truth, and which consequently lays itself open—except in the case of the Absolute Idea—to the demonstration that it is still imperfect, and will therefore develop fresh contradictions. It may be said that the idea looks, before the collapse, to the past, and, after it, to the future.

Such a time-reference must of course be merely metaphorical when we are dealing with the transitions of the Logic itself. But when we come to the applications of the dialectic to events in the time-process, we may expect to find it more than a metaphor. And this is just what we do find in this particular case. Amendment—as we see clearly in that special variety which is called Repentance—can only be defined with reference to the past. My nature is amended in so far as I have got rid of a sin which I previously committed. In so far as this amendment has taken place I am virtuous. But it is possible to define Virtue without reference to past Sin. It is the positive good content, taken not as a rejection of Sin, but as a simple fact.

176. We have thus gone through the entire dialectic process which leads from Innocence to Virtue. It is not, however, a process which occurs only once in each man. For Innocence and Virtue are not single and indivisible qualities. They have many aspects. And therefore a man may have passed out of the stage of Innocence in respect of one of his qualities, and not in respect of another, and the dialectic movement may therefore have to be repeated again, in respect of this latter. It is a matter of every-day observation that a man may be in a state of childlike submission to one element of morality, of explicit revolt against a second, and of free and reasoned acquiescence in a third.

And not only have Innocence and Virtue many aspects, but they are also capable of different degrees. For we saw above that a man could only be more or less innocent, since complete Innocence would require complete absence of will, and would therefore be impossible for any conscious being. It is therefore possible that the processes should only be partial. The revolt in Sin, and consequently the reconciliation in Virtue, may leave a certain residuum of the blind submission of mere Innocence, which will require to be removed by a repetition of the process.

177. We have now to consider two qualifications to the universality of the formula we have established. They were mentioned earlier in the chapter. The first of these lies in the fact that Virtue can be increased otherwise than through Sin and Amendment. It often happens that a man becomes conscious of some imperfection or defect in his morality, and forthwith amends it, so passing to a higher stage of Virtue. Indeed, this is often done unconsciously. With no deliberate resolve, with no knowledge of the process, a man rises, through the practice of virtue, to some higher level than that to which he had previously attained. Thus revolt and reconciliation are not the only road of moral advance.

This, however, does not at all conflict with Hegel's theory. Indeed it might have been anticipated. For he points out in his Logic that the form of the dialectic changes gradually as we move from the beginning to the end of the process[1]. The Antithesis becomes less and less the contrary of the Thesis, and more and more a union of the Thesis with its complementary element, so that its relation to the Thesis comes to resemble more and more closely the relation of a Synthesis. The advance from some particular imperfection no longer takes place by first emphasising the complementary imperfection, and then rising to a higher idea which transcends both. This

---

[1] Cp. *Studies in the Hegelian Dialectic*, Chap. IV.

is replaced by a direct advance from the original imperfection to the transcending idea. The process may be said to come nearer and nearer to a straight line though it never actually becomes one.

We may therefore anticipate, on *à priori* grounds, what we have seen actually happens. At first, when Innocence is nearly complete, the advance can only be upon the model of the transitions in the Doctrine of Being. From Innocence we must advance to Sin—its direct contrary. Only after passing through Sin can we arrive at Virtue. But as the general moral advance—or possibly the advance in some particular field of morality—progresses, the situation changes, and the transitions resemble those which are to be found in the Doctrine of the Notion. The man has attained to fuller self-consciousness. He can recognise the imperfection of the degree of Virtue to which he has attained by simple reflection. He does not require to have its imperfection driven home by the inability of that standpoint to keep from passing over into its opposite. He can see that it is imperfect even while he occupies it, and is therefore able to pass directly from it to a higher one which transcends it. It is, therefore, only when the position of the Thesis is relatively close to absolute Innocence that the process which we have sketched takes place. In proportion as the Thesis, in a later stage, sums up many advances of the past, and so is more virtuous than innocent, further transitions can be made without Sin and Amendment.

178. The inherent necessity of the process, then, is not for Virtue, since Virtue can be increased (though not indeed in the earlier stages) without it. Hegel does regard the process as inherently necessary, but only for the other members. Where there is Innocence there must necessarily follow Sin, and where there is Sin there must necessarily follow Retribution, Amendment, and Virtue.

179. But is even this in accordance with the facts? And this question brings us to the second qualification which we have to make. It is quite clear, if we only take individual cases, as we see them in this world between birth and death, that, though the process often does take place, it often does not.

We have only to look round us to see instances of Innocence which does not pass into Sin, of Sin which does not meet with Retribution, of Retribution which does not lead to Amendment. It is impossible to suppose that Hegel had forgotten this. Whatever the philosophical importance which he attributed to the facts of everyday life, his knowledge of them was profound, and his practical interest in them was acute. What then are we to suppose that he believed about these apparent exceptions to his theory ?

It seems clear that he did not believe in a mere tendency which would work itself out if not checked, but which might be checked so that it could not work itself out. His language indicates that he was dealing with a process which we were entitled to say not only might take place but would take place. Two alternatives remain.

180. He may have considered that there was not only a tendency, but an actual and inevitable process, in the race or the universe, while in the case of particular individuals there was merely a tendency, which might possibly be counteracted. The passages quoted above, and the rest of that part of the Philosophy of Religion from which they are taken, bear out this view, since Hegel's attention seems devoted to the progress of the race as a whole, and not of the individuals. Indeed, he shows everywhere a strong inclination to treat ethical problems as matters for mankind, and not for this or that man. He is not far from the belief—a belief it might be difficult to defend —that, when mankind has conquered a moral difficulty in one generation, all succeeding generations will enjoy the fruits of the victory as fully as each man does those of his own past struggles. Here, as elsewhere, the indifference to the individual shown in the applications of the Logic stands in striking contrast to the emphasis laid on individuality in the Logic itself.

181. But there is another way in which this difficulty might be avoided. Hegel believed in immortality. And he might therefore have explained the apparent incomplete moral processes by asserting that it was our field of vision which was incomplete. All the transitions in the process require time.

And it is only because death has intervened too soon that, in some cases, Innocence does not lead to Sin, Sin to Retribution, Retribution to Amendment, or Amendment to Virtue. But death only stops our observation of the process. It does not stop the process itself. The Innocence which we see in one life may pass into Sin in the next, and the Retribution which seems fruitless here may produce Amendment hereafter.

It would not be necessary, for the validity of this explanation, that the events of one life should be remembered in the next. For Retribution, in the sense in which it has been used here, does not depend for its efficiency on remembrance of the Sin, nor does Amendment depend on the remembrance of Retribution. All that is required is that actions done on one side of death shall affect the character on the other. And this must be so. If it were not, there would be no identity of the two existences, and, therefore, no immortality.

It is difficult to say which of these two alternatives Hegel would have adopted. It is especially difficult to know what he would have thought of the second, for, as has been remarked in Chapter II, he always declines to take the slightest account of the immortality in which he professes to believe. On the whole, it appears to me more probable that he would have adopted the first alternative, and admitted that there was only a tendency in the individual, while there was an inevitable process in the race. At the same time, I cannot help thinking that the other alternative might provide a better solution in the hands of any Hegelian who did not share his master's objection to taking immortality seriously.

182. We have now seen what Hegel's theory of Sin is, and we have seen on what basis a belief in that theory must rest. We have before us the fact of Sin—the fact that a being who forms part of the universe can put himself in opposition to the principles which underlie the true nature of that universe, and of himself in particular. And we have also before us the fact that such a being is yet, from the point of view of the very morality to which he opposes himself, a higher object in the scale of values than the stone or tree

which is a perfectly submissive instrument to the general purpose. And besides these facts we have the conclusions as to the general nature of reality which are demonstrated by the Logic. Our present theory rests (a) on the consideration that it is not only compatible with the conclusions of the Logic, but is one which those conclusions would by themselves render probable though not certain. Its further support is more or less negative, since it consists in (b) its claim to explain the facts better than any other explanation that has been put forward which is compatible with the conclusions of the Logic.

183. The peculiarity of this theory is the relatively high place which it gives to Sin. There are two other theories, with which it may be confounded, but it goes further than either of them. The first is the doctrine, which is so prominent in the philosophy of Leibniz, that evil is the condition of good, since it is impossible that good should exist unless evil existed also. The second is the doctrine that sin may be made an instrument of a greater good than would have existed without it—that men may rise, not only in spite of their repented sins, but by means of them.

Hegel's position differs from the first of these in making Sin not only a necessary concomitant of Virtue, but a necessary element in it. All Virtue is based on transcended Sin, for although, as we have seen, Virtue can advance in other ways than through Sin, this is only in the higher and later stages. The beginning of it must always be by such a process as that which has been described in this chapter. In thus making transcended Sin an element in Virtue, Hegel's position resembles the second theory mentioned above. But it differs from it in making the process universal and necessary. It is not merely that Sin may lead to increase of Virtue, and that Virtue may be based on Sin. Hegel's view is that Sin *must* lead to increase of Virtue, and that there is no Virtue which is not based on Sin.

184. The result of this is that moral evil and moral good are not absolutely opposed for Hegel, as they are for many philosophers. There can be no absolute opposition—however important the relative opposition may be for practical purposes

—between two terms, one of which is the Synthesis of the other. And again, which is perhaps the most paradoxical part of the system, a man draws nearer to Virtue when he commits a sin. For Sin, as the second in time of the two stages, has the advantage over Innocence. In passing to Sin from Innocence the sinner has taken a step on the only road which can lead him to Virtue, and morality has therefore gained.

Ordinary morality has accepted the position that even a sinful man is higher than a stone, which cannot commit sin. But many people would regard the view that a sinful man was higher than an innocent man as a dangerous falsehood.

Even if Hegel's position were detrimental to ordinary morality, it would not be thereby refuted. It is true that his system leads us to the conclusion that all reality is rational and righteous, and that it would be inconsistent if any part of the system led us to a contrary conclusion. But to say that it is righteous is one thing, and to say that it agrees with our previous conceptions of morality is another. If it did not do so, the fault might lie in those conceptions, and not in reality. I do not, however, believe that in the acceptance of Hegel's doctrine of Sin any change in the ordinary canons of morality would be logically involved, or that any logical ground would arise for disobedience to those canons.

185. It may be said, perhaps, that the consideration that a sin marks a moral advance on the state of innocence would be a ground for disregarding the sinful nature of an act to the commission of which we were tempted. But an argument of this nature would, I think, be sophistical. It is not true that under all circumstances a sin would mark a moral advance. It would not do so in any case in which the result—the state of Virtue—had been already reached, or in which we could reach it without sinning. It is only when we are in such a stage of relatively rudimentary Innocence that we cannot advance except by negation, that the sin is indispensable to the gaining of Virtue, and so is a moral advance.

Now how can I know that I am, at a particular time, and with regard to a particular virtue, in such a state? It seems to me that I could know it only by experience. I cannot be certain that I am unable to resist temptation except by finding that, in fact, I do not resist it. Thus it follows that, until my sin has been committed, I can never know it to be a necessary step to virtue, and therefore to be a moral advance. And thus the knowledge that it would be a moral advance can never be a factor in determining me to commit it.

And, again, in proportion as my knowledge of my own character showed me a probability more or less approximating to a certainty that advance in the case in question was only possible through sin, what would this amount to? To a belief, more or less certain, that I could not resist the temptation. For, if I could resist it, it would prove that I was no longer on the level of mere Innocence, but had risen to Virtue. I should therefore only have ground to believe that it would be good to commit the sin, in proportion as I was convinced it was inevitable that I should commit it. And thus our theory could have no effect in deciding my action, since it could only make me regard a sin as an advance in a case in which I considered my action as already certain.

On this theory, indeed, I can always say to myself, when tempted, "If I yield to this temptation, my sin will be a moral advance." But it will be equally true to say, "If I do not yield to it, then my resistance will be a moral advance." And thus there is no ground here for choosing either course. To suppose that there was a ground for either would be to fall into the same fallacy as that which asserts that Determinism must destroy all resistance to temptation, because a Determinist believes that, if he did commit the sin, it would be eternally necessary that he should commit it.

186. Thus Hegel's theory offers no logical ground for choosing sin rather than virtue. And it must also be remembered that it is not sin alone which forms the moral advance, but sin which is followed by retribution and amendment. This makes a considerable difference in the psychological effect of the belief. Should a schoolboy be convinced that, if he played truant, playing truant would be morally healthy for him, it would be illogical, but perhaps not unnatural, that he should take this as an argument for doing so. But if he were told that his moral advantage would consist in the fact that the offence would bring on a punishment sufficiently effective to cure him of any tendency to repeat the fault, it is not probable that the theory would make the temptation any greater than it had been before the metaphysical question was raised.

187. It is true that this theory does not lend itself to the deification of Virtue—it would scarcely be Hegel's if it did. It does not permit us to regard the difference between Virtue and Sin as the fundamental difference of the universe, for there are conditions much worse than Sin. Nor is it an ultimate difference, for the whole meaning of Sin is that it is a stage which leads on to Virtue, and a moment which is transcended in it. Hegel goes even further than this. For even Virtue is only a moment in a still higher perfection[1]. And again, whatever does happen to a moral being, whether it be Sin or Virtue, is, when it happens, a moral advance.

Such results are not adapted for moral declamations, but it may be doubted if they have any more serious defect. If a man feels Virtue to be a greater good for him than Sin, he will choose Virtue and reject Sin, even though he should think that Sin is not wholly bad, nor the worst possible state. All that is required of a theory of Sin, therefore, in order that it may be harmless to morality, is that it should not deny the difference between Virtue and Sin, or assert that Sin is the greater good of the two. Hegel's theory does not do either. To go further, and to condemn Sin as absolutely and positively bad, is useless to morality, and fatal to religion[2].

188. We may notice that this theory provides a justification for a belief which has flourished for a long period, especially in the English race, without any metaphysical support. It has very commonly been held that it is desirable that children should do certain things, for which, when they have done them, it is desirable that they should be punished. On most ethical

---

[1] To consider this point would be beyond the limits of the present chapter. Cp. Chap. IX.; also *Studies in the Hegelian Dialectic*, Sections 202—206.

[2] Cp. *Appearance and Reality*, Chap. xxv. p. 440.

theories this appears to be hopelessly unreasonable. Either, it is said, an act deserves punishment, and then it ought not to be done, or else it ought to be done, and then it cannot deserve punishment. Some systems of education accept the first alternative, and some the second, but they agree in rejecting the hypothesis that both the acts and their punishment could be desirable. In spite of this, however, the old view continues to be held, and to be acted on, perhaps, by some who do not explicitly hold it..

If we follow Hegel, we may come to the conclusion that the unreflective opinion of the race has, either by chance or by a judicious common sense, grasped the truth with more success than its critics. For it is evident that children, in relation to the morality of adults, are very often exactly in the position which Hegel calls Innocence. And it may therefore be anticipated that, in the majority of cases, they will rise to that morality most simply and completely by the process of alternate defiance and suppression.

Such words as Sin, Retribution, and Amendment seem, no doubt, unduly serious and pompous in this connection. But it must be remembered that we are watching the process from the standpoint of the Synthesis in a way which is seldom, if ever, possible when we are observing the struggles of our fellow adults. (It is to this exceptional point of observation, I suppose, that we must ascribe the fact that many people who would shrink from recognizing a moral advance in a night's drunkenness are quite able to see a moral advance in a forbidden pillow-fight.) To one who fully comprehends the facts, Sin would always appear too futile to be taken seriously. It is necessary, no doubt, to take our own sins and those of our neighbours very seriously, but that is because we do not fully comprehend. For those who do, if there are such, the most atrocious of our crimes may reveal themselves to have the same triviality which even we can perceive in a schoolboy's surreptitious cigarette. In heaven "they whistle the devil to make them sport who know that sin is vain[1]."

---

[1] Kipling, *Barrack-room Ballads*, Dedication.

It would seem, then, that in this matter a system of education cannot be judged by the same tests as a system of government. The punishments of the state can scarcely hope to be anything more than deterrent and preventive, and, since this is so, that state is in the most healthy condition in which the fewest punishments are deserved. But if punishment has, in education, the higher function of a stage in a necessary moral process, it would follow that a system of education is none the worse because it does not prevent children from deserving punishment—provided, of course, that it affords a reasonable probability that they will get what they deserve.

CHAPTER VII.

THE CONCEPTION OF SOCIETY AS AN ORGANISM.

189. HEGEL'S tendency to exalt the state, and society generally, at the expense of the individual citizen, is one of the most striking characteristics of his system. It is one, moreover, in which Hegelians, as a rule, have faithfully followed their master.

The exaltation in question is not identical with a desire to increase very largely the functions exercised by the state. It involves indeed, almost necessarily, the extension of those functions beyond the limits allowed them by the stricter Individualists. But it would be quite consistent with an amount of individual liberty which would prevent the result being classified as Socialism or Communism. And, on the other hand, it is quite possible to propose a system of the most rigid Socialism or Communism, and yet to disagree entirely with Hegel's view of the dignity of the state. This was, to a large extent, the position of the older Socialists, such as Robert Owen.

We may best define Hegel's position by contrasting it with its opposite. That opposite is the theory that the state and society are merely external mechanisms for promoting the individual welfare of the individual citizens. This theory does not, of course, involve that each citizen cares only about his own welfare. But, if he cares about the welfare of others, he regards them as an aggregate, each of whom has a welfare of his own, not as a whole, whose welfare is one and the same. Again, this theory does not assert that the state was formed by the agreement of individuals who were before isolated, nor that the machinery, which the state and society give, could possibly be dispensed with by the individual. But, in whatever way the union was first formed, and however indispensable it may be, we can only justify its existence on the ground that it is a common means to the separate ends of the citizens. To this view Hegel opposes the assertion that society is more than a merely external means.

I maintain that there is nothing in Hegel's metaphysics which logically involves this view of society. On the contrary, it seems to me that such a system of metaphysics involves the view that the present condition of society, and any possible form of the state, can only be looked on as means to the welfare of the individuals who compose them. That welfare, indeed, can never be found in isolation, but may be found in very different combinations.

190.   Hegel's own view on the subject is generally expressed by saying that the nature of society is organic. This phrase, so far as I know, is not used by Hegel himself. And it does not seem to be very accurate. An organic unity is, in the ordinary meaning of the term, such a unity as binds together the different parts of a living body. And, whatever may be the unity which exists in society, it would seem clear that it cannot, on Hegelian principles, be the same as that of the parts of a body. Self-conscious persons, such as make up society, are far more individual than a hand or a foot. Now, according to Hegel, the greater is the individuality of parts, the closer is the unity which *can* be established between them, and the deeper must we go to establish it. It follows that self-conscious persons will need a deeper and more fundamental principle of union than suffices for the parts of a body, and, if they *are* joined by a principle adequate for the purpose, will form a unity far closer than that of the parts of a body. And to call such a principle organic seems unreasonable. It is true that it comprehends and surpasses the principle of organic unity. But, if this were a reason for calling it organic, it would be an equally good reason for calling an organic unity mechanical, and for calling a mechanical unity a mathematical aggregate.

The use of the word organic, therefore, seems to me incorrect, and, not improbably, misleading. But since it is used by most of the writers of the present day who follow Hegel in this question, I shall adopt their phraseology while I am considering their views.

Hegel takes the State (Der Staat) as a higher form of society than the Civic Community (Die bürgerliche Gesellschaft). He expresses the distinction between them as follows : " Were the state to be considered as exchangeable with the civic community, and were its decisive features to be regarded as the security and protection of property and personal freedom, the interests of the individual as such would be the ultimate purpose of the social union. It would then be at one's option to be a member of the state. But the state has a totally different relation to the individual. It is the objective spirit, and he has his truth, real existence, and ethical status only in being a member of it. Union, as such, is itself the true content and end, since the individual is intended to pass a universal life. His particular satisfactions, activities, and way of life have in this authenticated substantive principle their origin and result[1]."

Hegel does not, however, make any distinct attempt to prove the superiority of the State to the Civic Community. He points out that the unity is more close and vital in the State, and there he leaves the matter, the line of thought being, apparently, that since it has been proved in the Logic that true reality is a perfect unity, the closer unity is always the higher form. For a more detailed treatment of the subject we must look to his followers. In particular, Professor Mackenzie, in his " Introduction to Social Philosophy," maintains the organic nature of society with such force and clearness that our best method of dealing with the subject will be to examine his exposition of it.

191. Professor Mackenzie defines an organism by saying that in it " the relations of the parts are intrinsic; changes take place by an internal adaptation; and its end forms an

---

[1] *Philosophy of Law*, Section 258, lecture note.

essential element in its own nature[1]." Here are three characteristics. The second does not require special consideration.
Its truth, and the sense in which it is to be taken, seem to
depend on the truth, and on the precise meaning, of the
previous statement that the relations of the parts are intrinsic.
The other two points of the definition seem to me to be
ambiguous. If they are taken to imply that society is an
end to the individuals who compose it, they would form an
adequate definition of organism; but in that sense I do not
think that Professor Mackenzie has proved them to be true
of society. On the other hand, in the sense in which he has
proved them to be true of society, they appear to me to be
quite compatible with a theory which should regard society
as a merely mechanical unity, and as simply a means to the
separate ends of its constituent individuals.

192. Let us take first the intrinsic relations of the parts
to the whole. If this were to mean, as it might possibly be
taken to mean, that to be in these relations was the end of
the individual who was in them, and that this was his end,
not from any further quality of the relations, but simply
because they were the relations which united him to society,
then, indeed, we should have an organic unity.

But this is not what Professor Mackenzie proves. He
appears to be satisfied when he has pointed out that the
individual's nature is *determined* in every direction by the
society in which he lives, and that there is no part of his
nature to which this determination does not extend[2]. This
is unquestionably true. No man, indeed, is *only* the product
of society, for it would be impossible to account for the
differentiated result, if it did not contain an originally differentiated element. The coexistence of individuals in a whole
may modify their differences, but cannot construct them out
of nothing. But this, I imagine, would not be denied by
Professor Mackenzie, and it is impossible to dispute his assertion that no individual, and no part of any individual's nature,

---

[1] *An Introduction to Social Philosophy*, Chap. III. p. 164. My references are
to the edition of 1895.

[2] *op. cit.* Chap. III. p. 166—171.

would be what it now is, except for the influence of the society
to which that individual belongs.

But what does this come to, when it is admitted? Surely
to nothing else than the assertion of complete reciprocal determination, which is involved in organic connection, but is by
no means equivalent to it. As soon as we realise that causal
determination is complete and reciprocal, and that the distinction between essence and appearance is illegitimate, we
are able to assert about any two things in the universe the
relation which Professor Mackenzie has pointed out between
the individual and society. No Englishman would, in any
respect, be quite what he is now, if the Reform Bill had not
been carried, or if Dr Pusey had joined the Roman Communion.
Granted. And no Englishman would be, in any respect, quite
what he is now, if there were one more herring in the Atlantic.
The influence in the first case is more important than in the
second; but that is not a difference of kind, and will not entitle
us to say that society joins individuals in any way which is
qualitatively different from the way in which everything in
the universe is joined to everything else.

What possible theory of the state does this truth exclude?
It would exclude, certainly, any theory which denied that the
individual was affected at all by living in society. But does
anyone hold—could anyone hold—such a view? It has been
asserted that society is the end of the individual. It has been
asserted that it is a means to that end. It has even been
asserted, by anchorites, that it was simply a hindrance to
that end. But has anyone ever said that man was exactly
the same in society as he would be out of it? It has been
maintained, no doubt, that the associated man is only superficially different from the isolated man, and that the two are
fundamentally the same. But it has never been denied that
they *are* different. The assertion which would be denied by
Professor Mackenzie's demonstration of "intrinsic relations"
is not that society makes no fundamental difference in the
individual, but that it makes no difference in him at all. And
when we have disposed of this absurdity, all sane theories of
the state are still left to choose from.

193. The intrinsic relations of individuals would also, no doubt, be incompatible with the theory which Professor Mackenzie calls mechanical. "A mechanical or dualistic view, again," he says, "would regard the individual as partly dependent and partly independent; as to some extent possessing a life of his own, and yet to some extent dependent on his social surroundings[1]." It is impossible, certainly, to divide any individual into isolated compartments, and if any part of a man's life is affected by the society of which he is a member, no part of his life can be wholly unaffected by it. But although the view here rejected may fitly be called mechanical, it is not the only view which deserves that name. It answers to the category to which Hegel has given the name of Formal Mechanism, but there still remains the higher category which he calls Absolute Mechanism. In Absolute Mechanism, if I interpret the Logic rightly, we discard the supposition that the internal nature of anything can be independent of the relations into which it enters with other things. We see that the two sides are inseparably connected. On the one hand, the internal nature of anything is meaningless except in connection with its relations to other things, since it is only in those relations that the inner nature can manifest itself. On the other hand, relations to other things are meaningless except in relation to the internal nature of the thing. A merely passive subject of relations is impossible, as the category of Reciprocity has already taught us. If A is mn, because it is related to BC, this is not a merely external relation. For it must be ascribed to the nature of A that BC produces upon it the result mn rather than the result op.

Now the admission of intrinsic relations—that there is nothing whatever in A which is independent of its relations to B, C, &c.—need not involve more than the category of Absolute Mechanism. And, in admitting this category, we have by no means reached the idea of organic unity. No unity, it is clear, can be organic which is a mere means to the separate ends of its constituent individuals. And there is

[1] *op. cit.* Chap. III. p. 150.

nothing in the category of Absolute Mechanism to hinder this from being the case. Each individual, it is true, is, under this category, determined throughout by the unity in which he stands with the other individuals of the same system. But ends, means, and hindrances to ends, all exercise causal determination over objects. A man is causally determined alike by the moral ideal which he holds, by the dinner which he eats, and by the hatreds which he feels. But this need not prevent us from saying that the first of these is an end, good in itself, the second a means, which has value only in so far as it enables us to carry out the end, and the third a hindrance to carrying out the end, and, therefore, positively bad.

Accordingly we find that those theories of society which carry individualism furthest are quite consistent with the category of Absolute Mechanism, and with the admission of intrinsic relations between the members of society. The hermits of the early Church regarded society as detrimental to man's highest interests, and consequently as an evil to be avoided as far as possible, and to be steadily resisted when unavoidable. A hedonist regards society as only justifiable in so far as it produces, for each of the individuals who compose it, a greater amount of private happiness than he would otherwise have enjoyed. Both these positions are quite compatible with the intrinsic relations which we have been considering. For each of them would have admitted that some society was indispensable, and each of them would have admitted that the whole man was modified by the society of which he formed a part.

194. I have endeavoured to prove that the intrinsic relation of the parts of society gives us no help towards establishing its organic nature, since the proposition would be equally true of any real system, whether organic or not. We must now consider the third clause of Professor Mackenzie's definition of an organism: "its end forms an essential element in its own nature."

Here again there seems to me to be a dangerous ambiguity. If this proposition meant, as it might mean, that the existence of the society as society was its own end, and also the end of the individuals who compose it, then, indeed, the unity in which it would bind those individuals would be so close that it might fairly be called organic, or even more than organic. But when we come to enquire into the precise meaning which Professor Mackenzie attaches to the phrase, we shall find that, in one part at least of his work, he gives it a much narrower meaning, which, however true, gives us no reason to regard it as an organism.

"That the growth of social conditions has reference to an inner end," he says, "is a point on which we need not here enlarge. That the movements of social development are purposeless, no one supposes; and that the purpose which it subserves lies within itself is equally apparent. What the end is, it may be difficult to determine; but it is easy to perceive that it is some form of human well-being[1]."

Professor Mackenzie seems here to assume that "some form of human well-being" must lie within society itself. But this, though it may be true, is by no means necessary. All human beings are at present within society, but it is possible that they may cease to be so in the future, and that the human well-being which it is the object of society to promote may be one in which society is broken up, and the individuals isolated. (I am not, of course, arguing that this *is* the case. I am only maintaining that the fact that the present and actual human being is in society, does not of itself prove that the future and ideal human being will also be in society[2].)

195. The end of a school, for example, is the well-being of the boys, and the boys form the school. Nevertheless, the school is not an end in itself. For boys leave school when they grow up, and the end of the school is their welfare throughout

---

[1] *op. cit.* Chap. III. p. 176.

[2] Professor Mackenzie appears, in one paragraph at least, to recognize this. For in the concluding passage of Chap. III. (p. 203) he admits, if I understand him rightly, that before we can properly call society an organism we must enquire whether the ideal human well-being, which is the end of society, is itself social. But since, in the passage quoted above from p. 176, he appears to assert explicitly that human well-being is, as such, social, I thought it well to deal with both positions separately. The view stated on p. 203, and developed in Chap. IV., will be considered later.

life, when they will certainly have left school, and may easily be completely isolated from all their old school-fellows.

Now what is undoubtedly true of this fraction of society may be, according to some theories, true of society as a whole. Let us take the case of a man who believed that society existed for the promotion of true holiness, as the highest end of man, while at the same time he defined holiness as a relation which existed between God and a particular individual, and which was independent of—even incompatible with—any relations between the individuals themselves. Now any one who believed this—and something very like it has been believed—would quite admit that the end of society was nothing else than human well-being, since he would conceive that the greatest human well-being lay in holiness. But the end of society would not be in itself; on the contrary, it would be something which could only be realized when society itself had ceased to exist.

Again, consider the case of a hedonist who should hold that the one end of society was to make the sum of pleasures felt by its individual members, taken as isolated beings, as large as possible. Such a man would hold that the end of society was a form of human well-being, while he would not regard society as an organic unity, but merely as a means for the respective ends of the various individuals who compose it.

196. My contention has been, so far, that it is useless and misleading to call any unity organic unless we are prepared to maintain that it (and not merely something at present contained in it) is an end to itself, and to its own parts. Otherwise we shall include among organic unities systems which exist as bare means for the carrying out of ends which are indifferent, or even hostile to the unity. To call such systems organic would be improper, in the first place, because that word has always been employed to denote a relatively close unity, while such a use would extend it to all unities whatever. Every aggregate of individuals which were not absolutely isolated from each other, and in which the connection was not reduced to the level of mere delusion, would be classed as organic.

And, in the second place, not only would such a definition depart completely from the ordinary usage, but it would render the term useless. When we said that a unity was organic, we should only say that it was a unity. It would be useless, for example, to say that society was organic. For we should only thereby deny the assertion that the individual, or any part of him, is uninfluenced by being in society. If any person does hold this remarkable view, I am unable to say; but it is certainly not of sufficient weight to render it worth while to appropriate such a convenient word as organic to express disbelief in it. Meanwhile, the distinction—of such cardinal importance in political theory—between those who admit and those who deny that society is an end in itself would remain without a suitable name.

I should suggest that the most suitable definition of an organic unity for our present purpose might be something like this: "a unity which is the end of its parts." This clearly distinguishes it from a unity which is merely mechanical. It also distinguishes it from a chemical unity, to use Hegel's phrase, in which the parts are regarded as mere means which may be discarded or merged, if that would conduce to the realisation of the end. For here the end is the unity of the parts, and the parts therefore are an element in the end, as well as the means to it.

This definition has the merit of coinciding with tolerable exactness with the ordinary use of the word organic, which is an important advantage when it can be gained without sacrifice of accuracy. Organic is commonly used of animal and vegetable life. Now the definition I have proposed would include animals and vegetables, and would not include anything which did not bear a tolerably close resemblance to biological unity.

Such a definition would mark a division in our present subject-matter which would be worth making. There are two theories at the present day as to the nature of society, and especially of the state, each of which has considerable practical influence, and for each of which much can be said that must be carefully considered by any student. They differ by the admission or rejection of the idea of society as an end in itself, and it would be convenient to refer to them as the organic and inorganic views of society.

Hegel's example would be on our side. For in the Logic he makes scarcely any distinction between the idea of an immanent end and the idea of life. And I imagine that this definition would not be disapproved by Professor Mackenzie[1].

197. Is society the end of man? This is the question which we have now to answer. Let us enquire, in the first place, what general information we possess regarding our supreme end.

If we turn to Hegel, we find that for him the supreme end is another name for Absolute Reality, which, *sub specie aeternitatis*, is eternally present, but, *sub specie temporis*, presents itself as an ideal and a goal. Now Hegel's conception of Absolute Reality is one which, as we have seen, might very fitly be called a society[2]. It is a differentiated unity, of which the parts are perfectly individual, and which, for that very reason, is a perfect unity. To call such a unity organic would only be incorrect because it was inadequate. And thus Absolute Reality would be the most perfect of all societies. Just because the individual was such a complete individual, he would have all his perfection, and all his reality, in nothing else but in his relations to other individuals. Or, to quote Professor Mackenzie, "no attainment of the ideal of our rational nature is conceivable except by our being able to see the world as a system of intelligent beings who are mutually worlds for each other[3]."

The end of man, then, is a society. But we are now considering "social philosophy" and not theology, and what we want to know is not our relation to the kingdom of heaven, but our relation to society as it is now around us, and as it may be expected to be in an earthly future. Now it is quite clear that, whatever this ideal society, which Hegel makes

---

[1] Cp. above Section 194, note, and the *Introduction to Social Philosophy*, Chap. iii. p. 203.

[2] Cp. above Sections 216—218.

[3] *op. cit.* Chap. iv. p. 260.

our end, may be, it is not the society which we have round us to-day. Absolute Reality, according to Hegel, is eternal, and cannot be fully realised in any state of the world which is still subject to succession in time. Absolute Reality must see and be seen under the highest category only, and is not realised while any reality is unconscious of itself, or appears to others under the form of matter. Absolute Reality, finally, is incompatible with pain or imperfection.

This is clearly not the society in which we live, and we are not entitled to argue that the society of the present is an organic unity, because the ideal society is such a unity. But although they are not identical, the society of the present and the ideal certainly stand in some relation to one another. Can we, by a closer investigation of this relation, find any reason to consider the society of the present organic?

198. It might seem as if we had made an important step in this direction when we reflected that in a system like society, whose parts are self-conscious individuals, one of the strongest forces towards making the system organic is the conviction that it ought to be so. For it will be an organism if the individuals make it their end. Now it must be admitted that our conviction of what ought to be our end will not always decide what our end actually is. A man's end may be above or below his theoretical opinion about it. He may acknowledge the higher, and yet pursue the lower. Or he may explicitly acknowledge only the lower, and yet pursue the higher, moved by some vague impulse, which he can neither justify nor resist. Still, on the whole, the belief that anything would be a worthy end has a great influence in making it a real one.

Can we, then, establish the organic nature of present society as an ideal, if not as a fact? Can we say that the society of this world ought to be organic, and that we shall do well in proportion as we make it so by regarding the various relations, natural and civic, which constitute it, as the end of our individual lives? The ultimate end, indeed, it cannot be. Nothing but the heavenly society can be that, and, since anything earthy must be different from absolute reality, our present society, even if improved as far as possible, could never be anything higher than the means to the ultimate end.   But, in reference to all the activities and interests of our individual lives, it might be said that present society might be rightly considered as the end, since it is only by working in it and through it that we can progress towards the ultimate ideal which alone can fully satisfy us.

This, if I understand him rightly, is something like the position which Professor Mackenzie adopts. Having said, in the passage quoted above, that "no attainment of the ideal of our rational nature is conceivable, except by our being able to see the world as a system of intelligent beings who are mutually worlds for each other," he continues, "now, how far it is possible to think of the whole world in this way is a question for the Philosophy of Religion to discuss. It is enough for us here to observe that, in so far as we come into relations to other human beings in the world, we are attaining to a partial realisation of the ideal which our rational nature sets before us.   And there is no other way by which we come to such a realisation. In so far as the world is merely material, it remains foreign and unintelligible to us.   It is only in the lives of other human beings that we find a world in which we can be at home. Now in this fact we obviously find a much deeper significance for the organic nature of society than any that we have yet reached. For we see that the society of other human beings is not merely a means of bringing our own rational nature to clearness, but is the only object in relation to which such clearness can be attained[1].

199.   I must confess, however, that I am unable to see that this argument is valid. It is true that the ultimate ideal is a state of society which is organic.   It is true, too, that only through our present society can that ideal be reached.   For we must begin from where we are, and at present we are in society. It may be granted, too, that it is almost incredible that a period of absolute social chaos should intervene between us and the goal, and that the progress to that goal may safely be considered as made continuously through society.

Yet it does not follow, I submit, that it would be well to

------

[1] *op. cit.* Chap. iv. p. 260.

regard our present society as an end. For although our progress
to the ideal is through it, that progress is often negatively
related to it. Our advance often—to some extent, always—
consists in breaking up and rising above relations which, up to
that point, had been part of the constitution of society. And
so these relations cannot be regarded as an end. The fact that
their value is purely derivative should be ever before us—at
least, in so far as we reflect at all. We must express ourselves
by them as long as we find them the best expression of the
absolute end, or the best road to' it, but only under the
reservation that we are to throw them aside as worthless,
when we find a more adequate expression or a more direct
road.

The abstract form of society, indeed, remains. In whatever
way we work out our destiny, we work it out in one another's
company. But if the particular relations which constitute our
present society at any moment are to be looked on as means, to
be discarded when better ones can be found, this is sufficient
to destroy the claims of our present society to be considered
organic. For the abstract fact that individuals are somehow
connected, can never be sufficient to unite them in an organic
unity. Individuals can never find their end, which must be
something concrete, not abstract, in the bare fact of their
connection with one another. It is only some particular
connection that they can accept as their end, and it is only
in respect of some particular connection that they are organic.
And if, as I suggested above, any particular relations which
we find in the society of the present day must be looked on as
mere means, it will be impossible to regard that society itself
as organic.

200. The correctness of this statement remains to be
considered. My object has been so far to assert, not that
our present society cannot be regarded as an organism, but
that there is nothing in the Hegelian metaphysics which can
fairly be taken as proving, or even as suggesting, the organic
nature of that society. It will be for the other side to prove,
if they can, that the perfect society of Absolute Reality will be
found to be constituted on the same plan as our present society,

joining and sundering in heaven those who are joined and sundered on earth.

No attempt has been made, so far as I know, to prove this, nor is it easy to see how it could be proved. Indeed, there is a strong presumption, to say the least, that the opposite is true. For when we come to consider what determines the actual relations in which men find themselves in society—the relations of family, of school, of profession, of state, of church—we find that overwhelming influence is exercised by considerations which we cannot suppose will have overwhelming influence in that ideal society in which all our aspirations would be satisfied. Birth of the same parents, birth on the same side of a river, a woman's beauty, a man's desire—such are the causes which often determine, in our present society, what individuals shall be most closely related together. All these things are no doubt real, in some degree, and therefore are to some degree represented in the ideal; but to suppose that they are as important there as they are here, would be to forget that in that ideal we are to find "a world in which we can be at home." No doubt the society of the present is the natural and inevitable introduction to the society of the future, but it is so only in the same way as everything else is. Of everything which has ever happened in the world, of anarchy as well as of society, of sin as well as of virtue, of hatred as well as of love, the fact that it has happened proves that it was a necessary incident in the movement towards the ideal. But this can give it no more than a derivative value. I find myself associated with Smith in a Parish Council. This no doubt is a stage in our progress towards the ideal society of heaven. But there is no à priori reason to regard it as more vitally connected with that goal of all our ambitions than anything else, good or bad, social or isolated, which happens to either of us. Whatever heaven may be like, it cannot closely resemble a Parish Council, since the functions of the latter involve both matter and time. And it is by no means improbable that the result of my joint labours with Smith on earth may be the attainment of a state in which I shall be linked most closely in heaven, not to Smith, but to Jones, who comes from another parish.

201.   The vast majority of the relations which make up
our present society are of this kind—relations which have their
origin and meaning only with reference to the conditions of our
present imperfect existence, and which would be meaningless
in the ideal.   It is possible that we might find, on further
consideration of the nature of Absolute Reality, and of our own
lives, some element in the latter which seemed to belong
directly to the former—something which did not merely lead
to heaven, but *was* heaven[1].   Supposing that this were so, and
that we found in our present lives some element of absolute
value, then it would be more hopeless than ever to regard our
present society as an end.   For, if such elements do exist, they
certainly are not able to exercise an uncontested influence over
the world.   And it is perhaps for this reason that the deepest
emotions are apt, if they have any effect on society, to have a
negative and disintegrating effect, at least as far as our present
observation will carry us.   They may bring peace on earth in
the very long run, but they begin with the sword.

Nothing, surely, could so effectively degrade present society
from the position of an end to that of a means, only valuable as
leading on to something else, than such a state of things, if
it should prove to be true.   If we have, here and now, partial
experience of something whose complete realisation would give
us utter and absolute satisfaction, how can we avoid a relation
of partial hostility to a state of society which refuses us that
supreme good ?   For it will scarcely be denied that utter and
absolute satisfaction is not an invariable accompaniment of social
life as we find it at present.

202.   To sum up the argument so far.   I have endeavoured
to prove, in the first place, that we gain nothing by calling
society an organism unless we are prepared to assert that
it is the end of the individuals composing it.   And, in the
second place, I have endeavoured to prove that there is nothing
in Hegel's metaphysical conclusions which entitles us to believe
that our present society is, or ought to be, an end for its
individual citizens.   But we can go further, and say that the

---

[1] Cp. Chap. IX.

true lesson to be derived from the philosophy of Hegel is that earthly society can never be an adequate end for man. For Hegel has defined for us an absolute and ultimate ideal, and this not as a vain aspiration, but as an end to which all reality is moving. This ideal we can understand—dimly and imperfectly, no doubt, but still understand. And to any one who has entertained such an ideal, society, as it is, or as it can be made under conditions of time and imperfection, can only be external and mechanical. Each of us is more than the society which unites us, because there is in each of us the longing for a perfection which that society can never realise. The parts of a living body can find their end in that body, though it is imperfect and transitory. But a man can dream of perfection, and, having once done so, he will find no end short of perfection. Here he has no abiding city.

I do not think that this view leads either to asceticism or to the cloister. Not to asceticism; for there is nothing in it inconsistent with the great truth, so often neglected, that a limited good is still good, though limited. The beatific vision is good; and so is a bottle of champagne. The only reason why we should not take the satisfaction produced by champagne as our end is that it is not one with which our nature could be eternally content. But the fact that we cannot stop till we get to heaven will not make our champagne on the road less desirable, unless, of course, we should see reason to regard it as a hindrance to the journey.

Nor have we found any reason to suppose that our proper course would be to isolate ourselves from the imperfect society of this world. For if that society is only a means, at least it is an indispensable means. If it is not a god to be worshipped, it is none the less a tool which must be used.

203. But has philosophy any guidance to give us as to the manner in which we shall use such a tool? It might be supposed that it had. "Let us grant," it might be said, "that the fact that the Absolute is an organic society does not prove that our present society is or ought to be organic. Yet our present society will become perfect in so far as it approaches the Absolute. And therefore we have gained an *à priori*

McT. 13

criterion of social progress. Whatever makes society more organic is an advance. Whatever makes society less organic is retrograde."

This argument seems to me fallacious. We must remember that, while the Absolute is a perfect unity, it is a perfect unity of perfect individuals. Not only is the bond of union closer than anything which we can now even imagine, but the persons whom it unites are each self-conscious, self-centred[1], unique, to a degree equally unimaginable. If, on the one side, we are defective at present because we are not joined closely enough together, we are defective, on the other side, because we are not sufficiently differentiated apart.

These two defects, and the remedies for them, are not, of course, incompatible. Indeed, Hegel teaches us that they are necessarily connected. None but perfect individuals could unite in a perfect unity. Only in a perfect unity could perfect individuals exist. But Hegel also points out that our advance towards an ideal is never direct. Every ideal can be analysed into two complementary moments. And in advancing towards it we emphasise, first, one of these, and then, driven on in the dialectic process by the consequent incompleteness and contradiction, we place a corresponding emphasis on the other, and finally gain a higher level by uniting the two.

This is the Hegelian law of progress. To apply it to the present case, it tells us that, in advancing towards an ideal where we shall be both more differentiated and more united than we are now, we shall emphasise first either the differentiation or the union, and then supplement it by the other; that we shall reach thus a higher state of equilibrium, from which a fresh start must be made, and so on, through continually repeated oscillations, towards the goal.

It would follow, then, that it would be impossible for us to say that a change in the constitution of society was only good if it drew men more closely together. For an advance in either direction will appear, till the corresponding advance

---

[1] Self-centred does not, with Hegel, mean isolated. Indeed, the two qualities are incompatible.

is made in the other, to amount to a positive decrease in the latter, which has become relatively less important. If, in any state of society, the unity increases while the differentiation is as yet unchanged, it will appear to have crushed individuality. If, on the other hand, differentiation increases while the unity is unchanged, society will appear to have lost unity. And yet in each case there will be a real advance in the only way in which advance is possible, because the emphasis laid on one side furnishes the possibility—indeed the necessity—for the eventual advance of the other side, which, for the time, it throws into the background.

204.   Philosophy, then, can afford us no guidance as to the next step to be taken at any time. It can tell us that we are far below the ideal, both in unity and differentiation. It can tell us that we cannot advance far in one without advancing also in the other. But it also tells us that the steps are to be taken separately, and it can give us no information as to which, here and now, we have to-take next. That must depend on the particular circumstances which surround us at the moment—our needs, dangers, resources. It can only be decided empirically, and it will just as often be a step which throws the unity into the background as it will be one which brings it forward into increased prominence.

There is no want of historical examples which illustrate this alternate movement of society. The institution of private property, the first establishment of Christianity, and the breaking up of the feudal system—each involved an increased emphasis on the individual. And each tended to make society, as it was, not more but less of an organism, by giving the individual claims and ideals which could not be satisfied in society as it was, and some of which—such as parts of the Christian ideal—cannot be satisfied on earth at all. Yet they were all steps in a real advance; for they gave an increased individuality to the parts of society on which have been based unities far closer than could have been attained without them. And we can see now that, if the Hegelian conception of the Absolute had been known when any of these changes was happening, it would have been a mistake to have condemned the change on the ground that it diminished instead of increasing the unity of society.

So, too, with the present. We are confronted to-day with schemes both for increasing and diminishing the stringency of social ties. On the one hand we are invited to nationalize the production of wealth. On the other hand, it is suggested that the relations of husband and wife, and of parent and child, should be reduced to the minimum which is physiologically necessary. I have no intention of suggesting that the second tendency is right, or—here at least—that the first is wrong. But I maintain that the question is one upon which philosophy throws no light, and which must be decided empirically. The ideal is so enormously distant that the most perfect knowledge of the end we are aiming at helps us very little in the choice of the road by which we may get there. Fortunately, it is an ideal which is not only the absolutely good, but the absolutely real, and we can take no road that does not lead to it.

205. The result seems to be that philosophy can give us very little, if any, guidance in action. Nor can I see why it should be expected to do so. Why should a Hegelian citizen be surprised that his belief as to the organic nature of the Absolute does not help him in deciding how to vote ? Would a Hegelian engineer be reasonable in expecting that his belief that all matter is spirit should help him in planning a bridge ? And if it should be asked of what use, then, is philosophy ? and if that should be held a relevant question to ask about the search for truth, I should reply that the use of philosophy lies not in being deeper than science, but in being truer than theology—not in its bearing on action, but in its bearing on religion. It does not give us guidance. It gives us hope.

CHAPTER VIII.

206. My object, in the present chapter, is more purely historical than in the rest of this work. I shall endeavour principally to determine the relation in which Hegel actually stood to the Christian religion, and not the relation which logically follows from the main principles of his philosophy. I believe it will be found, however, that, on this question at least, his conclusions are quite consistent with his fundamental premises.

In the course of this enquiry I shall quote with some frequency from Hegel's Philosophy of Religion. But I would ask the reader to look on these quotations rather as illustrations of my interpretation than as attempts to prove that it is correct. For such a purpose isolated quotations must always be inadequate. In the first place, Hegel's views on this subject are not so much expressed in distinct propositions, as in the tendency and spirit of page after page. If I were to quote all that is relevant in this way, I should have to transcribe at least half of Part III. of the Philosophy of Religion. And, in the second place, isolated passages which support one view may perhaps be balanced by others supporting the opposite view still more clearly. Whether I am right in supposing that this is not the case with the theory I shall advocate can only be determined by each enquirer through his own study of the text. In short, if this Chapter is of any utility to the student of Hegel, it must be by suggesting to him a point of view which is to be judged by his own knowledge of Hegel's works, and especially of the Philosophy of Religion.

207.   Hegel repeatedly speaks of Christianity as the highest of all religions, as the Absolute Religion, and as true.   This is a fact of the first importance to our study of the question before us.   But it is not, as is sometimes supposed, a sufficient answer to it.   We must ask two preliminary questions.   First—did even the highest religion express, according to Hegel, absolute truth ?   Second—was Hegel using the word Christianity in a sense which bears any similarity to the ordinary signification of the word ?   Most of this Chapter will be employed in investigating the second of these questions, and the perplexities in which our answer may involve us will perhaps be solved by considering the first.

Christianity is a word of ambiguous meaning.   By such as count themselves Christians it is, of course, applied especially to that system of religion which each of them, since he holds it to be true, holds to be truly Christian.   But it is also applied, both by Christians and others, in a wider sense.   It is used as a general name for various systems, more or less differing from one another, but having a general resemblance.   No reasonable person would refuse the name of Christian either to Calvinists or to Arminians, either to the Church of Rome or to the Church of England.

The precise limits of theological belief, however, within which the word is applicable, are very uncertain.   No one, indeed, would deny that Berkeley ought to be called a Christian, and that Spinoza ought not.   But what amount of variation from the more common forms of Christianity is compatible with a proper application of the term ?   This is a question on which not many Christians seem to be certain, and on which still fewer seem to be agreed.   Any attempt on the part of outsiders to determine the question would be not only arduous, but impertinent.   I shall therefore confine myself to an endeavour to show what views Hegel entertained on certain theological subjects of cardinal importance, without venturing an opinion as to the propriety of calling such a religious system by the name of Christian.

208.   The points on which Hegel's system appears to have, *primâ facie*, the most striking resemblance to Christianity are three: the doctrines of the Trinity, of the Incarnation, and of Original Sin. In connection with each of these we have to discuss a second. With his belief as to the Trinity of God is closely connected his belief as to God's personality. His treatment of the Incarnation as a general truth will compel us to enquire also into his view of Jesus as a historical person. And his doctrine of Original Sin will suggest the question of the similarity of his ethical system to that generally associated with Christianity. We have thus six points to determine.

209. With regard to the Trinity and Personality of God, the most significant point in Hegel's philosophy of religion is his analysis of reality into a triad of which the first member is again analysed into another triad. Of these categories of the primary triad he says, "According to the first of these, God exists in a pure form for the finite spirit only as thought... This is the Kingdom of the Father. The second characteristic is the Kingdom of the Son, in which God exists, in a general way, for figurative thought in the element of mental pictures... Since, however, the Divine comes into view, and exists for Spirit in history of this kind, this history has no longer the character of outward history; it becomes divine history, the history of the manifestation of God Himself. This constitutes the transition to the Kingdom of the Spirit, in which we have the consciousness that Man is implicitly reconciled to God, and that this reconciliation exists for Man[1]."

The importance of this primary triad is mainly for the doctrine of the Personality of God, and we must therefore postpone it till we have dealt with the doctrine of the divine Trinity. This is connected by Hegel with the secondary triad into which he analyses the Kingdom of the Father. "Within this sphere or element," he says, "(1) Determination is necessary, inasmuch as thought in general is different from thought which comprehends or grasps the process of Spirit. The eternal Idea in its essential existence, in-and-for-self, is present in thought, the Idea in its absolute truth. ...

"For sensuous or reflective consciousness God cannot exist

---

[1] *Philosophy of Religion*, ii. 221—223 (trans. iii. 4—6).

as God, *i.e.*, in His eternal and absolute essentiality. His manifestation of Himself is something different from this, and is made to sensuous consciousness....Spirit exists for the spirit for which it does exist, only in so far as it reveals and differentiates itself, and this is the eternal Idea, thinking Spirit, Spirit in the element of its freedom. In this region God is the self-revealer, just because He is Spirit; but He is not yet present as outward manifestation. That God exists for Spirit is thus an essential principle.

"Spirit is what thinks. Within this pure thought the relation is of an immediate kind, and there exists no difference between the two elements to differentiate them. Nothing comes between them. Thought is pure unity with itself, from which all that is obscure and dark has disappeared. This kind of thought may also be called pure intuition, as being the simple form of the activity of thought, so that there is nothing between the subject and the object, as these two do not yet really exist. This kind of thought has no limitation, it is universal activity, and its content is only the Universal itself; it is pure pulsation within itself.

" (2) It, however, passes further into the stage of absolute Diremption. How does this differentiation come about? Thought is, *actu*, unlimited. The element of difference in its most immediate form consists in this, that the two sides which we have seen to be the two sorts of modes in which the principle appears, show their difference in their differing starting-points. The one side, subjective thought, is the movement of thought in so far as it starts from immediate individual Being, and, while within this, raises itself to what is Universal and Infinite....In so far as it has arrived at the stage of the Universal, thought is unlimited; its end is infinitely pure thought, so that all the mist of finitude has disappeared, and it here thinks God; every trace of separation has vanished, and thus religion, thinking upon God, begins. The second side is that which has for its starting-point the Universal, the result of that first movement, thought, the Notion. The Universal is, however, in its turn again an inner movement, and its nature is to differentiate itself within itself, and thus to preserve within itself the element of difference, but yet to do this in such a way as not to disturb the universality which is also there. Here universality is something which has this element of difference within itself, and is in harmony with itself. This represents the abstract content of thought, and this abstract thought is the result which has followed from what has taken place.

"The two sides are thus mutually opposed or contrasted. Subjective Thought, the thought of the finite spirit, is a Process too, inner mediation; but this process goes on outside of it, or behind it. It is in only so far as subjective thought has raised itself to something higher that religion begins, and thus what we have in religion is pure motionless abstract thought. The concrete, on .the other hand, is found in its Object, for this is the kind of thought which starts from the Universal, which differentiates itself, and consequently is in harmony with itself. It is this concrete element which is the object for thought, taking thought in a general sense. This kind of thought is thus abstract thought, and consequently the finite, for the abstract is finite; the concrete is the truth, the infinite object.

"(3) God is Spirit; in His abstract character He is characterised as universal Spirit which particularises itself. This represents the absolute truth, and that religion is the true one which possesses this content[1]."

210. It is this triple nature in God which Hegel identifies with the triple nature expounded in the doctrine of the Trinity. Thus he says, " This eternal Idea, accordingly, finds expression in the Christian religion under the name of the Holy Trinity, and this is God Himself, the eternal Triune God[2]." And, in the next paragraph, " This truth, this Idea, has been called the dogma of the Trinity. God is Spirit, the activity of pure thought, the activity which is not outside of itself, which is within the sphere of its own being[2]."

And certainly the two doctrines have something in common. Both of them make God's nature to be triune, and both of them

---

[1] *op. cit.* ii, 224—226 (trans. iii. 7—10).
[2] *op. cit.* ii. 227 (trans. iii. 11).

make each member of the triad to be vitally and inherently connected with the other two. And thus Hegel is certainly right when he points out that his philosophy resembles Christian orthodoxy in rejecting the Deistic conception of God as an undifferentiated unity. And, again, he is justified when he ranks his system together with Christianity as possessing a deeper notion of the triplicity of God than the Hindoo religion. For in the latter (at any rate as expressed by Hegel) the relation of the three moments of the Godhead towards one another is comparatively external[1].

211. But it must be noticed that the three moments of the divine nature form, for Hegel, a triad in a dialectic process. The division into the three moments is not the external judgment of an external observer as to something intrinsically undivided. It is, on the contrary, the deepest nature of God. Nor are the three moments merely juxtaposed or externally combined in God. Each has only meaning in relation to the others, and the existence of one of the three presupposes the existence of the other two. From the existence of one, that is, we can deduce *à priori* the existence of the others. Now the only way in which our thought can reach, *à priori*, a conclusion which is not contained in the premises from which it starts, is, according to Hegel, the dialectic method.

The following passages may serve to illustrate the fact that Hegel regarded the three moments of the Godhead as the terms of a dialectic triad. Immediately after giving the account of the three moments quoted above, he continues, "Spirit is the process referred to; it is movement, life; its nature is to differentiate itself, to give itself a definite character, to determine itself; and the first form of the differentiation consists in this, that Spirit appears as the universal Idea itself[2]." Here the process from moment to moment of the divine nature is identified with the movement of Spirit as a whole; and this movement can, for Hegel, be nothing else but a dialectic process.

---

[1] Cp. Hegel's account of the Hindoo religion in Part II. of the *Philosophy of Religion*; also ii. 242 (trans. iii. 28).

[2] *op. cit.* ii. 226 (trans. iii. 10).

Again he says that God "is the eternal Process...that this should be consciously known as the entire and absolute truth, the truth in-and-for itself, is, however, just the work of philosophy, and is the entire content of philosophy. In it it is seen how all that constitutes Nature and Spirit presses forward in a dialectic form to this central point as to its absolute truth. Here we are not concerned to prove that the dogma, this silent mystery, is the eternal Truth. That is done, as has been said, in the whole of philosophy[1]." The "eternal Process" in question had been explained just before to be that of Father, Son, and Spirit. Now if this is "the entire content of philosophy," and to it all Nature and Spirit "presses forward in a dialectic form," the process must be dialectic.

Still speaking of the Trinity, he says, "It is characteristic of the logical sphere in which this shows itself that it is the nature of every definite conception or notion to annul itself, to be its own contradiction, and consequently to appear as different from itself, and to posit itself as such[2]." This is a description which exactly corresponds with the description of the dialectic process to be found in the Logic.

Once more, when speaking of the objections brought by the understanding against the triplicity of the divine nature, he says "If...we regard the matter from the point of view of logic, we see that the One has inner *dialectic* movement, and is *not* truly independent[3]" (The italics are Hegel's.)

The Trinity, therefore, is for Hegel a dialectic process. It is not one of the chain of triads which form the Logic. A dialectic process can begin wherever pure thought asserts an inadequate idea—in this case, the idea of God the Father—of reality. And this particular inadequate idea is not one of those through which we pass from Being to the Absolute Idea. But all dialectic processes, if complete, must have the same end. For there is only one Absolute Idea, and none but the Absolute Idea is free from contradiction. And accordingly we can see that the third moment of the Trinity—the Synthesis—is

---

[1] *op. cit.* ii. 229 (trans. iii. 13).
[2] *op. cit.* ii. 232 (trans. iii. 16).
[3] *op. cit.* ii. 238 (trans. iii. 23).

identical with the Absolute Idea, which is the final Synthesis of the Logic. (The Philosophy of Religion as a whole does not stop where the Logic does. It proceeds to more concrete forms. But it does this in the Kingdoms of the Son and of the Spirit. The Kingdom of the Father, which contains the *abstract ideas* of all three moments of the Trinity, is, like the subject matter of the Logic, pure thought only.)

212. In every dialectic triad it is certain that the Synthesis contains all the truth which there is in the triad at all. The Thesis and Antithesis are not devoid of all truth. But then the Thesis and Antithesis are transcended and reconciled in the Synthesis. In so far as they are true, they are contained in the Synthesis. In so far as they assert themselves to be anything more than moments in the Synthesis, in so far as they claim to be independent terms, only externally connected with the Synthesis—in so far they are false. There can be no doubt, I think, that this was Hegel's view, and that, on any other view, the dialectic process is invalid[1].

213. According to Hegel's exposition, the Father and the Son are the Thesis and Antithesis of a triad of which the Holy Ghost is the Synthesis. It will follow from this that the Holy Ghost is the sole reality of the Trinity. In so far as the Father and the Son are real, they are moments in the nature of the Holy Ghost. In so far as they are taken as correlative with the Holy Ghost, and as on the same level with the latter, they are taken wrongly and are not real. In other words, the Father and the Son are simply abstractions which the thinker makes from the concrete reality of the Holy Ghost.

This may be the correct doctrine of the Trinity, but it is not the usual one. It must be noticed that it does not merely place the Holy Ghost above the other two members of the Trinity, but merges these latter in the Holy Ghost, which is therefore not only the supreme reality, but the sole reality of God. And, again, the doctrine is more than the assertion that the relation of the members of the Trinity is not merely external. Doubtless it is not merely external, but internal and essential.

---

[1] Cp. *Studies in the Hegelian Dialectic*, Sections 6, 94.

But the point is as to the particular sort of relation. The Father and the Son are related to the Holy Ghost as something which is they, and more than they. But the Holy Ghost is related to the Father and the Son—if it is to be called a relation—in a very different manner. Each of them, so far as it is real at all, is the Holy Ghost. But each of them is less than the Holy Ghost. And so are both of them taken together.

The fact is that, although the movement of the dialectic is properly described as triple, its results are not. The result of a triad is a single truth in which two complementary moments can be distinguished. To call this triple is incorrect, as it places the whole and its parts on the same level. It would be absurd to say‘ that the nature of Parliament was quadruple, on the ground that it consisted of Sovereign, Lords, Commons, and Parliament. And although the Synthesis of a triad is more independent of its moments than Parliament is of its three parts, yet those moments are less independent of the Synthesis than the parts are of Parliament, so that the impropriety of counting whole and parts in one aggregate is as great in one case as in the other. In all this there is nothing, I think, which makes Hegel at all inconsistent with himself. But it takes us a good way from the ordinary doctrine of the Trinity.

214. We now pass to our second question—the Personality of God. We must begin by considering the nature of the primary triad of the Philosophy of Religion, which we temporarily postponed. Of this Hegel says, " We have, speaking generally, to consider the Idea as the divine self-revelation, and this revelation is to be taken in the sense indicated by the three categories just mentioned.

"According to the first of these, God exists in a pure form for the finite spirit only as thought. This is the theoretical consciousness in which the thinking subject exists in a condition of absolute composure, and is not yet posited in this relation, not yet posited in the form of a process, but exists in the absolutely unmoved calm of the thinking spirit. Here, for Spirit, God is thought of, and Spirit thus rests in the simple conclusion that He brings Himself into harmony with Himself by means of His difference—which, however, here exists only in the form of pure ideality, and has not yet reached the force of externality—and is in immediate unity with Himself. This is the first of these relations, and it exists solely for the thinking subject which is occupied with the pure content only. This is the Kingdom of the Father.

" The second characteristic is the Kingdom of the Son, in which God exists, in a general way, for figurative thought in the element of mental pictures or ideas. This is the moment of separation or particularisation in general. Looked at from this second standpoint, what in the first place represented God's Other or object, without, however, being defined as such, now receives the character or determination of an Other. Considered from the first standpoint, God as the Son is not distinguished from the Father, but what is stated of Him is expressed merely in terms of feeling. In connection with the second element, however, the Son is characterised as an Other or object, and thus we pass out of the pure ideality of Thought into the region of figurative thought. If, according to the first characterisation, God begets only one Son, here he produces Nature. Here the Other is Nature, and the element of difference thus receives its justification. What is thus differentiated is Nature, the world in general, and Spirit which is related to it, the natural Spirit. Here the element which we have already designated Subject comes in, and itself constitutes the content. Man is here involved in the content. Since Man is here related to Nature, and is himself natural, he has this character only within the sphere of religion, and consequently we have here to consider Nature and Man from the point of view of religion. The Son comes into the world, and this is the beginning of faith. When we speak of the coming of the Son into the world we are already using the language of faith. God cannot really exist for the finite spirit as such, for in the very fact that God exists for it is directly involved that the finite spirit does not maintain its finitude as something having Being, but that it stands in a certain relation to Spirit and is reconciled to God. In its character as the finite spirit it is represented as in a state of revolt and separation with regard to God. It is thus in contradiction with what is its own object and content, and in this contradiction lies the necessity for its abolition and elevation to a higher form. The necessity for this supplies the starting-point, and the next step in advance is that God exists for Spirit, that the divine content presents itself in a pictorial form to Spirit. Here, however, Spirit exists at the same time in an empirical and finite form, and thus what God is appears to Spirit in an empirical way. Since, however, the Divine comes into view, and exists for Spirit in history of this kind, this history has no longer the character of outward history; it becomes divine history, the history of the manifestation of God Himself. This constitutes the transition to the Kingdom of the Spirit, in which we have the consciousness that Man is implicitly reconciled to God, and that this reconciliation exists for Man[1]."

215. These three stages, like the three subdivisions of the Kingdom of the Father, which we have considered above, are for Hegel a dialectic process. For he clearly holds that the movement from the first to the second, and from the second to the third, is intrinsically necessary, and can be deduced *à priori.* And, as was remarked above, the dialectic method is for Hegel the only way in which our thought can reach *à priori* to a conclusion which is not contained in the premises from which it starts.

The following passages will illustrate the view which Hegel takes of the connection between the three " Kingdoms." " The Notion as well as Being, the world, the finite, are equally one-sided determinations, each of which changes round into the other, and appears at one time as a moment without independence, and at another as producing the other determination which it carries within itself[2]."

Again, when he is speaking of the transition from the Kingdom of the Son to the Kingdom of the Spirit, he says, " These are the moments with which we are here concerned, and which express the truth that Man has come to a conscious-

---

[1] *Philosophy of Religion,* ii. 221—223 (trans. iii. 4—6).
[2] *op. cit.* ii. 210 (trans. ii. 349).

ness of that eternal history, that eternal movement which God Himself. is.

"This is the description of the second Idea as Idea in outward manifestation, and of how the eternal Idea has come to exist for the immediate certainty of Man, *i.e.*, of how it has appeared in history. The fact that it is a certainty for man necessarily implies that it is material or sensuous certainty, but one which at the same time passes over into spiritual consciousness, and for the same reason is converted into immediate sensuousness, but in such a way that we recognize in it the movement, the history of God, the life which God Himself is[1]."

The fact is that the triad we are considering is identical with the triad of Logic, Nature, and Spirit which forms the whole content of the Encyclopaedia, and this triad is unquestionably dialectic[2].

216. Now if this triad is a dialectic process which exhibits the nature of God, it will follow that if God is really personal, He must be personal in the Kingdom of the Spirit. For that is the Synthesis, and in that alone, therefore, do we get an adequate representation of God's nature. If He were personal as manifested in the first and second Kingdoms, but not in the third, it would mean that He was personal when viewed inadequately, but not when viewed adequately—*i.e.*, that He was not really personal.

In support of the statement that God is only adequately known when He is known in the Kingdom of the Spirit, we may quote the following passages, "In the Ego, as in that which is annulling itself as finite, God returns to Himself, and only as this return is He God. Without the world God is not God[3]."

And again, "God regarded as Spirit, when He remains above, when He is not present in His Church as a living Spirit, is Himself characterised in a merely one-sided way as object[4]."

---

[1] *op. cit.* ii. 308 (trans. iii. 100).

[2] Cp. *Studies in the Hegelian Dialectic*, Sections 98—100, 131—132.

[3] *Philosophy of Religion*, i. 194 (trans. i. 200).

[4] *op. cit.* ii. 197 (trans. ii. 334).

Again, "It is not in immediate Appearance or manifestation, but only when Spirit has taken up its abode in the Church, when it is immediate, believing Spirit, and raises itself to the stage of thought, that the Idea reaches perfection[1]."

And, again, "Spirit is infinite return into self, infinite subjectivity, not Godhead conceived by means of figurative ideas, but the real present Godhead, and thus it is not the substantial potentiality of the Father, not the True in the objective or antithetical form of the Son, but the subjective Present and Real, which, just because it is subjective, is present, as estrangement into that objective, sensuous representation of love and of its infinite sorrow, and as return, in that mediation. This is the Spirit of God, or God as present, real Spirit, God dwelling in His Church[2]"

217. It is in the Kingdom of the Spirit, then, that we must look for an adequate representation of God's nature. Now is God represented here as personal?

The Kingdom of the Spirit, according to Hegel, is the Church. Thus he says, "The third stage is represented by the inner place, the Spiritual Community, existing at first in the world, but at the same time raising itself up to heaven, and which as a Church already has" God "in itself here on earth, full of grace, active and present in the world." And in the next paragraph, "The third element is the present, yet it is only the limited present, not the eternal present, but rather the present which distinguishes itself from the past and future, and represents the element of feeling, of the immediate subjectivity of the present spiritual Being. The present must, however, also represent the third element; the Church raises itself to Heaven too, and thus the Present is one which raises itself as well and is essentially reconciled, and is brought by means of the negation of its immediacy to a perfected form as universality, a perfection or completion which, however, does not yet exist, and which is thereupon to be conceived of as future. It is a Now of the present whose perfect stage is before it, but this perfect stage is distinguished

---

[1] *op. cit.* ii. 242 (trans. iii. 28).

[2] *op. cit.* ii. 315 (trans. iii. 107).

from the particular Now which is still immediacy, and it is thought of as future[1]."

The Kingdom of the Spirit, then, consists in the Spiritual Community, or Church (Die Gemeinde). Of course, the Church as we have it now and here is far too imperfect to be considered as an adequate representation of God. But then this Church is only, Hegel tells us, an imperfect form of that perfected Community, which from one point of view is eternally present, while from another point of view it must be conceived as being in the future. It is this perfect community which is the true Kingdom of the Spirit. But in becoming perfect it does not, for Hegel, cease to be a community.

218. God, then, if represented adequately is a community. Can a community be a person? Surely the answer to this is certain. A community is composed of persons. A perfect community may be as complete a unity as any person. But a community cannot be a person, and the fact that it is a perfect community, and a perfect unity, does not make it at all more possible for it to be a person[2].

There is no reason to doubt that Hegel saw this. For he never speaks of the Community in such a way as to suggest that it is a person. And his choice of words is significant. For his vocabulary was rich with terms for a unity, which would suggest, or at least not exclude the suggestion of, a personal unity. He chose, however, a word—Gemeinde—whose ordinary meaning quite excludes any idea of personal unity. It is surely a fair inference that he wished to exclude that idea.

Again, in speaking of the unity by which the individuals who compose the Community are united, he always calls it Love. Now, if the Community, besides being a unity of persons, was itself a person, its members, though they might be connected by love, would also be connected by something very different—a personal unity. And the fact that no bond but love is mentioned is therefore in favour of the theory that he did not conceive the Community as a person.

[1] *op. cit.* ii. 221 (trans. iii. 3—4).
[2] Cp. above, Sections 79—83.

219. It is to be noticed in connection with this, that Hegel, unlike many philosophers and theologians, uses the word love, in his philosophical writings, in the same sense in which he and other men use it elsewhere. It may be useful to quote what he says on this subject. In the first place, since love is what unites men into the Community which is God, as God really is, we shall get a more definite notion of the Community by seeing precisely what is meant by love. In the second place, we may be able to get some fresh light on the charge against Hegel of substituting cold and impersonal abstractions for the vivid and personal realities of popular religion.

"Love thy neighbour as thyself. This command," says Hegel, "thought of in the abstract and more extended sense as embracing the love of men in general, is a command to love *all* men. Taken in this sense, however, it is turned into an abstraction. The people whom one can love, and for whom our love is real, are a few particular individuals; the heart which seeks to embrace the whole of humanity within itself indulges in a vain attempt to spread out its love till it becomes a mere idea, *the opposite of real love*[1]."

What, then, is this love which the individuals of the Community feel for one another? This love, he tells us later, "is neither human love, philanthropy, the love of the sexes, nor friendship. Surprise has often been expressed that such a noble relationship as friendship is does not find a place amongst the duties enjoined by Christ. Friendship is a relationship which is tinged with particularity, and men are friends not so much directly as objectively, through some substantial bond of union in a third thing, in fundamental principles, studies, knowledge; the bond, in short, is constituted by something objective; it is not attachment as such, like that of the man to the woman as a definite particular personality. The love of the Spiritual Community, on the other hand, is directly mediated by the worthlessness of all particularity. The love of the man for the woman, or friendship, can certainly

---

[1] *op. cit.* ii. 292 (trans. iii. 83). The italics are Hegel's.

exist, but they are essentially characterised as subordinate; they are characterised not indeed as something evil, but as something imperfect; not as something indifferent, but as representing a state in which we are not to remain permanently, since they are themselves to be sacrificed, and must not in any way injuriously affect that absolute tendency and unity which belongs to Spirit[1]."

220. It may seem at first sight rather difficult to tell what this love can be, since it must be for particular individuals, and yet is neither to be friendship nor sexual love. But we must notice that Hegel gives a curiously narrow definition of friendship, excluding from it all affection which is fixed on the friend himself, and not on his qualities and relations—that affection which neither finds nor seeks any justification beyond its own existence. This, which many people would call friendship, is, I think, the love which Hegel regards as the bond which holds God together. It is, of course, compatible at present with friendship, in the Hegelian sense, as it is compatible at present with sexual attraction, but it has, as Hegel remarks in the last quoted passage, a significance *sub specie aeternitatis* which does not extend to them.

221. It will be remembered that in the first of these two passages it is said that a man can only love " a few particular individuals" (einige Besondere), while in the second he states love to be "mediated by the worthlessness of all particularity" (die Werthlosigkeit aller Besonderheit). The inconsistency is, I think, only apparent. In the first passage he was differentiating true love from the spurious universality of a love for humanity, and here he seems to use " Besonderheit " simply as generally opposed to "alle Menschen." His object is to point out that the love of each man must be for this and that other man, and that the number of these for each of us is limited. It is impossible that he should have meant that our love is real only when we love men in their particularity, in the special sense in which he uses Particularity in the Logic. For Particularity in that sense is always used by Hegel to

---

[1] *op. cit.* ii. 314 (trans. iii. 106).

denote inadequacy and error. It would be equivalent to saying that the only real love was love of men as they really are not.

In the second passage, however, he appears to use Particularity in this more definite sense, according to which it is distinguished, not only from Universality, but also from Individuality. In this sense, to regard a person as particular is to regard him as contingently and externally determined, not as a self-determining unity with an immanent universality. In this sense of the word, all real love would have to be mediated by the worthlessness of Particularity. But the result attained would be the conception of every person as a true Individual—a conception which unites and transcends Universality and Particularity. And this agrees with the previous assertion that true love can only be for another person as that person.

222. To return from this digression. We have thus come to the conclusion that Hegel holds that view as to the personality of God which I endeavoured (Chapter III)· to show was the logical consequence of his views on the general nature of reality. God is not personal. For God is identical with Absolute Reality, and Absolute Reality can only be adequately conceived as a society of persons, which itself is a perfect unity, but not a person.

Several circumstances have combined to prevent this interpretation of Hegel's meaning being generally accepted. The first of these is his use of the word God to designate Absolute Reality. In ordinary language, we mean by God a person. We most emphatically do *not* mean a society. And there is a vague idea, which has not been without influence on the interpretation of Hegel, that a man who talked so much about God must have believed God to be a person. But this error is gratuitous. For Hegel tells us plainly and repeatedly that by God he means simply Absolute Reality, whatever that may be. And it is our own fault if we take his language as implying a particular theory about the nature of Absolute Reality.

223. There is a similar, but less obvious mistake, which often leads enquirers into a similar error. If God is simply

Absolute Reality, then, it is said, everything which exists must be God. But such pantheism is a belief against which Hegel continually and most emphatically protests.

We must, however, make a distinction. The pantheism against which Hegel protests is that which deifies the mass of our everyday experience, taken as a mere aggregate of separate units, and taken in the inadequate and contradictory forms in which it presents itself in everyday experience. This is certainly not Hegel's conception of God. God, according to him, is a perfect unity, and is Spirit. God is certainly not the aggregate of "facts" of uncritical experience. But it does not follow that God is not identical with the whole of Absolute Reality. For Absolute Reality is by no means, for Hegel, the aggregate of these facts. Such facts are merely a mistaken and inadequate view of Absolute Reality, not devoid, of course, of *all* truth, but requiring enormous transformation and reconstruction before they can be fully true. And therefore the undoubted truth that God is not identical with them, when they are taken in this way, is no argument against the identity of God with Absolute Reality.

224. Again, it is supposed that if Hegel holds God to be Spirit—which he unquestionably does—he must also consider God to be a person, or else hold that Spirit—at any rate in its highest form—is not personal. But this is not an exhaustive dilemma. For, as I have endeavoured to show, Hegel regards God as a unity of persons, though not as a person. All Spirit is personal, but it is many persons, not one person, although it is as really one Spirit as it is many persons.

In illustration of this we may quote the following passages: "We have now reached the realised notion or conception of religion, the perfect religion, in which it is the notion itself that is its own object. We defined religion as being in the stricter sense the self-consciousness of God. Self-consciousness in its character as consciousness has an object, and it is conscious of itself in this object; this object is also consciousness, but it is consciousness as object, and is consequently finite consciousness, a consciousness which is distinct from God, from the Absolute. The element of determinateness is present in this form of consciousness, and consequently finitude is present in it; God is self-consciousness, He knows Himself in a consciousness which is distinct from Him, which is potentially the consciousness of God, but is also this actually, since it knows its identity with God, an identity which is, however, mediated by the negation of finitude. It is this notion or conception which constitutes the content of religion. We define God when we say, that He distinguishes Himself from Himself, and is an object for Himself, but that in this distinction He is purely identical with Himself, is in fact Spirit. This notion or conception is now realised, consciousness knows this content and knows that it is itself absolutely interwoven with this content; in the Notion which is the process of God, it is itself a moment. Finite consciousness knows God only to the extent to which God knows Himself in it; thus God is Spirit, the Spirit of His Church in fact, *i.e.*, of those who worship Him. This is the perfect religion, the Notion becomes objective to itself[1]." I should like to point out in passing that this passage forms the best comment on the definition of the Absolute Idea in the Smaller Logic. (Encyclopaedia, Section 236.)

Again, "Man knows God only in so far as God Himself knows Himself in Man. This knowledge is God's self-consciousness, but it is at the same time a knowledge of God on the part of Man, and this knowledge of God by Man is a knowledge of Man by God. The Spirit of Man, whereby he knows God, is simply the Spirit of God Himself[2]."

225. The third question which we have to consider is Hegel's treatment of the Incarnation. It is the nature of the Absolute Spirit to manifest itself in a multiplicity of individuals, each of whom is a self-conscious person. This is an eternal and adequate characteristic of Spirit. But, besides this, Spirit, Hegel tells us, manifests itself in the form of finitude. It must be remembered that finitude, for Hegel, does not merely mean that the finite thing has something else outside it, and is not unlimited. It means that its limits

[1] *op. cit.* ii. 191 (trans. ii. 327).
[2] *op. cit.* ii. 496 (trans. iii. 303).

are imposed on it from without, and are not a consequence of its own nature—that it is determined by another, and not determined by self. This is an inadequate and untrue description of reality, and accordingly the manifestation of God in this form of finitude is not to be found in the Kingdom of the Spirit—the sphere in which God's true nature is known. It finds a place in the Kingdom of the Son[1].

"We thus," Hegel says, "enter the sphere of determination, enter space and the world of finite Spirit. This may be more definitely expressed as a positing or bringing into view of the determinations or specific qualities, as a difference which is momentarily maintained; it is an act of going out on the part of God into finitude, an act of manifestation of God in finitude, for finitude, taken in its proper meaning, implies simply the separation of that which is implicitly identical, but which maintains itself in the act of separation. Regarded from the other side, that of subjective Spirit, this is posited as pure thought, though it is implicitly a result, and this has to be posited as it is potentially in its character as the movement of thought, or to put it otherwise, pure thought has to go into itself, and it is in this way that it first posits itself as finite[2]."

226. This view certainly has striking resemblances to the Christian doctrine of the Incarnation. For it rejects, in the first place, the view that matter, while created by God and subordinate to God, is completely alien to God's nature, so that God can never be incarnate in it. Then it also rejects the two contrary heresies which arise out of lingering traces of the last mentioned view. For, while Hegel admits that God when known as incarnate is not known in His perfection, he maintains on the other hand that it is the true and perfect God who is incarnated, and thus rejects all suggestion that the Son is inferior to the Father. On the other hand he asserts

---

[1] The *incarnation* of God in the Kingdom of the Son must be carefully distinguished from God's *manifestation* in Individuals. This latter is the absolute truth of God's nature, and persists in the Kingdom of the Spirit. These Individuals are perfect Individuals, and are not, in Hegel's terminology, finite.

[2] *op. cit.* ii. 251 (trans. iii. 38).

that God is really incarnate in matter—in so far as matter can be said to be real at all—and so excludes the Docetic theory that the body of the incarnate God was only a phantasm imitating matter.

Here, as always, Hegel reconciled opposites by uniting them in a higher reality which included and transcended both. He saw the inadequacy of trying to bridge over a difference which, so far as it existed at all, was qualitative, by quantitative concessions. To hold that the incarnate God was not fully God, or not really incarnate, was to destroy all the significance of the incarnation, while removing none of its difficulties. It is as hopeless as the similar attempt to bridge over the gulf between God and Nature by the length of a chain of emanations.

As against such views Hegel asserts the incarnation of very God in very Man. "In the Church Christ has been called the God-Man. This is the extraordinary combination which directly contradicts the Understanding; but the unity of the divine and human natures has here been brought into human consciousness and has become a certainty for it, implying that the otherness, or, as it is also expressed, the finitude, the weakness, the frailty of human nature is not incompatible with this unity, just as in the eternal Idea otherness in no way detracts from the unity which God is.... It involves the truth that the divine and human natures are not implicitly different[1]."

227. But there are other characteristics of Hegel's doctrine of the Incarnation which are not unimportant. God is incarnate not in one man only, nor in men only, but in everything finite. (Men are not intrinsically finite, in Hegel's sense of that word. But men are finite in so far as they appear in the Kingdom of the Son which is the sphere of finitude, and in which God only exists as incarnate.) The world of finitude is nothing but God in one moment of the dialectic process of His nature, and to say that a thing is finite, and to say that it is the incarnation of God, are identical. For

---

[1] *op. cit.* ii. 286 (trans. iii. 76).

there is no reality but God, and if the reality has the imperfect
form of finitude, this can only mean that it is God in the
imperfect form of incarnation.

228. It is true that Hegel is very far from holding that
God is equally incarnate in all finite objects. In proportion
as the finitude is overcome, the incarnation is to be considered
more perfect. God is more perfectly incarnate in a dog than
in a stone, more perfectly again in a wicked and foolish man,
still more perfectly in a wise and good man. But if God is
less incarnate in some finite things than in others, this is only
because those things are less real. All the reality in each
thing is only in the incarnation of God. For Hegel's view
is not that matter was first created as something else than
the incarnation of God, and that afterwards God became
incarnate in it. There is no such priority, whether logical
or temporal. For the matter is nothing else than the incarnation of God.

Defects, error, sin, are for Hegel only imperfectly real.
But nothing which is evil is pure and unmixed abstract evil,
and therefore all evil things have *some* reality. And in so far
as they are real they are incarnations of God. It is only of
pure abstract evil that you could say that it was not a form of
God. And pure abstract evil is non-existent. (All sin, for
example, is for Hegel relatively good[1].)

Here, again, we may say that whatever truth Hegel's view
of the Incarnation may have, it presents not unimportant
differences from the ordinary idea. The Incarnation is identical
with the Creation. To say that God is incarnate in the finite
is misleading. We should rather say that the finite is the
incarnation of God.

229. Now for the Christian religion the incarnation of God
in one particular human body is of unique significance. This
leads us to our fourth question. What does Hegel think as to the
divinity of Jesus ? It is clear that, on Hegel's theory, he must
have been God incarnate, since he was a man. It is equally clear
that he was not the sole incarnation of God. Yet Hegel does

---

[1] Cp. Chap. vi.

not reject the special prominence of Jesus in historical Christianity as a simple error. We must examine his treatment of it.

He points out that there are two separate questions to be considered. " The question as to the truth of the Christian religion directly divides itself into two questions: 1. Is it true *in general* that God does not exist apart from the Son, and that He has sent Him into the world ? And 2. Was *this man*, Jesus of Nazareth, the carpenter's son, the Son of God, the Christ ?

" These two questions are commonly mixed up together, with the result that if this particular person was not God's Son sent by Him, and if this cannot be proved to be true of Him, then there is no meaning at all in His mission. If this were not true of Him, we would either have to look for another, if indeed, one is to come, if there is a promise to that effect, *i.e.*, if it is absolutely and essentially necessary, necessary from the point of view of the Notion, of the Idea; or, since the correctness of the Idea is made to depend on the demonstration of the divine mission referred to, we should have to conclude that there can really be no longer any thought of such a mission, and that we cannot further think about it.

" But it is essential that we ask first of all, Is such a manifestation true in-and-for-itself[1] ?"

We have already seen what is Hegel's answer to the first question—that which relates to the general truth of the doctrine of Incarnation. But the second question divides into two. (*a*) In what way, and for what reasons, is it necessary to take the incarnation of God in one particular man as possessing a special significance ? (*b*) Why should the particular man taken be Jesus ?

230. To the first of these new questions Hegel's answer is that the selection of the incarnation in one particular man has reference, not to anything in the nature of the incarnation of God, but to the inability of mankind in general to grasp the idea of that incarnation in its truth. " If Man is to get a consciousness of the unity of divine and human nature, and

---

[1] *Philosophy of Religion*, ii. 318 (trans. iii. 110).

of this characteristic of Man as belonging to Man in general; or if this knowledge is to force its way wholly into the consciousness of his finitude as the beam of eternal light which reveals itself to him in the finite, then it must reach him in his character as Man in general, *i.e.*, apart from any particular conditions of culture or training; it must come to him as representing Man in his immediate state, and it must be universal for immediate consciousness.

"The consciousness of the absolute Idea, which we have in thought, must therefore not be put forward as belonging to the standpoint of philosophical speculation, of speculative thought, but must, on the contrary, appear in the form of certainty for man in general. This does not mean that they think this consciousness, or perceive and recognise the necessity of this Idea; but what we are concerned to show is rather that the Idea becomes for them certain, *i.e.*, this Idea, namely the unity of divine and human nature, attains the stage of certainty, that, so far as they are concerned, it receives the form of immediate sense-perception, of outward existence—in short, that this Idea appears as seen and experienced in the world. This unity must accordingly show itself to consciousness in a purely temporal, absolutely ordinary manifestation of reality, in one particular man, in a definite individual who is at the same time known to be the Divine Idea, not merely a Being of a higher kind in general, but rather the highest, the Absolute Idea, the Son of God[1]."

231. "Man in general" cannot rise to the philosophical idea that all finitude is an incarnation of God. He requires it in the form of "immediate sense-perception." This sense-perception must take the form of one single man, and not of several men. For if more than one were taken, they would have some common quality which was not common to all other men, and it would be thought that it was in virtue of that quality that they were incarnations of God. But if only one individual is taken, then the very particularity and immediacy of that individual, if taken in his own right, forces on us the conviction

---

[1] *op. cit.* ii. 282 (trans. iii. 72).

that he is not taken in his own right, but only as an example of a truth which is absolutely universal.

This seems to be what Hegel means when he says, " This individual,...who represents for others the manifestation of the Idea, is a particular Only One, not some ones, for the Divine in some would become an abstraction. The idea of some is a miserable superfluity of reflection, a superfluity because opposed to the conception or notion of individual subjectivity. In the Notion once is always, and the subject must turn exclusively to one subjectivity. In the eternal Idea there is only one Son, and thus there is only One in whom the absolute Idea appears, and this One excludes the others. It is this perfect development of reality thus embodied in immediate individuality or separateness which is the finest feature of the Christian religion, and the absolute transfiguration of the finite gets in it a form in which it can be outwardly perceived[1]."

232. We have thus seen the reason why the universal incarnation of God should be presented in the form of a particular man. It is not a reason which would induce Hegel to treat this particular presentation as anything of great worth or significance. It is due to no characteristic of the incarnation, but only to the failure of the unphilosophic majority to fully comprehend that incarnation. And Hegel had very little respect for the philosophic difficulties of the unphilosophic man. Anyone who is familiar with his language knows that he is using his severest terms of condemnation when he says that this particular form of the doctrine comes from the necessity of abandoning " the standpoint of speculative thought " in favour of " the form of outward existence." The philosopher may recognise the necessity that his doctrine should be transformed in this way, but he will regard the change as a degradation. Nothing is further from Hegel than the idea that the highest form of a doctrine is that in which it appeals to the average man. If he admits that some glimpse of the kingdom of heaven may be vouchsafed to babes, he balances the admission by a most emphatic assertion of the distorted and inadequate character of the revelation.

---

[1] *op. cit.* ii. 284 (trans. iii. 75).

233. We see then why a particular man is to be taken as the type of the incarnation. But why Jesus more than any other particular man? To this question also Hegel supplies an answer.

According to Hegel, as we have seen, different men are incarnations of God differing in their perfection. One man is more of an incarnation of God than another. Is this the explanation? Was Jesus the most perfect man—and therefore the most perfect incarnation of God—who has lived on earth, or at any rate who has been known to history? And is he the fitting *representative* of the incarnation, for those who need a representation, because he is, in truth and intrinsically, the most perfect *example* of it?

This is not Hegel's view. It would be improbable, to begin with, that he should have thought that Jesus was the most perfect man of whom history tells us. His conception of human nature was not one which would lead him to accept as his ideal man one who was neither a metaphysician nor a citizen.

But whatever may have been Hegel's opinion on this point, it is quite certain that it was not in the perfection of the character of Jesus that he found the reason which made it appropriate to take Jesus as the type of the incarnation. For it is not the life, but the teaching on which he lays stress. Not in the perfection of his character, but in the importance of the teaching expressed in his words, or implied in his life, consists the unique importance of Jesus to the history of religious thought. Hegel treats of the Passion at some length. But he says nothing of courage, of gentleness, of dignity—qualities which he would have been the last to ignore if they had been relevant. He is entirely occupied with the metaphysical significance of the " death of God[1]."

234. But it was not in the truth and purity of his moral precepts that, according to Hegel, the importance of Jesus' teaching was to be found. His precepts, like his life, would have appeared one-sided to Hegel—and one-sided in the direction with which Hegel had least sympathy. On this point

---

[1] *op. cit.* ii. 295—307 (trans. iii. 86—99).

we are not left to conjecture. It has been explained that the unity of God and man "must appear for others in the form of an individual man marked off from or excluding the rest of men, not all individual men, but One from whom they are shut off, though he no longer appears as representing the potentiality or true essence which is above, but as individuality in the region of certainty."

He then continues, "It is with this certainty and sensuous view that we are concerned, and not merely with a divine teacher, nor indeed simply with morality, nor even in any way simply with a teacher of this Idea either. It is not with ordinary thought or with conviction that we have got to do, but with this *immediate* presence and certainty of the Divine; for the immediate certainty of what is present represents the infinite form and mode which the "Is" takes for the natural consciousness. This Is destroys all trace of mediation; it is the final point, the last touch of light which is laid on. This Is is wanting in mediation of any kind such as is given through feeling, pictorial ideas, reasons; and it is only in philosophical knowledge, by means of the Notion only in the element of universality, that it returns again[1]."

235. The special significance of Jesus, then, is that he bears witness to a metaphysical truth—the unity of God and man.

But he bears witness to this not *as* a metaphysical truth—not as a proposition mediated and connected with others in a reasoned system—but as a "certainty and sensuous view," as the "immediate presence and certainty of the Divine." Nor is he, as Hegel remarks, in the strictest sense a teacher of this Idea. It is rather that this immediate certainty of the unity of God and Man runs through all his teaching, than that it is often explicitly enunciated.

The speeches of Jesus, which are presented by Hegel for our admiration, are those which imply this immediate certainty of unity with God. For example, "Into this Kingdom" of God "Man has to transport himself, and he does this by directly

---

[1] *op. cit.* ii. 283 (trans. iii. 73).

devoting himself to the truth it embodies. This is expressed
with the most absolute and startling frankness, as, for instance,
at the beginning of the so-called Sermon on the Mount:
' Blessed are the pure in heart, for they shall see God.' Words
like these are amongst the grandest that have ever been uttered.
They represent a final central point in which all superstition
and all want of freedom on Man's part are done away with[1]."

Again, he says, " The fact that this possession of this life
of the spirit in truth is attained without intermediate helps,
is expressed in the prophetic manner, namely that it is God
who thus speaks.   Here it is with absolute, divine truth, truth
in-and-for-itself, that we are concerned; this utterance and
willing of the truth in-and-for-itself, and the carrying out of
what is thus expressed, is described as an act of God, it is the
consciousness of the real unity of the divine will, of its harmony
with the truth.   It is as conscious of this elevation of His spirit,
and in the assurance of His identity with God, that Christ says
' Woman, thy sins are forgiven thee.' Here there speaks in
Him that overwhelming majesty which can undo everything,
and actually declares that this has been done.

" So far as the form of this utterance is concerned, what has
mainly to be emphasised is that He who thus speaks is at the
same time essentially Man, it is the Son of Man who thus
speaks, in whom this utterance of the truth, this carrying into
practice of what is absolute and essential, this activity on God's
part, is essentially seen to exist as in one who is a man and not
something superhuman, not something which appears in the
form of an outward revelation—in short, the main stress is to
be laid on the fact that this divine presence is essentially
identical with what is human[2]."

And again, " The Kingdom of God, and the idea of purity
of heart, contain an infinitely greater depth of truth than the
inwardness of Socrates[3]."

236. The appropriateness of the selection of Jesus as the
typical incarnation of God is thus due to the way in which his

---

[1] *op. cit.* ii. 290 (trans. iii. 81).

[2] *op. cit.* ii. 293 (trans. iii. 84).

[3] *op. cit.* ii. 295 (trans. iii. 86).

teaching implied and rested on the unity of the human and the divine. This, Hegel says, is a great truth. But is it the only fundamental truth of religion? According to Hegel it is not, and according to his exposition, the principle as exemplified by Jesus had two cardinal errors. Each of these may be defined as an excess of immediacy. It was a merely immediate assertion of a merely immediate unity.

That the assertion is merely immediate, is evident from what has been already said. There is no metaphysical system; there is no dialectic process leading from undeniable premises to a conclusion so paradoxical to the ordinary consciousness. It is simply an assertion, which needed no proof to those who felt instinctively convinced of its truth, but which had no proof to offer to those who asked for one.

Such a method of statement is, for Hegel, altogether defective. No philosophical error is more deadly, he teaches, than to trust to our instinctive belief in any truth—except, of course, one whose denial is self-contradictory. On this, indeed, he lays a rather exaggerated emphasis, impelled by his opposition to the advocates of "immediate intuition" who were his contemporaries in German philosophy. Again and again, through all his writings, recur the assertions that an instinctive conviction is just as likely to be false as true; that between the false and true only reason can discriminate; that the "humility" which trusts the heart instead of the head is always absurd and often hypocritical; and that the form and content of truth are so united that no truth can be held in a non-rational form without being more or less distorted into falsehood.

237. Moreover, the unity thus asserted was a purely immediate unity. "There is no mention of any mediation in connection with this elevating of the spirit whereby it may become an accomplished fact in Man; but, on the contrary, the mere statement of what is required implies this immediate Being, this immediate self-transference into Truth, into the Kingdom of God[1]."

Now such an immediate unity is, for Hegel, only one side

---

[1] *Philosophy of Religion*, ii. 291 (trans. iii. 81).

of the truth. It is true that man is eternally one with God, or he could never become one with God. But it is equally true that man is *not* one with God, unless he becomes so by a process of mediation, and that a man who rests in his immediacy would, so far as he did rest in it, not be divine, but simply non-existent. (We shall see how vital this side of the truth was for Hegel when we come to consider his treatment of Original Sin.) The reconciliation of these two aspects of the truth lies in the recognition that the unity of man and God is a unity which is immediate by including and transcending mediation. And this leaves the mere immediacy which ignores mediation as only one side of the truth.

238. Why then—the question recurs—is Jesus taken as the typical incarnation of God? True, he bore witness to the unity of man and God, but in such a way that both the form and the content of his testimony were inadequate, and, therefore, partially false.

As to the inadequacy of the form, the answer has been given already. If the form of his testimony had been more adequate, Jesus would have been a less fitting type of the incarnation. For a type, as we have seen, is only required for "men in general," who cannot attain to the "standpoint of speculative thought." For speculative thought no type is required, since it is able to see the incarnation in its universal truth[1]. But without rising to the standpoint of speculative thought it is impossible to see the unity of God and man as a necessary and demonstrated certainty. "Men in general," therefore, can only accept it as a matter of simple faith, or, at most, as demonstrated by external proofs, such as tradition or miracles, which do not destroy the intrinsic immediacy of the result. In proportion as men rise above the immediate reception of the doctrine, they rise above the necessity of a typical representative of it. And therefore no teacher for whom the doctrine is not immediate can be taken as a fitting type.

239. And we can see also that only a teacher whose immediate assertion was an assertion of a merely immediate unity could be taken as a type. For, as Hegel points out, a

---

[1] Cp. above, Section 230.

unity which is immediately asserted can only be an immediate unity. "The fact that this possession of the life of the spirit in truth is attained without intermediate helps, is expressed in the prophetic manner, namely, that it is God who thus speaks[1]." Form and content, in other words, are not mutually indifferent. A merely immediate assertion cannot express the true state of the case—that man's unity with God is both mediate and immediate. If this truth is put as an immediate assertion it appears a mere contradiction. It can only be grasped by speculative thought.

And thus a teacher speaking to men in general cannot embody in his teaching the whole truth as to the relation between man and God. He must teach the one side or the other—the immediate unity of Man and God, or their immediate diversity. It is not difficult to see why it should be a teacher of the first half-truth, rather than of the second, who should be selected as the typical incarnation of God.

In the first place, it was the doctrine of man's unity with God which was demanded by the needs of the time. "Jesus appeared at a time when the Jewish nation, owing to the dangers to which its worship had been exposed, and was still exposed, was more obstinately absorbed in its observance than ever, and was at the same time compelled to despair of seeing its hopes actually realised, since it had come in contact with a universal humanity, the existence of which it could no longer deny, and which nevertheless was completely devoid of any spiritual element—He appeared, in short, when the common people were in perplexity and helpless[2]."

Elsewhere he tells us that the rest of the world was also, at this time, in a state of alienation from self, and of spiritual misery[3]. It was useless to preach to such a world that it was separated from God. Of that fact it was conscious, and hence came its misery. What was wanted was to give it hope by insisting on the other side of the truth—that it was just as vitally united with God.

[1] *Philosophy of Religion*, ii. 293 (trans. iii. 84).
[2] *op. cit.* ii. 291 (trans. iii. 82).
[3] Cp. *Phenomenology*, iv. b. 158.

There is another reason, which is sufficiently obvious. A man who taught the immediate separation of man from God would be teaching a doctrine as true as the immediate unity of man with God, but he would be teaching a doctrine which could never suggest that he should be taken as a typical incarnation of God. On the other hand, we can see how easy it is to consider the teacher of the unity of man and God as a typical example of that unity, or even as the only example.

240. We are now able to reconcile two statements of Hegel's which might at first sight appear contradictory. On the one hand, he speaks of the position of Jesus as typifying the incarnation of God, as if that position had been determined by the choice of the Church. (By the Church here he does not mean the Spiritual Community of the future, or of the eternal present, which is found in the Kingdom of the Spirit, but the Church of the past, in the ages in which Christian dogma was formulated, which is still part of the Kingdom of the Son. In the Kingdom of the Spirit the unity of God and man would be seen in its full truth, and no longer in the inadequate form of sensuous certainty.)

On the other hand he speaks of the typification of the incarnation in Jesus as necessary. " It was to Christ only that the Idea, when it was ripe and the time was fulfilled, could attach itself, and in Him only could it see itself realised[1]."

There is nothing really contradictory in this. It is, as we have seen, the case that Jesus is only the special incarnation of God for the Church—for men in general who cannot rise to speculative thought. And, as we have also seen, the quality which renders it particularly fitting that Jesus should be taken as typical, is not any objective perfection in his incarnation of God, but is just the special manner in which his teaching meets the special needs, which are also the defects, of the Church militant on earth. Thus there is no reason for speculative thought to treat the incarnation of God in Jesus as anything of peculiar significance, except the fact that the

---

[1] *Philosophy of Religion,* ii. 320 (trans. iii. 113).

Church regards it as of peculiar significance. And thus it may be said that it is nothing but the choice of the Church which has attributed a specially divine character to Jesus.

But we must not regard that choice as capricious or accidental. No other man would have been so appropriate to choose—indeed, the choice could scarcely have been at all effective if it had fallen on anyone else. That a man should be accepted by men in general as God incarnate, it was necessary that his teaching should be penetrated by the idea of the unity of God and man, and that his teaching should have become prominent in the world in that age when the world felt, more intensely than it has ever felt at any other time, that it was alienated from its true reality, and when it required, more urgently than it has ever required at any other time, the assurance of its unity with the divine. No other man in history would answer to this description, and thus Hegel was justified in saying that in Jesus only could the Idea see itself realised.

241. Whether Hegel is altogether right in his analysis of the principles implicit in the teaching of Jesus we need not now enquire. Our object at present is not to determine the truth about Christianity but about Hegel's views on Christianity. And, to sum up his views as to the relation of Jesus to the incarnation of God, he holds (1) that Jesus was not the sole incarnation of God, nor an incarnation in a different sense to that in which everything is such an incarnation, (2) that his significance is that in him the Church symbolises, and appropriately symbolises, that universal incarnation which the Church has not sufficient speculative insight to grasp without a symbol, (3) that his appropriateness for this purpose does not lie in his being a more perfect incarnation of God, but in his being specially adapted to represent the divine incarnation to people who were unable to grasp its full meaning. In proportion as the incarnation is adequately understood, all exceptional character disappears from the incarnation in Jesus. Here again we must say that this doctrine may be true, and it may possibly deserve the name of Christian. But it does not much resemble the more ordinary forms of Christianity.

242. The fifth point which we had to consider was Hegel's doctrine of Original Sin, and of Grace. He asserts that there is a profound truth in the Christian doctrine of Original Sin. This truth is to be found in the following proposition : " Man is by nature evil; his potential (an sich) Being, his natural Being is evil." But how does he interpret this ?

" In man," he says, we " meet with ·characteristics which are mutually opposed: Man is *by nature good*, he is not divided against himself, but, on the contrary, his essence, his Notion, consists in this, that he is by nature good, that he represents what is harmony with itself, inner peace; and—Man is *by nature evil*. ...

" To say that man is by nature good amounts substantially to saying that he is potentially Spirit, rationality, that he has been created in the image of God ; God is the Good, and Man as Spirit is the reflection of God, he is the Good potentially. It is just on this very proposition and on it alone that the possibility of the reconciliation rests; the difficulty, the ambiguity is, however, in the potentiality.

" Man is potentially good—but when that is said everything is not said ; it is just in this potentiality that the element of one-sidedness lies. Man is good potentially, *i.e.*, he is good only in an inward way, good so far as his notion or conception is concerned, and for this very reason not good so far as his actual nature is concerned.

" Man, inasmuch as he is Spirit, must actually be, be for himself, what he truly is; physical Nature remains in the condition of potentiality, it is potentially the Notion, but the Notion does not in it attain to independent Being, to Being-for-self. It is just in the very fact that Man is only potentially good that the defect of his nature lies. ...

" What is good by nature is good in an immediate way, and it is just the very nature of Spirit not to be something natural and immediate; rather, it is involved in the very idea of Man as Spirit that he should pass out of this natural state into a state in which there is a separation between his notion or conception and his immediate existence. In the case of physical nature this separation of an individual thing from its law, from its substantial essence, does not occur, just because it is not free.

"What is meant by Man is, a being who sets himself in opposition to his immediate nature, to his state of being in himself, and reaches a state of separation.

"The other assertion made regarding Man springs directly from the statement that Man must not remain what he is immediately; he must pass beyond the state of immediacy; that is the notion or conception of Spirit. It is this passing beyond his natural state, his potential Being, which first of all forms the basis of the division or disunion, and in connection with which the disunion directly arises.

"This disunion is a passing out of this natural condition or immediacy; but we must not take this to mean that it is the act of passing out of this condition which first constitutes evil, for, on the contrary, this passing out of immediacy is already involved in the state of nature. Potentiality and the natural state constitute the Immediate; but because it is Spirit it is in its immediacy the passing out of its immediacy, the revolt or falling away from its immediacy, from its potential Being.

"This involves the second proposition : Man is by nature evil; his potential Being, his natural Being is evil. It is just in this his condition as one of natural Being that his defect is found; because he is Spirit he is separated from this natural Being, and is disunion. One-sidedness is directly involved in this natural condition. When Man is only as he is according to Nature, he is evil.

"The natural Man is Man as potentially good, good according to his conception or notion; but in the concrete sense that man is natural who follows his passions and impulses, and remains within the circle of his desires and whose natural immediacy is his law.

"He is natural, but in this his natural state he is at the same time a being possessed of will, and since the content of his will is merely impulse and inclination, he is evil. So far as form is concerned, the fact that he is will implies that he is no longer an animal, but the content, the ends towards which his acts of will are directed, are still natural. This is the standpoint we are concerned with here, the higher standpoint according to which Man is by nature evil, and is evil just because he is something natural.

"The primary condition of Man, which is superficially represented as a state of innocence, is the state of nature, the animal state. Man must (soll) be culpable; in so far as he is good, he must not be good as any natural thing is good, but his guilt, his will, must come into play, it must be possible to impute moral acts to him. Guilt really means the possibility of imputation.

"The good man is good along with and by means of his will, and to that extent because of his guilt. Innocence implies the absence of will, the absence of evil, and consequently the absence of goodness. Natural things and the animals are all good, but this is a kind of goodness which cannot be attributed to Man; in so far as he is good, it must be by the action and consent of his will[1]."

243. Hegel's doctrine of Original Sin, then, is that man in his temporal existence on earth has in his nature a contingent and particular element, as well as a rational and universal element, and that, while his nature is good in respect of the second, it is bad in respect of the first.

From this follow three corollaries. The first is that it is unsafe to trust to the fact that all or some men have an instinctive conviction that a proposition is true or a maxim binding. Such a conviction shows that the proposition or the maxim is agreeable to some part of human nature, but it proves nothing as to its truth or obligation. For it may be the contingent and particular side of human nature in which the conviction arises, and a conviction which springs from this can only be right by accident. Indeed, since form and content are not completely separable, it cannot be more than approximately right.

Again, since the rational and universal part of our nature is,

---

[1] *op. cit.* ii. 258—260 (trans. iii. 45—48).

to a large extent, merely latent until developed by thought, education, and experience, it follows that the old and educated are more likely, *caeteris paribus*, to be in the right than the young and ignorant. It is, therefore, illegitimate to appeal to the unsophisticated natural instincts of the plain man. Whatever presents itself simply as a natural instinct of a plain man presents itself in a form of contingency and particularity. It can only be right by chance, and it can never be quite right. From reason erroneous and sophisticated there is no appeal but to reason's own power of correcting its own errors.

And, again, each generation does not start fresh in the work of evolving its rational and universal nature. The world shows a steady, though not an unbroken, advance in this respect. It is therefore illegitimate to appeal to the opinions of the past, as if it were a golden age when the true and the good were more easily recognized. We are doubtless wrong on many points, but we are more likely to be right than simpler and less reflective ages.

244. Now all this may be true. It may be quite compatible with Christianity. It is possible that no other view on this subject is compatible with Christianity. But it is by no means a view which is exclusively Christian, or which originated with Christianity, or which involves Christianity, and the fact that Hegel accepts it does nothing towards rendering his position a Christian one. Human nature often leads us astray. Many men have had instinctive convictions of the truth of what was really false, and of the goodness of what was really bad. In spite of the many errors of the wise and prudent, it is safer to adopt their opinions than those of babes. The world had not to wait for Christianity to discover these truths. It would not cease to believe them if Christianity was destroyed. Indeed, when they have been denied at all, it has generally been in the supposed defence of Christianity. Hegel may be right when he points out that such a defence is suicidal. But he can scarcely be brought nearer to Christianity by holding a belief which hardly any one denies except one school of Christians.

The extreme emphasis which Hegel lays on this doctrine is polemic in its nature. Among his contemporaries there was a party of Intuitionists, who based their philosophy on various propositions which were asserted to be fundamental convictions of mankind. And he tells us that there was also a Pietist school who held that we could not know God, but must be content to adore him in ignorance. Both these views in different ways involved a trust in our own natures, without criticism or discrimination, simply because they are our own natures. And it was his opposition to these views which urged Hegel into an iteration of his doctrine of Original Sin, which at first sight seems somewhat inexplicable.

245. There is another feature of Hegel's treatment of Original Sin which we must mention. He regards conscious and deliberate sin as evil. But he regards it as less evil than that mere Innocence (Unschuldigkeit) which has its root, not in the choice of virtue, but in ignorance of vice. As compared with the deliberate choice of the good, the deliberate choice of the bad is contingent and particular—and therefore evil. But to make a deliberate choice even of the bad implies some activity of the reason and the will. And so it has a universality in its form, which Innocence has not. It is true that Innocence has a universality in its content, which Sin has not. So far they might seem to be on a level. But Sin is so far superior that it has advanced one step nearer to the goal of Virtue. The man who has sinned may not have mounted higher in doing so. But he has at any rate started on the only road which can eventually lead him upwards.

And the advance from Innocence to Virtue can only be through Sin. Sin is a necessary means to Virtue. " Man must (soll) be culpable; in so far as he is good, he must not be good as any natural thing is good, but his guilt, his will, must come into play, it must be possible to impute moral acts to him[1]."

246. This relative superiority of Sin is evident in the passage which I quoted above[2]. It is also evident in the whole of Hegel's treatment of the story of the Fall. Of this I will quote one extract. " It is knowledge which first brings out the contrast or antithesis in which evil is found. The animal, the

---

[1] *op. cit.* ii. 260 (trans. iii. 48) ; cp. above Chap. vi.

[2] *op. cit.* ii. 258—260 (trans. iii. 45—48).

stone, the plant is not evil; evil is first present within the sphere of knowledge; it is the consciousness of independent Being, or Being-for-self relatively to an Other, but also relatively to an Object which is inherently universal in the sense that it is the Notion or rational will. It is only by means of this separation that I exist independently, for myself, and it is in this that evil lies. To be evil means in an abstract sense to isolate myself; the isolation which separates me from the Universal represents the element of rationality, the laws, the essential characteristics of Spirit. But it is along with this separation that Being-for-self originates, and it is only when it appears that we have the Spiritual as something universal, as Law, what ought to be[1]."

Later in the book he says, "What is devoid of Spirit appears at first to have no sin in it, but to be innocent, but this is just the innocence which is by its very nature judged and condemned[2]."

After all this it is only to be expected that Hegel, while he considers that the story of the Fall embodies a great truth, considers also that the Fall was in reality a rise. In this respect the Devil only told the truth. "The serpent says that Adam will become like God, and God confirms the truth of this, and adds His testimony that it is this knowledge which constitutes likeness to God. This is the profound idea lodged in the narrative[3]." And again, "The serpent further says that Man by the act of eating would become equal to God, and by speaking thus he made an appeal to Man's pride. God says to Himself, Adam is become as one of us. The serpent had thus not lied, for God confirms what it said[4]."

If this is to be counted as Christianity, then it must be compatible with Christianity to hold that the lowest state in which man ever existed was in Paradise before the entrance of the serpent, and that Adam and Eve, in yielding to the temptations of the Devil, were in reality taking the first step towards realising the truest and highest nature of Spirit.

[1] op. cit. ii. 264 (trans. iii. 52).
[2] op. cit. ii. 316 (trans. iii. 108).
[3] op. cit. ii. 75 (trans. ii. 202).
[4] op. cit. ii. 265 (trans. iii. 54).

247. Hegel's doctrine of Grace is the correlative of his doctrine of Original Sin. ·In the latter we were reminded that man's temporal nature is infected with contingency and particularity. In the doctrine óf Grace the emphasis is laid on the rationality and universality of man's eternal nature.

"The very fact that the opposition" inherent in the nature of Spirit " is implicitly done away with constitutes the condition, the presupposition, the possibility of the subject's ability to do away with it actually. In this respect it may be said that the subject does not attain reconciliation on its own account, that is, as a particular subject, and in virtue of its own activity, and what it itself does ; reconciliation is not brought about, nor can it be brought about, by the subject in its character as subject.

"This is the nature of the need when the question is, By what means can it be satisfied ? Reconciliation can be brought about only when the annulling of the division has been arrived at ; when what seems to shun reconciliation, this opposition, namely, is non-existent ; when the divine truth is seen to be for this, the resolved or cancelled contradiction, in which the two opposites lay aside their mutually abstract relation.

"Here again, accordingly, the question above referred to once more arises. Can the subject not bring about this re-conciliation by itself by means of its own action, by bringing its inner life to correspond with the divine Idea through its own piety and devoutness, and by giving expression to this in actions ? And, further, can the individual subject not do this, or, at least, may not *all men* do it who rightly will to adopt the divine Law as theirs, so that heaven might exist on earth, and the Spirit in its graciousness actually live here and have a real existence ? The question is as to whether the subject can or cannot effect this in virtue of its own powers as subject. The ordinary idea is that it can do this. What we have to notice here, and what must be carefully kept in mind, is that we are dealing with the subject thought of as standing at one of the two extremes, as existing for itself. To subjectivity belongs, as a characteristic feature, the power of positing, and this means that some particular thing exists owing to me. This positing or making actual, this doing of actions, &c., takes place through me, it matters not what the content is; the act of producing is consequently a one-sided characteristic, and the product is merely something posited, or dependent for its existence on something else; it remains as such merely in a condition of abstract freedom. The question referred to consequently comes to be a question as to whether it can by its act of positing produce this. This positing must essentially be a pre-positing, a presupposition, so that what is posited is also something implicit. The unity of subjectivity and objectivity, this divine unity, must be a presupposition so far as my act of positing is concerned, and it is only then that it has a content, a substantial element in it, and the content is Spirit, otherwise it is subjective and formal; it is only then that it gets a true, substantial content. When this presupposition thus gets a definite character it loses its one-sidedness, and when a definite signification is given to a presupposition of this kind the one-sidedness is in this way removed and lost. Kant and Fichte tell us that man can sow, can do good only on the presupposition that there is a moral order in the world; he does not know whether what he does will prosper and succeed; he can only act on the presupposition that the Good by its very nature involves growth and success, that it is not merely something posited, but, on the contrary, is in its own nature objective. Presupposition involves essential determination.

"The harmony of this contradiction must accordingly be represented as something which is a presupposition for the subject. The Notion, in getting to know the divine unity, knows that God essentially exists in-and-for-Himself, and consequently what the subject thinks, and its activity, have no meaning in themselves, but are and exist only in virtue of that presupposition[1]."

248. Hegel's doctrine of Grace, then, comes to this, that man, as considered in his subjectivity,—that is, in his mere particularity—cannot effect the improvement which he needs. That improvement can only be effected through the unity of subjectivity and objectivity, "this divine unity." And, as this

---

[1] *op. cit.* ii. 277 (iii. 67).

238 HEGELIANISM AND CHRISTIANITY

unity is itself the goal to which the improvement aspires, this means that the goal can only be reached, *sub specie temporis*, because, *sub specie aeternitatis*, the runners have been always there. But this divine unity of the subjective and objective is just the manifestation of God in man, which is the whole nature of man. And, therefore, this eternal reality, on whose existence depends our temporal progress, is nothing outside us, or imparted to us. It is our own deepest nature—our only real nature. It is our destiny to become perfect, *sub specie temporis*, because it is our nature to be eternally perfect, *sub specie aeternitatis*. We become perfect in our own right. It is true that our perfection depends on God. But God, viewed adequately, is the community of which we are parts. And God is a community of such a kind that the whole is found perfectly in every part[1].

Whether this doctrine is compatible with Christianity or not, is a question, as I have already explained, which is not for our present consideration. But it can, at any rate, give us no grounds for calling Hegel a Christian, for it is by no means exclusively or especially Christian. All mystical Idealism is permeated by the idea that only the good is truly real, and that evil is doomed to be defeated because it does not really exist. In Hegel's own words—"the consummation of the infinite End...consists merely in removing the illusion which makes it seem yet unaccomplished[2]."

249. Hegel's doctrine of Grace, it will be noticed, is identical with the assertion of the immediate unity of the human and divine, which he tells us is the fundamental thought in the teaching of Jesus. But the doctrine of Grace is only the complement of the doctrine of Original Sin. It would seem, then, that Hegel's view was that the Christian Church remedied the one-sided character of its founder's teaching, by putting Original Sin by the side of Grace, and thus emphasising both the unity and the separation of the human and the divine. But the Church would not be able to see the true reconciliation and unity of these doctrines, since it

---

[1] Cp. above, Section 14.
[2] *Encyclopaedia*, Section 212, lecture note.

could never rise to the full height of speculative thought. It could only hold them side by side, or unite them by some merely external bond.

250. We now pass to the sixth and last point on which we have to compare the system of Hegel with Christianity— his views on morality. There is no doubt that Hegel's judgments as to what conduct was virtuous, and what conduct was vicious, would on the whole agree with the judgments which would be made under the influence of Christianity. But this proves nothing. Fortunately for mankind, the moral judgments of all men, whatever their religious or philosophical opinions, show great similarity, though not of course perfect coincidence. Different systems of religion may lead to different opinions, on the exact limits of virtue and duty in such matters as veracity or chastity. And they may, on the authority of revelation, introduce additional positive duties, such as to observe the seventh day, or to abstain from beef. But the great mass of morality remains unaffected in its content by dogmatic changes.

Different religions, however, may lay the emphasis in morality differently. They may differ in the relative importance which they attach to various moral qualities. And it is here that Hegel separates himself from Christianity. It is just that side of morality on which Christianity lays the most stress which is least important for Hegel. This appears in several ways.

251. (a) Christianity habitually attaches enormous importance to the idea of sin. The difference between vice and virtue is absolute, and it is of fundamental importance. It is unnecessary to quote examples of this, or to enlarge on the way in which the sense of sin, the punishment of sin, the atonement for sin, have been among the most prominent elements in the religious consciousness of the Christian world.

This idea is entirely alien to Hegel. I do not wish to insist so much on his belief that all sin, like all other evil, is, from the deepest point of view, unreal, and that *sub specie aeternitatis* all reality is perfect. It might be urged that this view was logically implied in any system which accepted the ultimate triumph of the good, and that Hegel had only developed a doctrine which was involved in Christianity, even if it was imperfectly understood by many Christians.

But the real difference lies in Hegel's treatment of sin as something relatively good, which we noticed above. Sin is for Hegel not the worst state to be in. Virtue is better than sin, but sin is better than innocence. And since, as we saw in dealing with Original Sin, the only path from innocence to virtue is through sin, it follows that to commit sin is, in some cases at least, a moral advance. I have tried to show in a previous chapter that such a belief does not obliterate the distinction between vice and virtue, or destroy any incentive to choose virtue rather than vice. But such a belief is clearly quite incompatible with an assertion that the distinction between vice and virtue is primal, and of supreme importance from the standpoint of the universe at large.

252. (b) Again, Christianity was the first religion to lay paramount stress in morals on the individual conscience of the moral agent. The responsibility of each man's actions was no longer taken—it was not even allowed to be shared—by the state or the family. And thus the central question for ethics became more subjective. The important point was not whether an action tended to realise the good, but whether it was inspired by a sincere desire to realise the good.

An unbalanced insistence on the duties and rights of the individual conscience may produce very calamitous results. This Hegel tells us with extraordinary force and vigour[1]. But he goes so far in his effort to avoid this error, that his system becomes defective in the reverse direction. For, after all, it must be admitted that, although a man may fall into the most abject degradation with the full approval of his conscience, yet he cannot be really moral without that approval. The subjective conviction is by no means the whole of morality, but it is an essential part.

Nor is morality altogether a social matter. It is very largely social. To live in a healthy society gives important

[1] Cp. *Phenomenology*, v. b. b. 275—284.

assistance, both by guidance and by inspiration, to the individual. Nor would a *completely* healthy moral life be possible in a diseased society. And yet it is possible to be better than the society you live in. It is even possible to be in fundamental opposition to it—to strive with all your might Eastwards when society is pushing towards the West—and yet to be in the right.

Such considerations as these Hegel ignores in his recoil from the morality of conscience. The great ethical question for him is not How shall I be virtuous, but What is a perfect society? It is an inadequate question, if taken by itself, but it is inadequate by reason of a reaction from the complementary inadequacy. And it is in the direction of this complementary inadequacy—of excessive subjectivity—that the morality of Christianity has always diverged in so far as it diverged at all.

253. (c) The exclusively social nature of Hegel's morality comes out in another way—in its limitation to the society of our present life. It may be doubted if this is to be attributed to a disbelief in individual immortality, or if—as I believe to be the case—he believed in our immortality but felt no great interest in it. But whatever may be the cause, the fact cannot be doubted. It would be difficult, I believe, to find a word in Hegel which suggests that our duties, our ideals, or our motives are in the least affected by the probability or possibility of our surviving the death of our bodies. And this is the more striking since a life in time could, according to Hegel, only express reality very inadequately, and could never be fully explained except by reference to something beyond it.

Here, again, the characteristic tendency of Christian morality is to over-emphasise the side which Hegel ignores. Whenever the Christian Church has failed to keep the balance true between time and eternity it has always been in the direction of unduly ignoring the former. Not content with treating temporal existence as imperfect, it has pronounced it intrinsically worthless, and only important in so far as our actions here may be the occasions of divine reward and punishment hereafter. I am not asserting, of course, that the Christian Church has always held such a view as this, but only that, when it did depart from the truth, it was into this extreme that it fell—exactly opposite to the extreme adopted by Hegel.

254. (*d*) Another form of the specially social character of Hegelian ethics is the preference which he gives, when he *does* consider individual characters, to social utility over purity of motive. A man's moral worth for Hegel depends much more on what he does, than on what he is. Or—to put it less crudely—he is to be admired if what he does is useful, even if he does it for motives which are not admirable. For Hegel the man who takes a city is better than the man who governs his temper, but takes no cities. And this consideration of result rather than motive is of course quite alien to the morality of conscience which is specially prominent in Christianity.

255. (*e*) Connected with this is the relative importance of morality as a whole. The Christian Church has always had a strong tendency to place virtue above all other elements of human perfection, not only as quantitatively more important, but as altogether on a different level. If a man is virtuous, all other perfections are unnecessary to gain him the divine approbation. If he is not virtuous, they are all useless. There is nothing of this to be found in Hegel. He does not show the slightest inclination to regard right moral choice as more important than right intellectual judgment. And moreover he was firmly convinced of the unity of human nature, and of the impossibility of cutting it up into unconnected departments. Within certain limits, no doubt, one man might be stronger morally, another intellectually. But it is impossible for failure in one direction not to injure development in another. Hegel would not only have admitted that every knave is more or less a fool—which is a fairly popular statement with the world in general. He would have insisted on supplementing it by a proposition by no means so likely to win general favour—that every fool is more or less a knave.

Christianity, again, is often found to hold that, in the

most important department of knowledge, truth can be attained without great intellectual gifts or exertions, by the exercise of a faith the possession of which is looked on as a moral virtue. Sometimes the further assertion is made that the exercise of the intellect is not only unnecessary for this purpose, but useless, and sometimes it is pronounced to be actually harmful. The more you reason about God, it has been said, the less you know.

This theory, even in its mildest form, is absolutely alien—indeed, abhorrent—to Hegel. The Kingdom of God may be still hidden in part from the wise and prudent. But of one thing Hegel is absolutely certain. It is not revealed to babes. You cannot feel rightly towards God, except in so far as you know him rightly. You cannot know him rightly, except in so far as you are able and willing to use your reason. If you arrived at the right conclusions in any other way, they would be of little value to you, since you would hold them blindly and mechanically. But in truth you cannot arrive at the right conclusions in their fulness in any other way. For all irrational methods leave marks of their irrationality in the conclusion.

256. (*f*) There is no trace in Hegel of any feeling of absolute humility and contrition of man before God. Indeed, it would be scarcely possible that there should be. Sin, for Hegel, is so much less real than man, that it is impossible for man ever to regard himself as altogether sinful. Sin is a mere appearance. Like all appearance, it is based on reality. But the reality it is based on is not sin. Like all reality, it is perfectly good. The sinfulness is part of the appearance.

Man's position is very different. God is a community, and every man is part of it. In a perfect unity, such as God is, the parts are not subordinate to the whole. The whole is in every part, and every part is essential to the whole[1]. Every man is thus a perfect manifestation of God. He would not be such a manifestation of God, indeed, if he were taken in isolation, but, being taken in the community, he embodies God perfectly.

Such a being is perfect in his own right, and sin is super-

---

[1] Cp. above, Section 34.

ficial with regard to him, as it is with regard to the Absolute. *Sub specie aeternitatis* he is sinless. *Sub specie temporis* he is destined to become sinless, not from any external gift of divine grace, but because he is man—and God.

It is true that Hegel speaks of man as sinful, while he does not ascribe sin to God. But this is merely a question of terminology. He uses man to describe the individuals who constitute reality, whether they are viewed in their real and eternal perfection, or their apparent and temporal imperfection. But he only speaks of reality as God when he speaks of its eternal and perfect nature. So man is called sinful and not God. But in fact both, man and God, part and whole, are in the same position. Neither, in truth, is sinful. Both are the reality on which the appearance of sin is based. And sin really only belongs to us in the same way that it belongs to God.

Again, as we have seen, sin is for Hegel not the absolutely bad. It is at any rate an advance on innocence. A man who knows himself to be a sinner is *ipso facto* aware that there are heights to which he has not reached. But Hegel tells him that it is equally certain that there are depths which he has left behind. No one who has sinned can be altogether bad.

I have tried to show in Chapter VI. that these conclusions do not destroy our incentives to virtue, nor diminish that relative shame and contrition—the only species which has influence on action—which we feel when we realise that our actions have fallen short of our own ideals, or of the practice of others. But they certainly seem incompatible with any absolute shame or contrition—with any humiliation of ourselves as evil before an all-good God. It is impossible for me to regard myself as absolutely worthless on account of my sins, if I hold that those sins are the necessary and inevitable path which leads from something lower than sin up to virtue. Nor can I prostrate myself before a God of whom I hold ·myself to be a necessary part and an adequate manifestation, and who is only free from sin in the sense in which I myself am free from it. "Hegel," it has, not unfairly, been said, "told the young men of Germany that they were God. This they found very pleasant."

257. Let us sum up the results to which we have attained. They are as follows. (*a*) According to Hegel's doctrine of the Trinity, the Holy Ghost is identical with the entire Godhead. The Father and the Son are either aspects in, or illegitimate abstractions from, the Holy Ghost. (*b*) God is not a person, but a community of persons, who are united, not by a common self-consciousness, but by love. (*c*) All finite things are incarnations of God, and have no existence except as incarnations of God. (*d*) The special significance of Jesus with regard to the incarnation is merely that he bore witness to that truth in a form which, while only partially correct, was convenient for popular apprehension. (*e*) Hegel's doctrines of Original Sin and of Grace are doctrines which do not belong especially to Christianity, even if they are compatible with it. (*f*) Hegel's morality has as little resemblance to that of the Christian Church as the morality of one honest man could well have to that of other honest men of the same civilization and the same epoch.

258. Such a system as this may or may not properly be called Christianity. But it is at any rate certain that it is very different from the mere ordinary forms of Christianity, and that a large number of Christians would refuse it the name. This was still more universally true in Hegel's time. The question remains why Hegel chose to call such a system Christian.

259. It is impossible to believe that it was a deliberate deception, prompted by a desire for his own interest. There is nothing whatever in Hegel's life which could give us any reason to accuse him of such conduct. And, moreover, if it were for such a purpose that the Philosophy of Religion was arranged, it was arranged very inadequately. It might possibly make people think that its author was a Christian. But it could not possibly conceal from them that, if so, he was a very unorthodox Christian. And unorthodoxy attracts persecution nearly as much as complete disbelief. If Hegel had been lying, he would surely have lied more thoroughly.

It might be suggested that the deception was inspired by a sense of duty. The Philosophy of Religion is not in itself a work for general reading. But its contents might become known to the general public at second-hand. And Hegel, it might be supposed, did not wish to upset the belief in Christianity of such people as were unable to rise to the heights of speculative thought.

But this seems rather inconsistent with Hegel's character. He has been accused of many things, but no one has accused him of under-estimating the importance of philosophy, or of paying excessive deference to the non-philosophical plain man. It is incredible that he should have consented to distort an academic exposition of some of his chief conclusions for the plain man's benefit. Nor, again, is there anything in his writings which could lead us to suppose that he thought that the plain man ought to have lies told him on religious matters. The eulogies which he passes on the work of the Reformation point to a directly contrary conclusion.

It is, no doubt, not impossible that Hegel may have been determined by the thought of the non-philosophical majority to use the terminology of Christianity, provided that he really thought it to some degree appropriate. But it is impossible to suppose that he used, either from benevolence or from selfishness, language which he held to be quite inappropriate. And we are left with the question—why did he hold it appropriate to call his system Christian?

260. It has been suggested that every man should be called a Christian who fulfils two conditions. The first is, that he believes the universe as a whole to be something rational and righteous—something which deserves our approval and admiration. The second is, that he finds himself in so much sympathy with the life and character of Jesus, that he desires to consecrate his religious feelings and convictions by associating them with the name of Jesus.

Of all the attempts to define the outer limits within which the word Christian may be applied, this is perhaps the most successful. Few other interpretations, certainly, stretch those limits so widely. And yet even this interpretation fails to include Hegel. For there are no traces in his writings of any such personal sympathy with the historical Jesus. We find no praise of his life and character—which indeed did not present the civic virtues by which Hegel's admiration was most easily excited. And of his moral teaching we find at least as much criticism as praise[1]. It is perhaps scarcely going too far to say that it is difficult to conceive how any reasonable and candid man could write about the Christian religion with less personal sympathy for its founder than is shown by Hegel.

261. We must return to the first of the two questions stated in Section 207. For the explanation of Hegel's use of the word Christianity lies, I believe, in this—that, according to him, not even the highest religion was capable of adequately expressing the truth. It could only symbolise it in a way which was more or less inadequate. This is partly concealed by the fact that in the last division of his Philosophy of Religion he treats of Absolute truth in its fulness, no longer concealed by symbols. But the subordinate position of religion is beyond all doubt.

In the Philosophy of Spirit, the last triad is Art, Religion, and Philosophy. Philosophy, then, is the synthesis of an opposition of which Religion is one of the terms. There must, therefore, be some inadequacy in Religion which is removed by Philosophy. Philosophy, says Hegel, "is the unity of Art and Religion. Whereas the vision-method of Art, external in point of form, is but subjective production, and shivers the sub-stantial content into many separate shapes, and whereas Religion, with its separation into parts, opens it out in mental picture, and mediates what is thus opened out; Philosophy not merely keeps them together to make a total, but even unifies them into the simple spiritual vision, and then in that raises them to self-conscious thought. Such consciousness is thus the intelligible unity (cognised by thought) of art and religion, in which the diverse elements in the content are cognised as necessary, and this necessary as free[2]."

And, in the Philosophy of Religion, "Religion itself is this

---

[1] For example, of the moral commands of Jesus he says, "for those stages in which we are occupied with absolute truth they contain nothing striking, or else they are already contained in other religions, and in the Jewish religion." *Philosophy of Religion*, ii. 291 (trans. iii. 82).

[2] *Encyclopaedia*, Section 572.

action, this activity of the thinking reason, and of the man who thinks rationally,—who as individual posits himself as the Universal, and annulling himself as individual, finds his true self to be the Universal. Philosophy is in like manner thinking reason, only that this action in which religion consists appears in philosophy in the form of thought, while religion as, so to speak, reason thinking naïvely, stops short in the sphere of general ideas (Vorstellung)[1].

262.   There can therefore be no question whether Christianity is the absolute truth. For there is no question that Christianity must be counted as religion, according to the definition of religion given in the passage quoted above from the Philosophy of Spirit. And therefore it cannot be completely adequate to express the truth.

But, on the other hand, all religions express the truth with more or less adequacy, and the degree of this adequacy varies. It increases, Hegel tells us, as we pass along the chain of religions given in the Philosophy of Religion, from the lowest Magic up to the religion of Ancient Rome. One religion only (according to Hegel's exposition, which practically ignores the inconvenient fact of Islam) succeeds to the Roman. This is the Christian. Of all the religions of the world, therefore, this is to be held the least inadequate to express the truth.

When Hegel calls Christianity the absolute religion, therefore, this cannot mean that it expresses the absolute truth. For, being a religion, it cannot do this. He means that it is as absolute as religion can be, that it expresses the truth with only that inaccuracy which is the inevitable consequence of the symbolic and "pictorial" character of all religion.

Does he mean, however, to limit this assertion to the past, and only to say that no religion *has* come so near to absolute truth as Christianity does? Or would he go further, and say that it would be impossible that any religion, while it remained religion, should ever express the truth more adequately than Christianity? I am inclined to think that he would have been prepared to make the wider assertion. Nothing less would

---

[1] *Philosophy of Religion*, i. 188 (trans. i. 194).

justify the strength of his language in calling Christianity the absolute religion. Moreover in all the applications of his philosophy to empirical facts, he shows a strong tendency to suppose that the highest manifestation of Spirit already known to us is also the highest which it is possible should happen—although the degree in which he yields to this tendency has been exaggerated[1].

This more sweeping assertion we must pronounce to be unjustified. We cannot be certain of the future except by an argument *à priori*, and arguments *à priori* can only deal with the *à priori* element in knowledge. No conclusion about the nature of the empirical element in knowledge can be reached *à priori*. Now the degree of adequacy with which a religion can express absolute truth depends on the precise character of its symbolism. And the precise character of the symbolism of any religion is an empirical fact, which cannot be deduced *à priori*.

It is therefore impossible to be certain that no religion will arise in the future which will express the truth more adequately than Christianity. It may be said, indeed, that such a religion would be improbable. It might be maintained that Christianity gets so near to absolute truth, that if people got any nearer they would have reached the truth itself, and require no symbols at all. But of this it is impossible to be certain. New religions cannot be predicted, but it does not follow that they are impossible.

263. The truth of Hegel's statement however, if it is confined to the past, cannot be denied. No religion in history resembles the Hegelian philosophy so closely as Christianity. The two great questions for religion—if indeed they can be called two—are the nature of the Absolute and its relation to the finite. The orthodox Christian doctrines of the Trinity and the Incarnation are not, as we have seen, compatible with Hegel's teaching. But they are far closer to that teaching than the doctrines of any other religion known to history.

In this way, and this way, I believe, alone, the difficult

---

[1] Cp. *Studies in the Hegelian Dialectic*, Chap. VI.

question of Hegel's relation to Christianity admits of a solution. The difficulty is increased by a change in Hegel's method of exposition when he reaches the Absolute Religion. In dealing with the lower religions, he had described those religions in the form in which they were actually held by those who believed them—or, at any rate, in what he believed to be that form—and had then pointed out in what degree they fell short of absolute truth. But, when he came to Christianity, he did not expound the Christian doctrines themselves, but that absolute truth which, according to him, they imperfectly symbolised. This not unnaturally produced the impression that the doctrines of Christianity not only symbolised the absolute truth, but actually were the absolute truth. But closer examination dispels this, for it shows, as I have endeavoured to show in this Chapter, that Hegel's doctrines are incompatible with any form of Christianity which has ever gained acceptance among men.

264. Thus the result is that Hegel does not regard his system as Christian, but holds Christianity to be the nearest approach which can be made to his system under the imperfect form of religion. And that he is right in both parts of this— the positive and the negative—may be confirmed from experience.

Christian apologists have not infrequently met the attacks of their opponents with Hegelian arguments. And so long as there are external enemies to meet, the results are all that they can desire. Against Scepticism, against Materialism, against Spinozistic Pantheism, against Deism or Arianism—nothing is easier than to prove by the aid of Hegel that wherever such creeds differ from orthodox Christianity, they are in the wrong. But this is not the end. The ally who has been called in proves to be an enemy in disguise—the least evident but the most dangerous. The doctrines which have been protected from external refutation are found to be transforming themselves till they are on the point of melting away, and orthodoxy finds it necessary to separate itself from so insidious an ally.

This double relation of Hegelianism to Christian orthodoxy can be explained by the theory which I have propounded. If orthodox Christianity, while incompatible with Hegelianism, is nevertheless closer to it than any other religion, it is natural that Hegelianism should support Christianity against all attacks but its own, and should then reveal itself as an antagonist—an antagonist all the more deadly because it works not by denial but by completion.

CHAPTER IX.

THE FURTHER DETERMINATION OF THE ABSOLUTE.

265. THE progress of an idealistic philosophy may, from some points of view, be divided into three stages. The problem of the first is to prove that reality is not exclusively matter. The problem of the second is to prove that reality is exclusively spirit. The problem of the third is to determine what is the fundamental nature of spirit.

The result of the second stage, though comprehensive, is still abstract, and is therefore defective even from a theoretical point of view. It does not enable us to see the ultimate nature of the universe, and to perceive that it is rational and righteous. We only know in an abstract way that it *must* be rational and righteous, because it fulfils the formal condition of rationality and righteousness—harmony between the nature of the universal and the nature of the individual. Such a skeleton is clearly not complete knowledge. And it is therefore, to some extent, incorrect and inadequate knowledge; for it is knowledge of an abstraction only, while the truth, as always, is concrete. The content of the universe has not been produced by, or in accordance with, a self-subsistent law. It is the individual content of the universe which is concrete and self-subsistent, and the law is an abstraction of one side of it, with which we cannot be contented. From a theoretical point of view, then, the assertion of the supremacy of spirit is comparatively empty, unless we can determine the fundamental nature of spirit.

266. The practical importance of this determination is
not less. As a guide to life, the knowledge of the absolutely
desirable end is, no doubt, not without drawbacks. A certain
degree of knowledge, of virtue, and of happiness, is appropriate
and possible for every stage of the process of spirit. By the
aid of reflection we may perceive the existence of a stage much
higher than that in which we are. But the knowledge that
we shall reach it some day is not equivalent to the power
of reaching it at once. We are entitled to as much perfection
as we are fit for, and it is useless to demand more. An
attempt to live up to the Supreme Good, without regard to
present circumstances, will be not only useless, but, in all
probability, actually injurious. The true course of our development at present is mostly by thesis and antithesis, and
efforts to become perfect as the crow flies will only lead us
into some blind alley from which we shall have to retrace
our steps.

Nevertheless, the knowledge of the goal to which we are
going may occasionally, if used with discretion, be a help in
directing our course. It will be something if we can find out
which parts of our experience are of value *per se*, and can
be pursued for their own sake, and which parts are merely
subsidiary. For however long it may take us to reach the
Absolute, it is sometimes curiously near us in isolated episodes
of life, and our attitude towards certain phases of consciousness,
if not our positive actions, may be materially affected by the
consideration of the greater or less adequacy with which those
phases embody reality.

And a more complete determination of the nature of spirit
would not be unimportant with regard to its effect on our
happiness. The position from which we start has indeed
already attained to what may be called the religious standpoint. It assures us of an ultimate solution which shall only
differ from our present highest ideals and aspirations by far
surpassing them. From a negative point of view, this is
complete, and it is far from unsatisfactory as a positive theory.
But it is probable that, if so much knowledge is consoling and
inspiriting, more knowledge would be better. It is good to

know that reality is better than our expectations. It might be still better to be able at once to expect the full good that is coming. If the truth is so good, our hopes may well become more desirable in proportion as they become more defined.

In other ways, too; more complete knowledge might conduce to our greater happiness. For there are parts of our lives which, even as we live them, seem incomplete and merely transitory, having no value unless they lead on to something better. And there are parts of our lives which seem so fundamental, so absolutely desirable in themselves, that we could not anticipate without pain their absorption into some higher perfection, as yet unknown to us, and that we demand that they shall undergo no further change, except an increase in purity and intensity. Now we might be able to show of the first of these groups of experiences that they are, in fact, mere passing phases, with meaning only in so far as they lead up to and are absorbed in something higher. And we might even be able to show of the second that they are actually fundamental, lacking so far in breadth and depth, but in their explicit nature already revealing the implicit reality. If we can do this, and can justify the vague longings for change on the one hand, and for permanence on the other, which have so much effect on our lives, the gain to happiness which will result will not be inconsiderable.

267. We have already found reason to hold that spirit is ultimately made up of various finite individuals, each of which finds his character and individuality in his relations to the rest, and in his perception that they are of the same nature as himself. In this way the Idea in each individual has as its object the Idea in other individuals[1]. We must now enquire in what manner those individuals will be able to express, at once and completely, their own individuality and the unity of the Absolute.

Human consciousness presents three aspects—knowledge, volition, and feeling, i.e., pleasure and pain. Knowledge and

---

[1] Cp. Sections 14, 15.

volition are correlative methods of endeavouring to obtain that unity between individuals which is the perfection of spirit, while feeling is not so much a struggle towards the goal as the result of the process, so far as it has gone. Through knowledge and volition we gain harmony, and, according as we have gained it more or less completely, our feeling is pleasurable or painful. The absence of any independent movement of feeling renders it unnecessary, for the present, to consider it separately.

I shall first enquire what general aspect would be presented by spirit, if we suppose knowledge and volition to have become as perfect as possible. It will then be necessary to ask whether knowledge and volition are permanent and ultimate forms of the activity of spirit. I shall endeavour to show that they are not, that they both postulate, to redeem them from paradox and impossibility, an ideal which they can never reach, and that their real truth and meaning is found only in a state of consciousness in which they themselves, together with feeling, are swallowed up and transcended in a more concrete unity. This unity I believe to be essentially the same as that mental state which, in the answer to our first question, we shall find to be the practically interesting aspect of knowledge and volition in their highest perfection as such. This state will thus have been shown to be, not only the supremely valuable element of reality, but also the only true reality, of which all other spiritual activities are but distortions and abstractions, and in which they are all transcended. It will not only be the highest truth but the sole truth. We shall have found the complete determination of spirit, and therefore of reality.

268. Let us turn to the first of these questions and consider what would be our attitude towards the universe, when both knowledge and volition had reached perfection. To answer this we must first determine in rather more detail what would be the nature of perfect knowledge and volition.

In the first place we must eliminate knowledge as the occupation of the student. The activity and the pleasure which lie in the search after knowledge can, as such, form no part of the Absolute. For all such activity implies that some knowledge has not yet been gained, and that the ideal, therefore, has not yet been reached. The ideal must be one, not of learning, but of knowing.

And the knowledge itself must be greatly changed. At present much of our knowledge directly relates to matter; all of it is conditioned and mediated by matter. But if the only absolute reality is spirit, then, when knowledge is perfect, we must see nothing but spirit everywhere. We must have seen through matter till it has disappeared. How far this could be done merely by greater knowledge on our part, and how far it would be necessary for the objects themselves, which we at present conceive as matter, to develop explicitly qualities now merely implicit, is another question, but it is clear that it would have to be done, one way or another, before knowledge could be said to be perfect.

Nor is this all. Not only all matter, but all contingency, must be eliminated. At present we conceive of various spirits—and even of spirit in general—as having qualities for which we can no more find a rational explanation than we can for the primary qualities of matter, or for its original distribution in space. But this must disappear in perfected knowledge. For knowledge demands an explanation of everything, and if, at the last, we have to base our explanation on something left unexplained, we leave our system incomplete and defective.

Explanation essentially consists of arguments from premises; and it would seem therefore that such perfection could never be attained, since each argument which explained anything must rest upon an unexplained foundation, and so on, *ad infinitum*. And it is true that we can never reach a point where the question " Why ? " can no longer be asked. But we can reach a point where it becomes unmeaning, and at this point knowledge reaches the highest perfection of which, as knowledge, it is susceptible.

The ideal which we should then have reached would be one in which we realised the entire universe as an assembly of spirits, and recognized that the qualities and characteristics, which gave to each of these spirits its individuality, did not

lie in any contingent or non-rational peculiarity in the individual himself, but were simply determined by his relations
to all other individuals. These relations between individuals,
again, we should not conceive as contingent or accidental, so
that the persons connected formed a mere miscellaneous crowd.
We should rather conceive them as united by a pattern or
design, resembling that of a picture or organism, so that every
part of it was determined by every other part, in such a
manner that from any one all the others could, with sufficient
insight, be deduced, and that no change could be made in any
without affecting all. This complete interdependence is only
approximately realised in the unity which is found in aesthetic
or organic wholes, but in the Absolute the realisation would
be perfect. As the whole nature of every spirit would consist
exclusively in the expression of the relations of the Absolute,
while those relations would form a whole, in which each part,
and the whole itself, would be determined by each part, it
follows that any fact in the universe could be deduced from
any other fact, or from the nature of the universe as a
whole.

269. If knowledge reached this point, the only question
which could remain unanswered would be the question, " Why
is the universe as a whole what it is, and not something else ? "
And this question could not be answered. We must not,
however, conclude from this the existence of any want of
rationality in the universe. The truth is that the question
ought never to have been asked, for it is the application of
a category, which has only meaning within the universe, to
the universe as a whole. Of any part we are entitled and
bound to ask " why," for, by the very fact that it is a part,
it cannot be self-subsistent, and must depend on other things.
But when we come to an all-embracing totality, then, with
the possibility of finding a cause, there disappears also the
necessity of finding one. Self-subsistence is not in itself a
contradictory or impossible idea. It *is* contradictory if applied
to anything in the universe, for whatever is in the universe
must be in connection with other things. But this can of
course be no reason for suspecting a fallacy when we find

ourselves obliged to apply the idea to something which has nothing outside it with which it could stand in connection.

To put the matter in another light, we must consider that the necessity of finding causes and reasons for phenomena depends on the necessity of showing why they have assumed the particular form which actually exists. The enquiry is thus due to the possibility of things happening otherwise than as they did, which possibility, to gain certain knowledge, must be excluded by assigning definite causes for one event rather than the others. Now every possibility must rest on some actuality. And the possibility that the whole universe could be different would have no such actuality to rest on, since the possibility extends to all reality. There would be nothing in common between the two asserted alternatives, and thus the possibility of variation would be unmeaning. And therefore there can be no reason to assign a determining cause.

The necessity which exists for all knowledge to rest on the immediate does not, then, indicate any imperfection which might prove a bar to the development of spirit. For we have seen that the impulse which causes us even here to demand fresh mediation is unjustified, and, indeed, meaningless. But we shall have to consider, in the second part of this chapter, whether the possibility of making even the unjustified demand does not indicate that for complete harmony we must go on to something which embraces and transcends knowledge.

270. Let us now pass on to the ideal of volition. We must in the first place exclude, as incompatible with such an ideal, all volition which leads to action. For action implies that you have not something which you want, or that you will be deprived of it if you do not fight for it, and both these ideas are fatal to the fundamental and complete harmony between desire and environment which is necessary to the perfect development of spirit.

Nor can virtue have a place in our ideal, even in the form of aspiration. Together with every other imperfection, it must be left outside the door of heaven. For virtue implies a choice, and choice implies either uncertainty or conflict. In the realised ideal neither of these could exist. We should desire our truest and deepest well-being with absolute necessity, since there would be nothing to deceive and tempt us away. And we should find the whole universe conspiring with us to realise our desire. The good would be *ipso facto* the real, and virtue would have been transcended.

The ideal of volition is rather the experience of perfect harmony between ourselves and our environment which excludes alike action and choice. This involves, in the first place, that we should have come to a clear idea as to what the fundamental demands and aspirations of our nature are. Till we have done this we cannot expect harmony. All other desires will be in themselves inharmonious, for, driven on by the inevitable dialectic, they will show themselves imperfect, transitory, or defective, when experienced for a sufficiently long time, or in a sufficiently intense degree. And, besides this, the very fact that the universe is fundamentally of the nature of spirit, and therefore *must* be in harmony with us when we have fully realised our own natures, proves that it *cannot* be permanently in harmony with us as long as our natures remain imperfect. For such a harmony with the imperfect would be an imperfection, out of which it would be forced by its own dialectic.

And this harmony must extend through the entire universe. If everything (or rather everybody) in the universe is not in harmony with us our ends cannot be completely realised. For the whole universe is connected together, and every part of it must have an effect, however infinitesimal, upon every other part. Our demands must be reconciled with, and realised by, every other individual.

And, again, we cannot completely attain our own ends unless everyone else has attained his own also. For, as was mentioned in the last paragraph, we cannot attain our own ends except by becoming in perfect harmony with the entire universe. And this we can only do in so far as both we and it have become completely rational. It follows that for the attainment of our ends it would be necessary for the entire universe to have explicitly developed the rationality which is its fundamental nature. And by this self-development every other individual, as well as ourselves, would have attained to the perfection of volition. Moreover, looking at the matter more empirically, we may observe that some degree of sympathy seems inherent to our nature, so that our pleasure in someone else's pain, though often intense, is never quite unmixed. And on this ground also our complete satisfaction must involve that of all other people.

271. We have now determined the nature of perfected knowledge and volition, as far as the formal conditions of perfection will allow us to go. What is the concrete and material content of such a life as this? I believe it means one thing, and one thing only—love. I do not mean benevolence, even in its most empassioned form. I do not mean the love of Truth, or Virtue, or Beauty, or anything else whose name can be found in a dictionary. I do not mean sexual desire. And I do mean passionate, all-absorbing, all-consuming love.

For let us consider. We should find ourselves in a world composed of nothing but individuals like ourselves. With these individuals we should have been brought into the closest of all relations, we should see them, each of them, to be rational and righteous. And we should know that in and through these individuals our own highest aims and ends were realised. What else does it come to? To know another person thoroughly, to know that he conforms to my highest standards, to feel that through him the end of my own life is realised—is this anything but love?

Such a result would come all the same, I think, if we only looked at the matter from the point of view of satisfied knowledge, leaving volition out of account. If all reality is such as would appear entirely reasonable to us if we knew it completely, if it is all of the nature of spirit, so that we, who are also of that nature, should always find harmony in it, then to completely know a person, and to be completely known by him, must surely end in this way. No doubt knowledge does not always have that result in every-day life. But that is incomplete knowledge, under lower categories and subject to unremoved contingencies, which, from its incompleteness, must leave the mind unsatisfied. Perfect knowledge would be different. How much greater would the difference be if, besides the satisfaction attendant on mere knowledge, we had realised that it was through the people round us that the longings and desires of our whole nature were being fulfilled.

This would, as it seems to me, be the only meaning and significance of perfected spirit. Even if knowledge and volition still remained, their importance would consist exclusively in their producing this result. For it is only in respect of the element of feeling in it that any state can be deemed to have intrinsic value. This is of course not the same thing as saying that we only act for our own greatest happiness, or even that our own greatest happiness is our only rational end. I do not deny the possibility of disinterested care for the welfare of others. I only assert that the welfare of any person depends upon the feeling which is an element of his consciousness. Nor do I assert that a quantitative maximum of pleasure is the Supreme Good. It is possible that there may be qualitative differences of pleasure which might make a comparatively unpleasant state more truly desirable than one in which the pleasure was far greater. But this does not interfere with the fact that it is only with regard to its element of feeling that any state can be held to be intrinsically desirable.

272. Perfected knowledge and volition, taken in connection with the consequent feeling, not only produce personal love, but, as it seems to me, produce nothing else. There are, it is true, many other ways in which knowledge and volition produce pleasure. There are the pleasures of learning, and of the contemplation of scientific truth; there are the pleasures of action, of virtue, and of gratified desire. But these all depend on the imperfect stages of development in which knowledge and volition are occupied with comparatively abstract generalities. Now all general laws are abstractions from, and therefore distortions of, the concrete reality, which is the abstract realised in the particular. When we fail to detect the abstract in the particular, then, no doubt, the abstract has a value of its own—is as high or higher than the mere particular. But when we see the real individual, in whom the abstract and the particular are joined, we lose all interest in the abstract as such. Why should we put up with an inadequate falsehood when we can get the adequate truth? And feeling towards an individual who is perfectly known has only one form.

273. But what right have we to talk of love coming as a necessary consequence of anything? Is it not the most unreasoning of all things, choosing for itself, often in direct opposition to what would seem the most natural course? I should explain the contradiction as follows. Nothing but perfection could really deserve love. Hence, when it comes in this imperfect world, it only comes in cases in which one is able to disregard the other as he is now—that is, as he really is not—and to care for him as he really is—that is, as he will be. Of course this is only the philosopher's explanation of the matter. To the unphilosophic object to be explained it simply takes the form of a conviction that the other person, with all his faults, is somehow *in himself* infinitely good—at any rate, infinitely good for his friend. The circumstances which determine in what cases this strange dash into reality can be made are not known to us. And so love is unreasonable. But only because reason is not yet worthy of it. Reason cannot reveal—though in philosophy it may predict—the truth which alone can justify love. When reason is perfected, love will consent to be reasonable.

274. Fantastic as all this may seem, the second part of my subject, on which I must now enter, will, I fear, seem much worse. I have endeavoured to prove that all perfect life would lead up to and culminate in love. I want now to go further, and to assert that, as life became perfect, all other elements would actually die away—that knowledge and volition would disappear, swallowed up in a higher reality, and that love would reveal itself, not only as the highest thing, but as the only thing, in the universe.

If we look close enough we shall find, I think, that both knowledge and volition postulate a perfection to which they can never attain; that consequently if we take them as ultimate realities we shall be plunged into contradictions, and that the only way to account for them at all is to view them as moments or aspects of a higher reality which realises the perfections they postulate. This perfection lies in the production of a complete harmony between the subject and the object, by the combination of perfect unity between them with perfect discrimination of the one from the other. And this, as I shall endeavour to prove, is impossible without transcending the .limits of these two correlative activities.

275. In the first place, is it possible that the duality which makes them two activities, rather than one, can be maintained in the Absolute ? For, if it cannot be maintained, then knowledge and volition would both be merged in a single form of spirit. The object of both is the same—to produce the harmony described in Hegel's definition of the Absolute Idea. What is it that separates them from one another, and is the separation one which can be considered as ultimate ?

276. The most obvious suggestion is that volition leads directly to action, while knowledge does so only indirectly, by effecting volition. If however we look more closely we shall find that this is not a sufficient distinction. We may perhaps leave out of account the fact that a desire, however strong, does not provoke us to action if it is for something which we know is perfectly impossible, or for something which no action can effect. No action is produced by a desire that two and two may make five, or by a desire that the wind may blow from the west. But even in cases where the process of development is taking place, and the harmony between desire and reality is being gradually brought about, it is by no means always the case that it is brought about by action. There are two other alternatives. It may be brought about by a discovery in the field of knowledge, which reveals a harmony which had previously escaped observation. Discovery is itself, certainly, an action. But it is not the act of discovery which here produces the harmony, but the truth which it reveals, and the truth is not an action. We have not gained the harmony because we have changed the environment, but because we have understood it. And the act of discovery is the result of our desire to understand, not of our desire for the result discovered.

The other possible means of reconciliation is by the desire changing itself into conformity with the environment, either through an intellectual conviction that the previous desire was mistaken, or by that process of dialectic development inherent in finite desires.

Let us suppose, for example, that a desire that vindictive justice should exhibit itself in the constitution of the universe finds itself in conflict with the fact, known by empirical observation, that the wicked often prosper. Some degree of harmony between desires and facts may be obtained in this case by means of action as affecting the political and social environment. But this alone could never realise the demand. We have, however, two other possible methods of reconciliation. Philosophy or theology may assure us that there is a future life, and that in it our desires will be fulfilled. Or our notions of the desirable may develop in such a way as no longer to require that the universe should exhibit vindictive justice. In either case we should have attained to harmony without action following as a consequence of our volition.

277. Or, secondly, it may be suggested that the distinction lies in the activity or passivity of the mind. In knowledge, it might be said, our object is to create a picture in our minds, answering to the reality which exists outside them, and based on data received from external sources. Since the test of the mental picture is its conformity to the external reality, the mind must be passive. On the other hand, in volition the mind supplies an ideal by means of which we measure external reality. If the reality does not correspond to our desires, we condemn it as unsatisfactory, and, if the thwarted desires belong to our moral nature, we condemn it as wrong. Here, it might be urged, the mind is in a position of activity.

There is unquestionably some truth in this view. The greater weight is certainly laid, in knowledge on the external object, in volition on the consciousness of the agent. But we must seek a more accurate expression of it. For the mind is not passive in knowledge, nor purely active in volition. In considering the last argument we saw that the harmony may be produced, wholly or in part, by the alteration of the desires till they coincide with the facts. In so far as this is the case, the mind is in a more or less passive position, and is altered by external facts, whether the result comes from arguments drawn from the existence of those facts, or by reaction from the contact with them in actual life.

We may go further, and say, not only that this may happen in some cases, but that it must happen in all cases to some extent. For otherwise in the action of mind on the environment we should have left no place for any reaction, and by doing so should deny the reality of that member of the relation which we condemn to passivity. But if the as yet unharmonized environment was unreal, as compared with the as yet unembodied ideal, the process would cease to exist. If the environment has no existence our demands cannot be said to be realised in it. If it has real existence, it must react on our demands.

Nor, again, can it be said that the mind is purely passive in knowledge. The data which it receives from outside are subsumed under categories which belong to the nature of the mind itself, and the completed knowledge is very different from the data with which it began. Indeed if we attempt to consider the data before any reaction of the mind has altered them we find that they cannot enter into consciousness—that is, they do not exist.

278. Let us make one more effort to find a ground of distinction. I believe that we may succeed with the following statement—in knowledge we accept the facts as valid and condemn our ideas if they do not agree with the facts; in volition we accept our ideas as valid, and condemn the facts if they do not agree with our ideas.

Suppose a case of imperfect harmony. The first thing, of course, is to recognize that there is something wrong somewhere. But, when we have realised this, what can we do? Since the two sides, the facts and our ideas, are not in harmony, we cannot accept both as valid. To accept neither as valid would be impossible—because self-contradictory—scepticism and quietism. We must accept one and reject the other. Now in knowledge we accept the facts as valid, and condemn our ideas, in so far as they differ from the facts, as mistaken. In volition, on the other hand, we accept our ideas as valid, and condemn the facts, in so far as they differ from our ideas, as wrong.   If, for example, it should appear to us that a rational and righteous universe would involve our personal immortality, while there were reasons to believe that we were not personally immortal, then we should have to take up a double position.   On the one hand we should be bound to admit that our longing for immortality would not be gratified, however intense it might be.   On the other hand we should be bound to assert that the universe was wrong in not granting our desires, however certain it was that they would not be granted.   Of course this assumes that every effort has been made to produce the harmony.   We are not entitled to condemn the universe as evil on account of an unfulfilled desire, until we have carefully enquired if it is a mere caprice, or really so fundamental a part of our nature that its realisation is essential to permanent harmony.   And we are not bound to condemn our ideas as untrue because the facts seem against them at first sight.

279.   I am far from wishing to assert that any want of harmony really exists.   Such a view would be quite contrary to Hegel's philosophy.   But we must all acknowledge that in a great number of particular cases we are quite unable to see *how* the harmony exists, although on philosophical grounds we may be certain that it must exist somehow.   And, besides, even in some cases where we may intellectually perceive the harmony, our nature may not be so under the control of our reason, as to enable us to feel the harmony, if it happens to conflict with our passions.   In all these cases it will be necessary to deal with an apparent want of harmony, and in all these cases we must give the facts the supremacy in the sphere of knowledge and the ideas the supremacy in the sphere of volition.

One of our most imperative duties is intellectual humility—to admit the truth to be true, however unpleasant or unrighteous it may appear to us.   But, correlative to this duty, there is another no less imperative—that of ethical self-assertion.   If no amount of "ought" can produce the slightest "is," it is no less true that no amount of "is" can produce the slightest "ought."   It is of the very essence of human will, and of that effort to find the fundamentally desirable which we call morality, that it claims the right to judge the whole universe. This is the categorical imperative of Kant. We find it again in Mill's preference of hell to worship of an unjust deity. Nor is it only in the interests of virtue as such that the will is categorical. Pleasure is no more to be treated lightly than virtue. If all the powers of the universe united to give me one second's unnecessary toothache, I should not only be entitled, but bound, to condemn them. We have no more right to be servile than to be arrogant. And while our desires must serve in the kingdom of the true, they rule in the kingdom of the good.

We must note in passing that we are quite entitled to argue that a thing is because it ought to be, or ought to be because it is, if we have once satisfied ourselves that the harmony does exist, and that the universe is essentially rational and righteous. To those who believe, for example, in a benevolent God, it is perfectly competent to argue that we must be immortal because the absence of immortality would make life a ghastly farce, or that toothache must be good because God sends it. It is only when, or in as far as, the harmony has not yet been established, that such an argument gives to God the things which are Caesar's, and to Caesar the things which are God's, to the embarrassment of both sides.

280. If we have now succeeded in finding the distinction between knowledge and volition, we must conclude that it is one which can have no place in the absolute perfection. For we have seen that the distinction turns upon the side of the opposition which shall give way, when there is opposition, and not harmony, between the subject and the object. In an Absolute there can be no opposition, for there can be no want of harmony, as the Absolute is, by its definition, the harmony made perfect. And not only can there be no want of harmony, but there can be no possibility that the harmony should ever become wanting. Everything must have a cause, and if it were possible that the harmony which exists at a given time should subsequently be broken, a cause must co-exist with the harmony capable of destroying it. When the harmony is universal, the cause would have to exist within it. Now when we speak of things which are only harmonious with regard to certain relations, or in a certain degree, we can speak of a harmony which carries within it the seeds of its own dissolution. Such is the life of an organism, which necessarily leads to death, or the system of a sun and planets, which collapses as it loses its energy. But when we come to consider a harmony which pervades objects in all their relations, and which is absolutely perfect, anything which could produce a disturbance in it would be itself a disturbance, and is excluded by the hypothesis. This will be seen more clearly if we remember that the harmony is one of conscious spirit. The consciousness must be all-embracing, and therefore the cause of the possible future disturbance must be recognized for what it is. And the possibility of such a disturbance must produce at once some degree of doubt, fear, or anxiety, which would, by itself and at once, be fatal to harmony.

It follows that, since not even the possibility of disturbance can enter into the Absolute, the distinction between knowledge and volition, depending as it does entirely on the course pursued when such a disturbance exists, becomes, not only irrelevant, but absolutely unmeaning. And in that case the life of Spirit, when the Absolute has been attained, will consist in the harmony which is the essence of both knowledge and volition, but will have lost all those characteristics which differentiate them from one another, and give them their specific character.

281. Before passing on to further arguments, we must consider an objection which may be raised to what has been already said. This is that no trace of the asserted union of knowledge and volition is to be found in our experience. We often find, in some particular matter, a harmony which is, at any rate, so far complete that no want of it is visible, in which the self and the environment show no perceptible discordance. And yet knowledge and volition, though in agreement, do not show the least sign of losing their distinctness. On the one hand we assert that a given content is real, and on the other that it is desirable. But the difference of meaning between the predicates " true " and "good " is as great as ever.

But no harmony to which we can attain in the middle of

a life otherwise inharmonious can ever be perfect, even over a limited extent. For the universal reciprocity which must exist between all things in the same universe would prevent anything from becoming perfect, until everything had done so. And a harmony between two imperfections could never be complete, since the imperfect remains subject to the dialectic, and is therefore transitory. Even supposing, however, that such a limited harmony could be perfect, it could never exclude the possibility of disturbance. The possibility was excluded in the case of a universal harmony, because the ground of disturbance could not exist within the harmony, and there was nowhere else for it to exist. But here such a ground might always be found outside. And while there is any meaning in even the possibility of a discrepancy between our ideas and the facts, there is no reason to expect the separation of knowledge and volition to cease.

282. Knowledge and volition, then, cannot remain separate in the Absolute, and therefore cannot remain themselves. Into what shall they be transformed? The only remaining element of consciousness is feeling, that is, pleasure and pain. This, however, will not serve our purpose. It has nothing to do with objects at all, but is a pure self-reference of the subject. And this, while it makes it in some ways the most intimate and personal part of our lives, prevents it from ever being self-subsistent, or filling consciousness by itself. For our self-consciousness only develops by bringing itself into relation with its not-self. The definition of the Absolute Idea shows that the appreciation of an object is necessary to spirit. Feeling therefore is only an element in states of consciousness, not a state by itself. We are conscious of relations to an object, and in this consciousness we see an element of pleasure or pain. But pleasure or pain by themselves can never make the content of our mind.

The one alternative left is emotion. For our present purpose, we may perhaps define emotion as a state of consciousness tinged with feeling, or rather, since feeling is never quite absent, a state of consciousness, in so far as it is tinged with feeling. Here we have all three elements of consciousness.

We are aware of the existence of an object; since we are brought into relation with it, we recognize it as harmonising more or less with our desires; and we are conscious of pleasure or pain, consequent on the greater or less extent to which knowledge and volition have succeeded in establishing a harmony. This state of mind may be a mere aggregate of three independent activities. In that case it will be useless for us. But it may turn out to be the concrete unity from which the three activities gained their apparent independence by illegitimate abstraction. If so, it may not impossibly be the synthesis for which we are searching.

283. It is clear that no emotion can be the ultimate form of spirit, unless it regards all objects as individual spirits. For the dialectic shows us that, till we regard them thus, we do not regard them rightly. And the dialectic shows us, also, that we do not regard them rightly till we know them to be in complete harmony with ourselves, and with one another. To regard all that we find round us as persons, to feel that their existence is completely rational, and that through it our own nature is realised, to experience unalloyed pleasure in our relations to them—this is a description to which only one emotion answers. We saw in the first part of this Chapter that the only value and interest of knowledge and volition, when pushed as far as they would go, lay in love. Here we go a step further. If anything in our present lives can resolve the contradictions inherent in knowledge and volition, and exhibit the truth which lies concealed in them, it must be love.

284. If this is to take place, love must transcend the opposition between knowledge and volition as to the side of the relation which is to be considered valid in case of discrepancy. Neither side in the Absolute must attain any pre-eminence over the other, since such pre-eminence has only meaning with regard to the possibility of imperfection.

Neither side has the pre-eminence in love. It is not essential to it that the subject shall be brought into harmony with the object, as in knowledge, nor that the object shall be brought into harmony with the subject, as in volition. It is sufficient that the two terms should *be* in harmony.

The subject refuses here to be forced into the abstract position of either slave or master. To conceive the relation as dependent on the conformity of the subject to the object would ignore the fact that the subject has an ideal which possesses its rights even if nothing corresponds to it in reality. To conceive the relation, on the other hand, as dependent on the conformity of the object to the subject, would be to forget that the emotion directs itself towards persons and not towards their relations with us. When, as in volition, the harmony results from the conformity of the object to the subject, any interest in the object as independent can only exist in so far as it realises the end of the subject, and is so subordinate. But here our interest in the object is not dependent on our interest in the subject. It is identical with it. We may as well be said to value ourselves because of our relation to the object, as the object because of its relation to ourselves.

This complete equilibrium between subject and object is the reason why love cannot be conceived as a duty on either side. It is not our duty to love others. (I am using love here in the sense in which it is used in every-day life, which was also Hegel's use of it[1].) It is not the duty of others to be loveable by us. In knowledge and volition, where one side was to blame for any want of harmony, there was a meaning in saying that the harmony ought to be brought about. But here, where the sides have equal rights, where neither is bound to give way, no such judgment can be passed. We can only say that the absence of the harmony proves the universe to be still imperfect.

And, as this harmony subordinates neither side to the other, it is so far qualified to express the Absolute completely. It needs for its definition no reference to actual or possible defects. It is self-balanced, and can be self-subsistent.

285. I now proceed to a second line of argument which leads to the same conclusion. Both knowledge and volition, I maintain, postulate an ideal which they can never reach, while they remain knowledge and volition. If this can be shown, it

---

[1] Cp. Sections 219, 220.

will follow that neither knowledge nor volition, as such, are compatible with the perfection of reality, but that, in that perfection, they will be transcended by some other state, which will realise the ideal of harmony which they can only demand.

286. It will be remembered that in Chapter II. we came to the conclusion that our selves were fundamental differentiations of the Absolute because no other theory seemed compatible with the fact that a conscious self was a part which contained the whole of which it was part. In other words, the self contains much that is not-self. Indeed, with the exception of the abstraction of the pure I, all the content of the self is not-self.

If we look at knowledge and volition, we see clearly that the element of the not-self is essential to them. To know implies that there is something known, distinct from the knowledge of it. To acquiesce implies that there is something in which we acquiesce, which is distinct from our acquiescence in it. Without the not-self, knowledge and volition would be impossible. But, with the not-self, can knowledge and volition ever be perfect ?

I do not think that they can ever be perfect, because they are incapable of harmonising the abstract element of not-self which, as we have seen, must always be found in their content. All the rest of the content of experience, no doubt, is capable of being harmonised by knowledge and volition. But what, as it seems to me, is impossible to harmonise is the characteristic of experience which makes it not-self—which makes it something existing immediately, and in its own right, not merely as part of the content of the knowing self.

This is, of course, only an abstraction. The pure not-self, like the pure self, cannot exist independently. It is a mere nonentity if it is separated from the other elements of experience—those which make the content of the not-self. But though, like the pure self, it is an abstraction, it is, like the pure self, an indispensable abstraction. Without it our experience would not be not-self as well as self. And, if the experience was not as truly not-self as self, it could not, we have seen, be our experience at all.

287. What results follow from this element of the not-self? Let us first consider what happens in the case of knowledge, postponing volition. The whole content of knowledge is permeated by an essential element which has only one characteristic—opposition to the self. It necessarily follows that a certain opposition seems to exist between the knowing self on the one hand, and the whole content of knowledge on the other.

But this opposition involves knowledge in a contradiction. For it is impossible to take them as really opposed. The knowing self is a mere abstraction without the content of knowledge, and the content of knowledge would not be knowledge at all without the knowing self. And yet, as was said above, it is impossible to get rid of the view that they are opposed. For the element of the abstract not-self, which is found in all the content of knowledge, is the direct contrary of the pure self.

288. It is to be expected that this contradiction will cause the mind, in the pursuit of knowledge, to encounter a difficulty which it at once sees to be unmeaning and yet cannot get rid of. And this is what does happen. We have seen above[1] that when knowledge should have reached the greatest perfection of which it is capable, there would still remain one question unanswered, Why is the whole universe what it is, and not something else? We saw also that this question was illegitimate, as the possibility on which it rested was unmeaning. For a possibility that the whole universe should be different from what it is would have no common ground with actuality, and is not a possibility at all. And yet this unmeaning doubt haunts all knowledge, and cannot be extirpated.

We are now able to see why this should be the case. The existence of the element of the not-self prevents a complete harmony between the self and the content of knowledge. The knowing self appears to stand on one side and the known universe on the other. And when the knowing self thus appears to be in a position of independence, there arises the

---

[1] Section 269.

THE FURTHER DETERMINATION OF THE ABSOLUTE

delusion that in that self would be found an independent fixed point which would be the same, even if the whole known universe were different. And then the possibility of a different known universe appears to be a real one. And, since no reason can, of course, be given why the universe is what it is, there appears to be a contingent and irrational element in reality.

We have seen that this is not a real possibility. And now we have another proof of its unreality. For the delusion that it is real is caused by the persistence of thought in considering its natural condition—the existence of the not-self—as its natural enemy. The existence of such a miscalled possibility, therefore, is no argument against the rationality of the universe. But it does tell against the adequacy of knowledge as an expression of the universe. By finding a flaw in perfection, where no flaw exists, knowledge pronounces its own condemnation. If the possibility is unmeaning, knowledge is imperfect in being compelled to regard it as a possibility.

289. It seems at first sight absurd to talk of knowledge as inadequate. If it were so, how could we know it to be so? What right have we to condemn it as imperfect, when no one but the culprit can be the judge? This is, no doubt, so far true, that if knowledge did not show us its own ideal, we could never know that it did not realise it. But there is a great difference between indicating an ideal and realising it. It is possible—and I have endeavoured to show that it is the fact—that knowledge can do the one and not the other. When we ask about the abstract conditions of reality, knowledge is able to demonstrate that harmony must exist, and that the element of the not-self is compatible with it, and essential to it. But when it is asked to show in detail *how* the harmony exists, which it has shown *must* exist, it is unable to do so. There is here no contradiction in our estimate of reason, but there *is* a contradiction in reason, which prevents us from regarding it as ultimate, and which forces us to look for some higher stage, where the contradiction may disappear.

290. An analogous defect occurs, from the same cause, in volition. The special characteristic of volition is, as we have seen, that it demands that the world shall conform to the ideals laid down by the individual. Volition, that is to say, demands that the content of experience shall be the means to the individual's end. Unless this is so, volition cannot be perfect.

The assertion that perfect satisfaction requires us to consider everything else as a means to our own end may be doubted. Is there not such a thing as unselfish action? And in that highest content of satisfaction which we call moral good, is it not laid down by high authority that the fundamental law is to treat other individuals as ends and not as means?

It is undoubtedly true that our satisfaction need not be selfish. But it must be self-regarding. Many of our desires are not for our own pleasure,—such as the desire to win a game, or to eat when we are hungry. But these are still desires for our own good. If the result did not appear to us to be one which would be desirable for us, we should not desire it. Put in this way, indeed, the fact that volition and its satisfaction are self-centred appears almost a truism. It is possible, again, that a sense of duty or a feeling of benevolence may determine as to unselfish action—to action painful to ourselves, which, apart from those feelings, we could not regard as our good. But such action implies that we do regard virtue, or the happiness of others, as our highest good. Even if we take Mill's extreme case of going to hell, we must conceive that the following of virtue as long as possible, although the eventual result was eternal misery and degradation, presented itself to him as his highest good. Self-sacrifice, strictly speaking, is impossible. We can sacrifice the lower parts of our nature. But if we were not actuated by some part of our nature, the action would cease to be ours. It would fall into the same class as the actions of lunacy, of hypnotism, of unconscious habit. The will is ours, and the motive which determines will must be a motive which has power for us. In other words our volition is always directed towards our own good, and has always ourselves for its end.

And this is not interfered with by the possibility and the obligation, which unquestionably exist, of regarding other individuals as ends. We may do this with the most absolute sincerity. But if we are asked why we do it, we do not find it an ultimate necessity. We insert another term. We may perhaps ascribe our conduct to a sense of sympathy with others. In this case the reference to self is obvious. Or, taking a more objective position, we may say that we do it because it is right. Now the obligation of virtue is admitted by all schools to be internal. This is maintained alike by those who imagine it to be an empirical growth, and by those who suppose it eternal and fundamental to spirit. That virtue must be followed for its own sake is only another way of saying that we conceive virtue to be our highest good. Kant made the treatment of individuals as ends the primary law of morals. But the existence of morals depended on the Categorical Imperative. And the obligation of this on the moral agent—his recognition of it as binding—was equivalent to an assertion that he adopted it. The adoption must not be conceived as optional, or morality would become capricious; but it must be conceived as self-realisation, or it would be unmeaning to speak of the agent, or his motive, as virtuous.

291. Now the element of the not-self prevents volition from completely realising its ideal. For the whole significance of that element is that the experience into which it enters is not dependent on the self. (Not dependent must not be taken here as equivalent to independent. The true relation of the self and the not-self is one of reciprocal connection. And so it would be misleading, according to the common use of words, to say either that they were independent, or that either was dependent on the other.) It is not a mere means to the end of the self, it has its own existence, its own end.

292. The end of the self is not therefore, as such, supreme in the universe. Even if the universe is such as perfectly realises the self's end, it does not do so because its purpose is to realise the self's end, but because its own end and the self's are the same. And this throws an appearance of contingency and sufferance over the satisfaction of the self which prevents it from being quite perfect.

As with the corresponding defect in knowledge, there is only an appearance of contingency. For the self and not-self are not isolated and independent. They are parts of the same universe, and the nature of each of them is to embody the unity of which they are both parts. Thus the relation of each to the other is not external and accidental, but of the very essence of both. And thus, again, the fact that the not-self realises the ends of the self is not contingent, but necessary to the very essence of the not-self.

The condemnation therefore does not fall on the nature of reality, but on volition, which is unable to realise the complete harmony, because it persists in regarding as a defect what is no defect. It is unable to realise the complete unity of the self with the not-self, and, since the not-self is not a *mere* means to the self, it can never get rid of the view that it is only accidentally a means, and so an imperfect means. Like knowledge, volition regards its essential condition—the existence of a not-self—as an imperfection. And therefore it can never realise its ideal.

293. To sum up. If this analysis has been correct, it will prove that neither knowledge nor volition can completely express the harmony of spirit, since their existence implies that spirit is in relation with a not-self, while their perfection would imply that they were not. At the same time the dialectic assures us that complete harmony must exist, since it is implied in the existence of anything at all. We must therefore look elsewhere to find the complete expression of the harmony which is the ultimate form of spirit.

The trouble has arisen from the fact that the self is unable, in knowledge and volition, to regard the element of the not-self except as something external and alien. I do not mean that everything which is not-self appears entirely external and alien. If that were the case there could be no harmony at all—and consequently no knowledge or volition—since all the content of experience, except the abstract pure self, comes under the not-self. But I mean that the characteristic which experience possesses of being not-self—its " not-selfness," if the barbarism is permissible,—will always remain as an external and alien element.

If we are to discover the state of spirit in which the harmony could be perfect, we must find one in which the element of not-self does not give an aspect of externality

and alienation to the content of experience.   In other words
we shall have to find a state in which we regard the not-self
in the same way as we regard the self.

294. Although we find it convenient to define the not-self
by its negative relation to the self, it is not entirely negative,
for then it would not be real.   It must have some positive
nature.   It is, of course, a differentiation of the Absolute.
Now we saw reason, in Chapter II, to believe that the only
fundamental differentiations of the Absolute were finite selves.
That, therefore, of which any self is conscious as its not-self,
is, from its own point of view, another self.   And that which
appears to the observing self as the element of not-selfness
in its object, will, from the object's own point of view, be
the element of selfness.

We can now restate our problem.   Can we find any state
of spirit in which A regards B in the same way as A regards
himself?

295. Now I submit that, when A loves B, he is concerned
with B as a person, and not merely with the results of B on A,
and that therefore he does look on B as B would look on
himself.   The interest that I feel in my own life is not due
to its having such and such qualities.   I am interested in it
because it is myself, whatever qualities it may have.   I am
not, of course, interested in myself apart from all qualities,
which would be an unreal abstraction.   But it is the self
which gives the interest to the qualities, and not the reverse.
With the object of knowledge or volition on the other hand
our interest is in the qualities which it may possess, and we
are only concerned in the object's existence for itself because
without it the qualities could not exist.   But in the harmony
which we are now considering, we do not, when it has been
once reached, feel that the person is dear to us on account
of his qualities, but rather that our attitude towards his
qualities is determined by the fact that they belong to him.

296. In support of this we may notice, in the first place,
that love is not necessarily proportioned to the dignity or
adequacy of the determining motive.   This is otherwise in
knowledge and volition.   In volition, for example, the depth
of our satisfaction ought to be proportioned to the completeness

with which the environment harmonizes with our ideals, and to the adequacy with which our present ideals express our fundamental nature. If it is greater than these would justify it is unwarranted and illegitimate. But a trivial cause may determine the direction of very deep emotion. To be born in the same family, or to be brought up in the same house, may determine it. It may be determined by physical beauty, or by purely sensual desire. Or we may be, as we often are, unable to assign any determining cause at all. And yet the emotion produced may be indefinitely intense and elevated. This would seem to suggest that the emotion is directed to the person, not to his qualities, and that the determining qualities are not the ground of the harmony, but merely the road by which we proceed to that ground. If this is so, it is natural that they should bear no more necessary proportion to the harmony than the intrinsic value of the key of a safe does to the value of the gold inside the safe.

Another characteristic of love is the manner in which reference to the object tends to become equivalent to reference to self. We have seen above that all volition implies a self-reference, that, however disinterested the motive, it can only form part of our life in so far as the self finds its good in it. Now here we come across a state of spirit in which the value of truth and virtue for us seem to depend on the existence of another person, in the same way as they unquestionably depend for us on our own existence. And this not because the other person is specially interested in truth and virtue, but because all our interest in the universe is conceived as deriving force from his existence.

297. And a third point which denotes that the interest is emphatically personal is found in our attitude when we discover that the relation has been based on some special congruity which has ceased to exist, or which was wrongly believed in, and never really existed at all. In knowledge and volition such a discovery would put an end to the relation altogether. To go on believing that a thing was rational or satisfactory, because it was so once, or because we once believed that it was so, would be immediately recognized as an absurdity. If the cause of the harmony ceases, the harmony

ceases too. But here the case is different. If once the relation
has existed, any disharmony among the qualities need not, and,
we feel, ought not, to injure the harmony between the persons.
If a person proves irrational or imperfect, this may make us
miserable about him. It may make us blame him, or, more
probably, make us blame God, or whatever substitute for God
our religion may allow us. But it will not make us less
interested in him, it will not make us less confident that
our relation to him is the meaning of our existence, less
compelled to view the universe *sub specie amati*. As well
might any imperfection or sin in our nature render us less
interested in our own condition, or convince us that it was
unimportant to ourselves.

It often happens, of course, that such a strain is too hard
for affection, and destroys it. But the distinction is that,
while such a result would be the only proper and natural
one in knowledge and volition, it is felt here as a condemnation.
Knowledge and volition ought to yield. But love, we feel, if
it had been strong enough, might have resisted, and ought
to have resisted.

298. It would seem, then, that we have here reached a
standpoint from which we are able to regard the object as
it regards itself. We are able to regard the history and
content of the object as a manifestation of its individuality,
instead of being obliged to regard the individuality as a dead
residuum in which the content inheres. We are able to see
the object from within outwards, instead of from without
inwards. And so its claims to independence and substantiality
become no more alien or inharmonious to us than our own.

This recognition of the independence of the object is
absolute. In knowledge and volition that independence was
recognized to some extent. In volition, in particular, and
more especially in those higher stages in which volition becomes moral, we saw that our own satisfaction depends on
realising the independence and the rights of others, and treating them, not as means, but as ends. But the reasons why
this was necessary were always relative to our own self-
realisation. Even with virtue, the ultimate ground of each
man's choice of it must always be that he prefers it to vice.

And hence this recognition as end was itself a subordination as means, and the absolute assertion of itself as end, which the object itself made, continued to be something alien and inharmonious.

The position here is different. The subject is no longer in the same position of one-sided supremacy. In knowledge and volition it exists as a centre of which the world of objects is the circumference. This relation continues, for without it our self-consciousness and our existence would disappear. But conjoined with it we have now the recognition of the fact that we ourselves form part of the circumference of other systems of which other individuals are the centre. We know of course that this must be so. But it is only in love that it actually takes place. We are not only part of someone else's world in his eyes, but in our own. And we feel that this dependence on another is as directly and truly self-realisation as is the dependence of others on us. All through life self-surrender is the condition of self-attainment. Here, for the first time, they become identical. The result seems, no doubt, paradoxical. But any change which made it simpler would render it, I think, less correspondent to facts. And if, as I have endeavoured to show, knowledge and volition carry in them defects which prevent our regarding them as ultimate, we need not be alarmed for our formula of the Absolute, because it appears paradoxical to them. It would be in greater danger if they could fully acquiesce in it.

With such a formula our difficulties cease. Here we have perfect unity between subject and object, since it is in the whole object, and not merely in some elements of it, that we find satisfaction. And, for the same reason, the object attains its rights in the way of complete differentiation, since we are able, now that we are in unity with the whole of it, to recognize it as a true individual. Again, even unmeaning doubts of the completeness and security of the harmony between subject and object must now vanish, since not even an abstraction is left over as alien, on which scepticism could fix as a possible centre of discord.

299. There is a third line of argument which can lead us to the same conclusion. We have seen that the nature of each individual consists in certain relations to other individuals. This view must not be confounded with that suggested by Green, that "for the only kind of consciousness for which there is reality, the conceived conditions are the reality[1]." For there is all the difference possible between attempting to reduce one side of an opposition to the other, and asserting, as we have done, that the two sides are completely fused in a unity which is more than either of them.

Experience can be analysed into two abstract, and therefore imperfect, moments—the immediate centres of differentiation and the relations which unite and mediate them. The extreme atomistic view takes the immediate centres as real, and the mediating relations as unreal. The view quoted by Green, as extreme on the other side, takes the relations as real and the centres as unreal. The view of the dialectic, on the contrary, accepts both elements as real, but asserts that neither has any separate reality, because each is only a moment of the true reality. Reality consists of immediate centres which are mediated by relations. The imperfection of language compels us to state this proposition in a form which suggests that the immediacy and the mediation are different realities which only influence one another externally. But this is not the case. They are only two sides of the same reality. And thus we are entitled to say that the whole nature of the centres is to be found in their relations. But we are none the less entitled to say that the whole nature of the relations is to be found in the centres.

300. Now it is clear that each individual must have a separate and unique nature of its own. If it had not, it could never be differentiated from all the other individuals, as we know that it is differentiated. At the same time the nature of the individuals lies wholly in their connections with one another; it is expressed nowhere else, and there it is expressed fully. It follows that the separate and unique nature of each individual must be found only, and be found fully, in its connections with other individuals—in the fact, that is, that all the other individuals are for it.

---

[1] *Works*, ii. 191.

This must not be taken to mean that the connection is the logical *prius* of the individual nature—that the latter is in any sense the consequent or the result of the former. Nor does it mean that the individual natures could be explained or deduced from the fact of connection. Such views would be quite contrary to Hegel's principles. His position is essentially that reality is a differentiated unity, and that either the differentiation or the unity by itself is a mere abstraction. And it would be contrary to all the lessons of the dialectic if we supposed that one moment of a concrete whole could be either caused or explained by the other moment. It is the concrete reality which must be alike the ground and the explanation of its moments.

What we have to maintain here is not that the characters of the individuals are dependent on their connections, but, on the contrary, that the characters and the connections are completely united. The character of the individual is expressed completely in its connections with others, and exists nowhere else. On the other hand the connections are to be found in the nature of the individuals they connect, and nowhere else, and not merely in the common nature which the individuals share, but in that special and unique nature which distinguishes one individual from another.

This completes our definition of the Absolute Idea. Not only has the nature of each individual to be found in the fact that all the rest are for it, but the nature which is to be found in this recognition must be something unique and distinguishing for each individual. The whole difference of each individual from the others has to be contained in its harmony with the others.

We need not be alarmed at the apparently paradoxical appearance of this definition. For all through the doctrine of the Notion, and especially in the Idea, our categories have been paradoxical to the ordinary understanding. Even if we could find nothing in experience which explicitly embodied this category, we should not have any right, on that ground, to doubt its validity. If the arguments which have conducted us to it are valid, we shall be compelled to believe that this, and this only, is the true nature of absolute reality. The only effect of the want of an example would be our inability to form a mental picture of what absolute reality would be like.

301. I believe, however, that we can find an example of this category in experience. It seems to me that perfect love would give such an example, and that we should thus find additional support for the conclusion already reached.

It is clear, in the first place, that our example must be some form of consciousness. For the nature of the individual is still to have all reality for it, and of this idea, as we have seen, we can imagine no embodiment but consciousness.

Knowledge, however, will not be what is required. We want a state such that the individuals' recognition of their harmony with one another shall itself constitute the separate nature of each individual. In knowledge the individual recognizes his harmony with others, but this is not sufficient to constitute his separate nature. It is true that knowledge not only permits, but requires, the differentiation of the individuals. Nothing but an individual can have knowledge, and if the individuals were merged in an undifferentiated whole, the knowledge would vanish. Moreover, in proportion as the knowledge of a knowing being becomes wider and deeper, and links him more closely to the rest of reality, so does his individuality become greater. But although the individuality and the knowledge are so closely linked, they are not identical. The individuality cannot lie in the knowledge. Men may, no doubt, be distinguished from one another by what they know, and how they know it. But such distinction depends on the limitations and imperfections of knowledge. A knows X, and B knows Y. Or else A believes X_1 to be the truth, while B believes the same of X_2. But for an example of a category of the Idea we should have, as we have seen above, to take perfect cognition. Now if A and B both knew X as it really is, this would give no separate nature to A and B. And if we took, as we must take, X to stand for all reality, and so came to the conclusion that the nature of A and B lay in knowing the same subject-matter, knowing it perfectly, and, therefore, knowing it in exactly the same way, we should have failed to find that separate nature for A and B which we have seen to be necessary.

Nor can our example be found in volition. Perfect volition would mean perfect acquiescence in everything. Now men can be easily differentiated by the fact that they acquiesce in different things. So they can be differentiated by the fact that they acquiesce in different sides of the same thing—in other words, approve of the same thing for different reasons. Thus one man may approve of an auto da fé on the ground that it gives pain to the heretics who are burned, and another may approve of it on the ground that it gives pleasure to the orthodox who look on. But there can only be one way of acquiescing in the whole nature of any one thing, and only one way, therefore, of acquiescing in the whole nature of everything, and the ground of differentiation is consequently wanting.

302. The only form of consciousness which remains is emotion. To this the same objections do not seem to apply. Perfect knowledge of X must be the same in A and B. Perfect acquiescence in X must be the same in A and B. But I do not see any reason why perfect love of X should be the same in A and B, or why it should not be the differentiation required to make A and B perfect individuals. The object in love is neither archetype, as in knowledge, nor ectype, as in volition, and hence there is no contradiction in saying that love of the same person is different in different people, and yet perfect in both.

303. We have thus been led by three lines of argument to the same conclusion. The Absolute can only be perfectly manifested in a state of consciousness which complies with three conditions. It must have an absolute balance between the individual for whom all reality exists, and the reality which is for it—neither being subordinated to the other, and the harmony being ultimate. It must be able to establish such a unity between the self and the not-self, that the latter loses all appearance of contingency and alienation. And, finally, in it the separate and unique nature of each individual must be found in its connections with other individuals. We have found that knowledge and volition comply with none of these conditions. There remains only one other alternative at present known to us—love. I have tried to show that in this case all three conditions are fulfilled.

304. One or two points require further explanation. It is no doubt true that love, as we now know it, never exists as the

whole content of consciousness. Its value, and indeed its possibility, depends on its springing from, being surrounded by, and resulting in, acts of knowledge and volition which remain such, and do not pass into a higher stage. This however is only a characteristic of an imperfect state of development. At present there is much of reality whose spiritual nature we are unable to detect. And when we do recognize a self-conscious individual we can only come into relation with him in so far as that other reality, still conceived as matter, which we call our bodies, can be made instrumental to our purposes. And finally, even when we have recognized reality as spirit, the imperfection of our present knowledge leaves a large number of its qualities apparently contingent and irrational. Thus every case in which we have established a personal relation must be surrounded by large numbers of others in which we have not done so. And as all reality is inter-connected, the establishment and maintenance of this relation must be connected with, and dependent on, the imperfect relations into which we come with the surrounding reality. And, again, the same inter-connection brings it about that the harmony with any one object can never be perfect, till the harmony with all other objects is so. Thus our relations with any one object could never be completely absorbed in love—leaving no knowledge and volition untranscended—until the same-result was universally attained.

But there is no reason why it should not be attained completely, if attained universally. It is entitled to stand by itself, for it is, as we have seen, self-contained. It does not require a reference to some correlative and opposed activity to make its own nature intelligible, and it does not require any recognition of the possibility of discord. It is the simple and absolute expression of harmony, and, when once the harmony of the whole universe has become explicit, it is capable of expressing the meaning of the whole universe.

305. Before this ideal could be attained, it is clear that sense-presentation, as a method of obtaining our knowledge of the object, would have to cease. For sense-presentation can only give us consciousness of reality under the form of matter, and in doing this, it clearly falls short of the perfect harmony, since it presents reality in an imperfect and inadequate form.

There seems no reason why the fact of sense-presentation should be regarded as essential to consciousness. Our senses may be indispensable to knowledge while much of the reality, of which we desire to be informed, still takes the shape of matter, and the rest is only known to us in so far as it acts through material bodies. But it seems quite possible that the necessity, to which spirits are at present subject, of communicating with one another through matter, only exists because the matter happens to be in the way. In that case, when the whole universe is viewed as spirit, so that nothing relatively alien could come between one individual and another, the connection between spirits might be very possibly direct.

306. Another characteristic of a perfect manifestation of the Absolute is that it must be timeless. In this, again, I can see no difficulty. If, in love, we are able to come into contact with the object as it really is, we shall find no disconnected manifold. The object is, of course, not a mere blank unity. It is a unity which manifests itself in multiplicity. But the multiplicity only exists in so far as it is contained in the unity. And, since the object has thus a real unity of its own, it might be possible to apprehend the whole of it at once, and not to require that successive apprehension, which the synthesis of a manifold, originally given as unconnected, would always require.

It is true, of course, that we cannot conceive the Absolute as connection with a single other person, but rather, directly or indirectly, with all others. But we must remember, again, that all reality must be conceived as in perfect unity, and, therefore, individuals must be conceived as forming, not a mere aggregate or mechanical system, but a whole which only differs from an organism in being a closer and more vital unity than any organism can be. The various individuals, then, must be conceived as forming a differentiated and multiplex whole, but by no means as an unconnected manifold. It might therefore be practicable to dispense with successive acts of apprehension in contemplating the complete whole of the universe, as much as in contemplating the relative whole of a single individual. And in that case there would be no reason why the highest form of spirit should not be free from succession, and from time.

I should be inclined to say, personally, that, even at present, the idea of timeless emotion is one degree less unintelligible than that of timeless knowledge and volition—that the most intense emotion has some power of making time seem, if not unreal, at any rate excessively unimportant, which does not belong to any other form of mental activity. But this is a matter of introspection which every person must decide for himself.

How such great and fundamental changes are to be made—how knowledge and volition are to pass into love, and a life in time into timelessness—may well perplex us. Even if we see the necessity of the transition, the manner in which it is to be effected would remain mysterious. But all such transitions, we may reflect, must necessarily appear mysterious till they have taken place. The transition is from two relatively abstract ideas to a more comprehensive idea which synthesises them. Till the synthesis has taken place, the abstractions have not yet lost the false appearance of substantiality and independence which they acquired by their abstraction from the whole. Till the synthesis has taken place, therefore, the process by which the two sides lose their independence must appear something, which, though inevitable, is also inexplicable. It is not till the change has been made that we are able to realise fully that all the meaning of the lower lay in the higher, and that what has been lost was nothing but delusion. So, in this case, we must remember that we are not constructing love out of knowledge and volition, but merely clearing away the mistakes which presented love to us in the form of knowledge and volition.

307. It may be said that the extent and intensity in which love enters into a man's life is not a fair test of his perfection. We consider some people who have comparatively little of it as far higher than others who have much. And again—and this is perhaps a more crucial instance—we find cases in which we regard as a distinct advance a change in a man's life which diminishes his devotion to individuals in comparison with his ardour for abstract truth or abstract virtue.

The existence of such cases cannot be denied, but need not, I think, be considered incompatible with what has been said. Any harmony which we can attain at present must be very imperfect, and postulates its own completion, at once because of its partial success and of its partial failure. Now the principle of the dialectic is that spirit cannot advance in a straight line, but is compelled to tack from side to side, emphasising first one aspect of the truth, and then its complementary and contradictory aspect, and then finding the harmony between them. In so far, then, as the harmony is at any time imperfect, because it has not fully grasped the opposites to be reconciled, it can only advance by first grasping them, and then reconciling them. The difference must be first recognized, and then conquered, and between the first stage and the second the harmony will be impaired. The opposition may be between the abstract generality of religion and the abstract particularity of passion, it may be between the abstract submission of the search for truth and the abstract assertion of the search for good, it may be between abstract intensity deficient in breadth and abstract extension deficient in depth. When any of these divisions happen the harmony will be broken, and yet the change will be an advance, since we shall have entered on the only path by which the harmony can be perfected. In that harmony alone we live. But here, as everywhere in this imperfect world, the old paradox holds good. Only he who loses his life shall find it.

308. The love of which we speak here cannot be what is generally called love of God. For love is of persons, and God, as we have seen, is a unity of persons, but not a personal unity. Nor can we say that it is God that we love in man. It is no more the merely divine than the merely human. The incarnation is not here a divine condescension, as in some religious systems. The abstractly universal is as much below the concrete individual as is the abstractly particular, and it is the concrete individual which alone can give us what we seek for.

Again, though differentiation has no right as against the concrete whole, it is independent as against the element of unity. And, therefore, if we could come into relation with the element of unity as such, it would not connect us with the differentiated parts of the universe, and could not therefore be a relation adequately expressing all reality.

M^{c}T.   19

We can, if we choose, say that our love is *in* God, meaning thereby that it cannot, at its highest, be conceived as merely subjective and capricious, but that it expresses the order of the universe, and is conscious that it does so. It is more than religion, but it must include religion. But this is not love of God. The relation is between persons, and God is conceived only as the unity in which they exist.

309. If we cannot, properly speaking, love God, it is still more impossible to love mankind. For mankind is an abstraction too, and a far more superficial abstraction. If God was only an abstraction of the element of unity, at least he was an abstraction of the highest and most perfect unity, able to fuse into a whole the highest and most perfect differentiation. But mankind represents a far less vital unity. It is a common quality of individuals, but not, conceived merely as mankind, a living unity between them. The whole nature of the individual lies in his being a manifestation of God. But the unity of mankind is not a principle of which all the differences of individual men are manifestations. The human race, viewed as such, is only an aggregate, not even an organism. We might as well try to love an indefinitely extended Post Office Directory. And the same will hold true of all subordinate aggregates—nations, churches, and families.

310. I have been using the word love, in this chapter, in the meaning which is given to it in ordinary life—as meaning the emotion which joins two particular persons together, and which never, in our experience, unites one person with more than a few others. This, as we have seen, was also Hegel's use of the word[1] At the same time we must guard against confounding it with the special forms which it assumes at present. At present it makes instruments of sexual desire, of the connection of marriage, or of the connection of blood. But these cannot be the ultimate forms under which love is manifested, since they depend on determining causes outside love itself. Love for which any cause can be assigned carries the marks of its own incompleteness upon it. For, when it is complete, all

---

[1] Cp. Sections 219, 220.

relations, all reality, will have been transformed into it. Thus there will be nothing left outside to determine it. Love is itself the relation which binds individuals together. Each relation it establishes is part of the ultimate nature of the unity of the whole. It does not require or admit of justification or determination by anything else. It is itself its own justification and determination. The nearest approach to it we can know now is the love for which no cause can be given, and which is not determined by any outer relation, of which we can only say that two people belong to each other—the love of the Vita Nuova and of In Memoriam.

311. No doubt an emotion which should be sufficient, both in extent and intensity, to grasp the entire universe, must be different in degree from anything of which we can now have experience. Yet this need not force us to allow any essential difference between the two, if the distinction is one of degree, and not of generic change. The attempt to imagine any communion so far-reaching—extending, as we must hold it to do, to all reality in the universe—is, no doubt, depressing, almost painful[1]. But this arises, I think, from the inability, under which we lie at present, to picture the ideal except under the disguise of a "false infinite" of endless succession. However much we may know that the kingdom of heaven is spiritual and timeless, we cannot help imagining it as in time, and can scarcely help imagining it as in space. In this case the magnitude of the field to be included naturally appears as something alien and inimical to our power of including it. We are forced, too, since our imagination is limited by the stage of development in which we at present are, to give undue importance to the question of number, as applied to the individuals in the Absolute. If we look at it from this standpoint the most casual contemplation is bewildering and crushing. But number is a very inadequate category. Even in everyday life we may see how number falls into the shade as our knowledge

---

[1] I see no necessity for considering the relations between each individual and all the others to be direct. It would seem quite as possible that the relation of each individual to the majority of the others should be indirect, and through the mediation of some other individuals.

of the subject-matter increases. Of two points on an unlimited field we can say nothing but that they are two in number. But if we were considering the relation of Hegel's philosophy to Kant's, or of Dante to Beatrice, the advance which we should make by counting them would be imperceptible. When everything is seen under the highest category, the Absolute Idea, this process would be complete. All lower categories would have been transcended, and all separate significance of number would have vanished. And with it would vanish the dead weight of the vastness of the universe.

We must remember too, once more, that the Absolute is not an aggregate but a system. The multiplicity of the individuals is not, therefore, a hindrance in the way of establishing a harmony with any one of them, as might be the case if each was an independent rival of all the rest. It is rather to be considered as an assistance, since our relations with each will, through their mutual connections, be strengthened by our relations to all the rest.

312.   The conclusions of this chapter are, no doubt, fairly to be called mystical. And a mysticism which ignored the claims of the understanding would, no doubt, be doomed. None ever went about to break logic, but in the end logic broke him. But there is a mysticism which starts from the standpoint of the understanding, and only departs from it in so far as that standpoint shows itself not to be ultimate, but to postulate something beyond itself. To transcend the lower is not to ignore it. And it is only in this sense that I have ventured to indicate the possibility of finding, above all knowledge and volition, one all-embracing unity, which is only not true, only not good, because all truth and all goodness are but distorted shadows of its absolute perfection—" das Unbegreifliche, weil es der Begriff selbst ist."

CAMBRIDGE : PRINTED BY J. AND C. F. CLAY, AT THE UNIVERSITY PRESS.

For EU product safety concerns, contact us at Calle de José Abascal, 56–1°,
28003 Madrid, Spain or eugpsr@cambridge.org.

www.ingramcontent.com/pod-product-compliance
Ingram Content Group UK Ltd.
Pitfield, Milton Keynes, MK11 3LW, UK
UKHW010349140625
459647UK00010B/939